The Good Fight

Why Conservatives Must Take Back America

Paul A. Ibbetson

www.EternalLightAndPowwerCompany.Com

The Good Fight

Why Conservatives Must Take Back America

Cover Design and Art Work by Dante Joseph

www.DanteJoseph.com

Cover Image 2011 Used under license from Shutterstock.com

Table of Contents

Acknowledgments   5

Introductions   6

Chapter 1   Why Do We Need A Conservative Movement?   7

Chapter 2   Avoiding Deceivers   17

Chapter 3   Taking Responsibility   50

Chapter 4   Why The Ron Paulies Hate Me   86

Chapter 5   The Homosexual Agenda   98

Chapter 6   Terrorism   124

Chapter 7   Women and the Conservative Movement   146

Chapter 8   Abortion   158

Chapter 9   Political Correctness   165

Chapter 10   A Moment for the Pharisees   173

Chapter 11   Border Security and Immigration   179

Chapter 12   A Conservative Movement: Goals, Rules, and Guidelines   188

Appendix A   The Ibbetson McGinn Debate   197

Appendix B   Bible Verses   220

References   223

Author's Note: Throughout this book I have used my own previously published articles. For the purpose of this book, these articles have been re-edited for punctuation, grammar, and minor word changes. The articles have not changed in form or content from my original published articles and I made these changes in a effort to make this book a more enjoyable reading experience for my audience. The original articles remain at their cited locations in their original format.

Acknowledgments

As I travel through this world, it becomes more apparent each day that God has placed people in my life at pivotal moments that have modeled values and taught me important lessons from which I have benefitted tremendously. I want to recognize four men who affected my thinking in positive ways. I would like to acknowledge my home town preacher Stan Bryan. Thank you, Stan, for your effectiveness at the pulpit and for modeling Christian values. I am blessed to know you. I would also like to acknowledge my uncles Ron, Richard, and David Ibbetson. Over the years they have been a powerful force in teaching me about hard work, innovation, and the capitalistic mentality that success can be achieved without guilt. Thank you all. I am a better, wiser, and stronger person for knowing these men.

Introduction

There comes a time in the course of world events when great movements are not only allowed to take shape, grow, and have a great impact on society, but also when the necessity of their success may fundamentally save a society from destruction. This is such a time. America, a truly blessed nation, is at a precipice. We are at a crucial place in its history when its people will either turn their backs on the ideological beliefs that have made this country great, or they will fight to defend this country from physical, social, economic, and spiritual destruction. A conservative movement has already begun, but without a sound strategic blueprint for tomorrow, its future success is not assured. This book is a wake-up call. Though some may consider these truths politically incorrect, conservatives need to take a long look at the problems in this country and our responsibility to fight for the values we hold dear. It's time to face the ideological foes of this nation, and beat them in the battlefield of ideas. It's time for conservatives to take a stand and be accountable. It's time to join the Good Fight!

Chapter 1

Why Do We Need A Conservative Movement?

The truth is a difficult thing to come by these days. It's not just that there are hoards of deceivers out there who wish to enslave the American people for their own nefarious purposes, the situation is more complex. Yes, deceivers are out there and this book will identify them, expose their deeds, make an argument for why they must be defeated, and show you how regular people can come together and defeat them. However, this is not the whole battle facing conservatives. You see, the truth is hard to come by because we conservatives often keep the truth from one another. This happens for many reasons which will be discussed in this book. In fact, in the greater scheme of things one of the bigger enemies conservatives have is often themselves. In this book, we will tackle the obstacles which come from both sides of the political aisle. Nothing should be out of bounds when one's telling the truth. Free speech and free thought is a frequent victim of political correctness, and this book will not be shackled by such constraints.

Liberals have been dominating the cultural scene in America for decades despite being a statistical minority. Many major issues, such as government spending, the traditional family, abortion, taxes, terrorism, border security, our adherence to the Constitution, our Biblical foundations, among many others, have been dominated by liberals. How could this happen? Liberals had a strategic plan, were organized to implement that plan, and when they entered the battlefield of ideas, conservative were a no show. Liberals have won many battles, and continue to win without a fight. This book will force Americans to take a hard look at some important cultural battles that have recently been lost without effective opposition from conservatives and the ramification of those losses. Equally important, we will look at battles that were fought, but fought with poor strategies by conservatives, and how similar defeats can be avoided in the future. In the end, this book will make amply evident that conservatives must strategically pick core value issues of importance and fight with every legal means to defeat the modern day liberal. It is my hope that this book will be educational and inspirational, but I have to say now that I am going to attempt to provoke readers into action and I am not going to worry about political correctness along the way. This country just does not have enough time left to avoid some serious tough love. I have given the warning. Let's move now to understanding, defining, and identifying the enemy.

In my 2009 book, *Feeding Lions: Sharing the Conservative Philosophy in a Politically Hostile World*, I laid the foundations for explaining differences between conservatives and liberals. It is only fitting to revisit a portion of the pivotal information from that book, because understanding the clear differences in ideology between these two groups is of absolute importance as we currently battle for the future of this nation. It also serves as a foundation to supporting a major push to the existing conservative movement. This is a major focus of the book. As stated in *Feeding Lions,* conservatives are identified by their adherence to the following principles: 1. God, 2. Family, 3. Country. These principles are tied together in order of importance, and have a cumulative effect on one another. Let's take a moment to break these principles down. Conservatives gravitate toward Judeo-Christian values. This is more than a belief in sacred documents such as the Bible, but is also a pervasive moral belief in personal accountability. This accountability is rooted in the acceptance of the fact that people will be judged by a supreme being for their life's deeds. Yep, we are talking about Judgment Day. Christianity is a belief system that holds firm to the sacred promise that there will be rewards and punishments at the end of one's life for following, or refusing to follow, God's law. This Judeo-Christian value system is found everywhere in American culture and directly effects all facets of conservatism. Did you get the significance of that statement? No matter what it is, God has an influence on EVERTHING in American culture.

When we look at the second principle of conservatism in Family, we can see the direct influence of God in how traditional American values are formed. The value of the unborn and the opposition to abortion is brought forth directly from the Bible, as is the battle to uphold traditional marriage as defined as a moral covenant between a man and a woman. These two battles seek to maintain a tradition of conservative Christian bedrock values here in America. The fundamental difference between liberals and conservatives on the issue of Family is that liberals can envision family relationships, unions, and contracts within an environment completely devoid of God. For conservatives, this reality is inconceivable. When these two beliefs system come together, conflicts arise. The world of the liberal homosexual and their encroachment on traditional society is a topic worthy of expanded discussion. An entire chapter is designated in this book to address the issue of the homosexual agenda in America.

The third principle of conservatism is that of Country. Simply put, conservatives see America as fundamentally good. That is, conservatives believe that our country has done more good in the world than bad, and that by following traditional values Americans have improved our country, and done substantial good in the world. Because of this, when conservatives see symbols of the United States such as the American flag, we feel pride and patriotism. When the conservative principles of 1. God, 2. Family, and 3. Country are applied as focal values to the issues of the day, their powerful positive cumulative effect on traditional America can accurately and consistently guide conservative strategies in addressing political issues and opponents.

When it comes to understanding today's liberals, it is not adequate to simply assume that they will act and think in direct opposition to conservatives on the same wide ranging set of issues, even though this is painfully true. First, we must separate the modern liberal from the classical definition of liberalism. In political philosophy, the classical liberal is the equivalent of what we might call the conservative of today. This bothers some individuals when people, such as me, use the term "liberal" to identify shifty politicians like Harry Reid and Nancy Pelosi who we know as big government, tax raising, pro-abortion, American apologists. What I tell people today when they start to get hung up on today's use of the word "liberal," remember that we live in the modern world and it is a place where sides must be taken. To do this, distinct classifications of political ideology must be made, and forces must be marshaled to fight for this country. The world continues to turn and we must turn with it as we describe the world around us. Just remember, the word "gay" used to mean a state of "happiness." Terms change and we must keep up.

In today's modern world, the term "liberal" embodies the belief systems of the Barack Obamas, Nancy Pelosis, and Harry Reids of the world, and we should not feel uneasy about letting this classification stand. We should learn what it means, understand its ramifications, and fight it with all our strength. Let's man and woman-up and get to understanding the modern liberal. The modern liberal places God in the category of myth and fairytale. Thus, the Bible is seen as fantasy at best, and a dangerous document at worst. Without the belief in a supreme being, liberals see the Bible as a book of restrictions which they have no personal obligation to follow. It is not that liberals do not understand the cumulative effect that religion has for conservatives, they simply reject it. They enjoy and revel in the freedom of being their own God, and believe they will be judged only by the standards of their cohorts. Liberals don't want to be labeled as Godless heathens, even when they act like it. So, to maintain the appearance of moral equality with their God-fearing conservative opposition, liberals will say they are "spiritual." The term "spiritual" is used by modern liberals as a way to maintain a semblance of religious "street cred" without having to go to church, read the Bible, submit to God, avoid sin, or, you know, doing all the things those lame redneck, backwoods, snake-handling, Bible thumpers do. For liberals, they can be "spiritual" about music, yoga, water bongs, etc.--they have a very versatile selection to pick from. Most importantly, they can deflect their non-religiosity when the issue is brought up by saying they are spiritual. Of course, back on this plane of existence, this is clearly nothing but moral relativism in its purist form and it allows the modern liberal to endorse the lowest denominator of human conduct. For example, having multiple sex partners for teens, same-sex partners for marriage, and killing babies in the womb is simply an issue to be justified within the liberal's own spiritual value system. To liberals, man is God, or woman is God, let's not forget the quasi-religious perspective of feminists. Either way, the liberal mindset inevitably leads to an ideological confrontation with conservatives.

In government, when man seeks to replace God's will with his own, inevitably he will be a dictator. Dictators by definition reject capitalistic free market principles, and would never accept a Constitution which is based on rule by the people, dignity, freedom, and private property. It is not a fluke that liberals throughout time find themselves romanticizing dictators from Stalin to Mao to Castro. These totalitarians shared similar belief systems with the modern liberal, first and foremost of which, is their hatred of America. That's right, the modern day liberal hates America. They may mumble their way through the Pledge of Allegiance, but pin them down in a discussion, or be a fly on the wall in the ballot box, and you will see that liberals are unable to hide their disdain for what conservative Americans hold dear, and what conservative Americans hold dear is this country and maintaining its historical values into the future. Liberals see the country as fundamentally flawed and in need of immediate radical change. Their hatred of America is also cumulative, starting with their rejection of God, followed by repulsion of the traditional nuclear family, and a renouncement of the free market system in a constitutionally representative republic. On the conservative principles of: 1.God, 2. Family, 3. Country, liberals see the world in absolute opposition to conservatives. No wonder they cannot get along.

There is no "good" or "bad" liberal in modern America. There is only the modern liberal, and he or she will be in diametric opposition to the conservative across the board on all political issues. If you cannot accept this fact, you and the conservative movement will continually be victimized by this lingering ignorance. Why do we need a conservative movement? We need it because liberals will never stop pushing their destructive policies within America until the country as we know and love it is destroyed. We must stop them. The charge to save America is completely on us. If we fail, we have only ourselves to blame. This is an important and painful truth to embrace.

You will hear, most often from liberals that in the spirit of unity conservatives should come together with liberals to "get things done." This is code for, "comply with the current liberal agenda" in the name of friendly bipartisanship, decency, and reasonableness. So-called Republicans like John McCain have been very proficient at doing this and at times, the liberal media will call him heroic names like "Maverick" or say that he, "walks to his own drumbeat." I have my own names for individuals like these, "turncoat," "sell-out," and "RINO." It is due to the GOP's recent failure to demand truly conservative candidates for high office that John McCain managed to become a 2008 Republican Presidential Candidate, which has brought the nation four, and possibly eight years of Barack Obama. Thanks, John McCain. Thanks, GOP. Fortunately, times change, and people are not only waking up to the futility of handing control to liberals under the guise of "coming together," they are also just plain tired of watching the country being destroyed. This frustration and anger are the seeds of a resurging conservative movement which this book seeks to foster. Our responsibility is to be part of a major counterstrike in 2012 which will help get our nation back to traditional values. To make this happen, we must have a clear picture of the current battlefield. To do that, we need to get honest about the political parties in America.

In *Feeding Lions*, I spoke about how the battle for the future of American culture is between conservative and liberal ideologies, and not between political parties. This remains true today. The fight is between conflicting ideologies and mental attitudes, and not simply between Democrats and Republicans, between donkeys and elephants. With that said, the conservative movement must have a political tent in which it is represented, and the Republican Party is the logical choice. The Democratic Party, by ideologically moving to the farthest point of the radical left today and embracing nothing short of pure socialism, has further solidified the necessity for the Republican Party to be the place where conservative values grow. When we look at the conservative movement, we can see it as an emerging political force which calls out deficiencies in both parties and in the two-party system. However, this book is not a call for a third party, though we will talk about third parties later in the book. It is an acknowledgement that currently we have a two party system in which one party is ideologically consistent, well-funded, and motivated for action while the other party is ideologically inconsistent, self-defeating, and all too often weak in the spine. If you haven't figured it out yet, Democrats are political party number one. Ideologically, they represent the radical left to the point of socialism, and they tow the Marxist line in almost perfect lockstep. There is almost no atrocity that a member of their ranks can be caught doing that will force them to eat their own. So, while the Republican Party suffers from not being consistently conservative, the Democrat Party has become almost completely consistently liberal. A safe rule of thumb in the current world in which we live: avoid all Democratic candidates like the plague. Republicans can be considered as potential carriers, but all Democrats are inherently infected. Liberals are bankrolled by ideological leftists with endless funds, such as George Soros, and they have a motivated plan to dismantle America and rebuild it into a Marxist utopia. They are winning and if not for sporadic opposition by the conservative majority, our country as we have known it and as the Founding Fathers created it, would already be gone.

The reason that conservatives are finally grouping together, calling their representatives, marching on Washington, and preparing to vote in record numbers is because of the inability of the other political party, the Republicans, to properly champion conservative values, and stand up to radicals on the left. In 2006, voters punished the Republican Party for uncontrolled spending, a failure to secure the border, and for simply selling out to Democrats for the purposes of "getting things done." In 2008, the Republican Party picked the most liberal member of the Party, John McCain, to be the GOP champion. This is a prime example of the ideological inconsistency of the Republican Party. The clear conservative values of Sarah Palin, the 2008 Vice-Presidential candidate, simply made John McCain's liberal stances more prominent, and made him even more unlikeable and unwinnable in the eyes of true conservatives. This was a perfect scenario for an up and coming liberal star like Barack Obama. Who among you knew John McCain could not win the election even before the Democrat primary was completed? If you were like me, it was a long painful road to the general election. We cannot afford another John McCain in 2012.

The inconsistency of the Republican Party to deliver has been a problem for longer than many would like to admit, and it brought forth the beginnings of a movement to get back to the conservative principles of God, Family, and Country. The process did not begin in 2008, but thanks to Barack Obama, the harbinger of "hope and change," the movement has been accelerated with the speed and power equivalent to the Energizer Bunny. As George W. Bush was critiqued in *Feeding Lions*, the actions of Barack Obama and his cohorts will be analyzed in detail in this book. As we begin our look at Barack Obama, a few things about the president should be clarified from the start.

Despite some concerns that still linger in certain circles, I can tell you with great certainty that Barack Obama is not the anti-Christ. The Devil is much more experienced and can operate without a teleprompter. Barack Obama is also not the mastermind of some secret cabal with a grand conspiracy to destroy the country. The President is nothing more insidious than a modern day liberal. Isn't that scary enough? In fact, Obama has been very straight-forward in laying out how he will destroy the country through a series of fundamental transformations. The fact that Americans elected a presidential candidate with radical socialist ties, who openly told the nation he would be the equivalent of a Marxist wrecking ball to America, should frighten people more than any conspiracy theory about the politician with the middle name "Hussein." Simply by making good on his campaign promises, Barack Obama has taken the country to the brink of destruction. He has done this by pushing liberal agendas which existed prior to his administration and advancing them at the expense of the American people. This book will discuss these agendas, their ramifications, and why they must be overcome at the ballot box and

13

through cultural victories. This will be accomplished by the overwhelming conservative majority if it can be unified under effective leadership and planning. Barack Obama has taken advantage of situational circumstances such as a declining economy to push record spending and a socialist healthcare program on the American people against their will. Yes, I have no problem holding Obama accountable for the conga line of terrible decisions he has made. However, we should never build Obama up to be more than what he is. We have to be real. Obama is not working alone. For every socialism expanding, constitutional slashing, freedom limiting directive he has put into motion, he has had a Democratic Party behind him, cheering him on and ideologically in step with all his actions. Did someone mention something about a birth certificate? Let's take a moment and deal with the hard truth of this issue. Has Barack Obama been purposely deceptive on this issue? Yes, no doubt he has. The President's staff has done everything to spur on this controversy. Does it tell the nation that future political candidates should be better vetted? I hope so, even though at this time, no states have adopted guidelines to stop this from happening again. Here is the painful truth for all the "birthers": I understand your frustration, but Obama will not be impeached, removed, or otherwise kicked out of office due to the lack of a long-form birth certificate. From the point of view of the modern day conservative movement which we must advance now, time spent on the birth certificate issue is wasted energy. That will make some people angry, I know, but here is the consolation prize: the "birthers" wish to see Barack Obama booted out of office, and that end goal can still be attained. Obama can still be sent home as a one-term President if we accomplish his direct defeat. Obama can be removed by voters at the ballot box. If our voting majority shows up at the polls, we can send this liberal President back to community organizing. This can be done. However, placing Hussein back on the train to Chicago is not the whole ballgame. Bigger than Barack--hear me now--bigger than this single president is the need for a strong conservative movement to flourish into the future, filling every level of society. We must look at the big picture; we must look far into the future. With that said, let's focus our attention on the progress of the conservative movement which needs to be the focus of our time and energy.

In reaction to Obama's aggressive liberal domestic agenda and utter disdain for mainstream America, the Tea Party movement was born. The Tea Party movement, which I embrace with the delicious joy of a man finding water in the dessert, is a truly conservative movement. Tea Partiers are simply people that love their country and want to see a future with limited government, restrained government spending, an adherence to the Constitution, and traditional American values. The beauty of the Tea Party movement is that it originated and has flourished without the financial backing of the two major political parties. Out of the gate, Democrats loathed the Tea Party attendees and viciously attacked these moms and dads of mainstream America. We all remember the venom spewed at Tea Party members by San Francisco liberal Nancy Pelosi, as reported by Fox News in 2009: "The Tea Party movement is being orchestrated from Republican headquarters, so isn't truly a grassroots movement." Pelosi continued to say, "The Republican Party directs a lot of what the Tea Party does, but not everybody in the Tea Party takes direction from the Republican Party. And so there was a lot of, shall we say, Astroturf, as opposed to grassroots" (Fox, 2009). If Pelosi had looked a little closer, she would have seen that the Republican Party also gave the Tea Party movement the cold shoulder until their numbers became huge and their voting power became undeniable.

In the end, the self sufficiency of the Tea Party has been, and will continue to be, a positive aspect of the conservative movement. I say this with full knowledge that the Republican Party will be the instrument by which liberals will be defeated and America will be saved. However, I do not think that all Republicans who are currently under this political tent should remain, or that tolerating their presence in it is healthy for a strong conservative movement. This book will point out some big name Republicans that should get the boot. Additionally, in the powerful and unified conservative movement which I envision, saving America will not be accomplished by the Tea Party alone. This group is one component of a much bigger picture, one force within a much larger potential arsenal. The full conservative movement requires all of the voting numbers which can be marshaled by awakening the conservative heart of the majority populace. That means that people who are not even aware of what is happening to their country have to be brought to reality. They have to educated, invigorated, and brought into the fight. The groundwork has been laid; now we will proceed to the hotly contested battle grounds where today's ideological warfare is taking place.

Chapter 2

Avoiding Deceivers

Don't be an idiot! Wow that seems like a harsh way to start out a chapter but please, don't be one. We conservatives have the advantage of statistical numbers and if we were fully organized, educated, and motivated we could dominate the political arena. However, we have to take a hard look at why that is not happening now. Conservatives often allow themselves to be tricked by the myriad of liberal deceivers that are out there. These shysters range from slimy Democrats to RINOs within the Republican Party. They also include the Hollywood elites who viewers watch on the movie screen, and whose celebrity status gives them too much influence on political matters. This group of deceivers also includes liberal magpies such as Bill Maher and Chris Matthews. Liberals have an agenda, as we have been discussing. I will provide a concise anthology of the issues in this agenda through my previously published articles. Liberals know that they cannot consistently overwhelm traditional America at the polls, but they can do things to trick people to their advantage. When you hear the liberal media repetitiously saying that their candidate is "unbeatable" or that a conservative candidate "doesn't really have a chance," that little voice in your head starts saying, "Well, it's a done deal already. Why should I even waste my time to go vote?" Watch as the next major elections start building up. The liberal controlled media will spend great effort telling America which conservatives can't be elected, while simultaneously spending time telling people why they should vote for the liberal candidate. Lastly, in an attempt to take this trickery full circle, the liberal media will pretend to "discover" certain Republican candidates that just might have some decent qualities--politicians worthy of future greatness. Beware! These diamonds in the rough, newly "discovered" and often given large portions of television face-time, are guaranteed losers for a conservative movement and the Republican Party and liberals absolutely know this. Rule of thumb: If liberals endorse a so-called "conservative" candidate, that candidate will be bad for the country.

When it comes to deceiving first time voters, Hollywood has an almost endless line of activists who pop up to be part of the liberal propaganda machine. During election cycles, teens and young adults get bombarded daily with the MTV "I smoke herb in my super-crib when not slapping around my harem of booty-poppin' hos," rappers along with the pre-pubescent baby-boy-Bieber-heartthrob-types who pretend in political commercials that they know more about politics than hairspray. These tools of the liberal machine also get quality face time in front of the TV camera to say little more than, "Hey, I'm cool and you know it. Now do the next stupid thing I say." It is a strong and steady infusion of liberal propaganda that works to push young voters towards liberal candidates and causes, and away from conservatives. The Hollywood influence promoting liberal propaganda is also not just a young person's game. Remember seeing old silver-haired Andy Griffith, a television icon to many my age, being dusted off and propped up in front of the cameras to tell us Obama's healthcare package was going to be just great! Well yeeees sir! I deeeeclare! Andy even plucked a chord on the old guitar to solidify a moment of TV nostalgia for viewers. I did not appreciate this attempt at political chicanery but I could not bring myself to feel much anger against good old Sheriff Andy Taylor. Doing that might make the sun refuse to shine in Mayberry. You see, it's easy to get sucked in. Conservatives get tricked all the time, and sometimes they end up right up beside the liberals doing stupid liberal things. In this chapter we will talk about the different forms of deception our conservative movement is likely to face. We will also look at how to recognize deception and avoid looking like an idiot in this culture war. I start by presenting my February 4, 2010, article on Stone Soup.

Stone Soup: What liberals are Cooking up for 2010

Most of us have heard the fairy tale *Stone Soup*. This children's story in its many versions gives an account of a hungry traveler in a time of economic hardship who enters a village with nothing more than a cooking pot and a stone. Through creative manipulation, the villagers are made to believe that a simple stone can produce a wonderful soup. Little by little, the villagers add vegetables and other tasty tidbits to the stone soup until finally, and almost magically, they have a bountiful, scrumptious pot of soup to eat.

Now, many that tell this story attempt to dig up a positive moral to what transpired around the bubbling pot. Some say that the people came together and shared resources and that this story shows that by ourselves, we may be able to nibble on a single vegetable, but working together, we can enjoy tasty soup. However, the truth is much darker and speaks of manipulation and trickery.

Think about it for a moment. If we are to find a fundamental truth in the story *Stone Soup,* it is that there is a sucker born every day. Yes, the people of the village were tricked, duped, hoodwinked, bamboozled. Taking this story to its truthful conclusion, the shyster of this story was probably wanted in several counties for soup fraud and conspiracy to market false condiments. The deeper lesson from this story is that deception has almost no limits, or places that it cannot flourish, if it is crafted well.

Liberal democrats are about to hit some very hard political times. I have a feeling that votes are going to be about as hard to find in many political races as food was in this story. So, as was the case with the trickster that worked to fill a pot with the labors and fruits of others, the American people are going to be offered bowl after bowl of good liberal cooking all the way to the mid-term elections in 2010.

This dish starts with the rejection of the current reality that democrats will most certainly lose their majority in the House and many seats in the Senate. From *USA Today* on down the line, liberals are attempting to slice and dice the historic loss of Ted Kennedy's seat in Massachusetts by saying that Scott Brown has a liberal aroma which mitigates the national implications of the democrats' defeat in one of the bluest of the blue states. This crushing defeat becomes part of a series of losses including elections in New Jersey and Virginia that democrats said were nothing more than local discontent. I can hear the falsehoods clanking at the bottom of the pot, and soon you will be asked to submit your contribution.

The largest of these salt-covered lies will be that Americans have given the President a mandate to do whatever he wants with this country and will not hold him or supporting members of congress accountable at the polls for the atrocious actions that have been heaped upon this nation from Washington. The President's State of the Union address in all its arrogance and condescension has more than filled the nostrils of the nation with the truth of the distasteful dishes this president still wishes to place on our plates. Only the "Stone Soupers" fail to smell what the "Barack" is cooking at this stage of the game. The question is whether people are going to order something better for this country or simply lie back and leave it to the cooks that are currently in the kitchen. If voters decide to go with the latter, they had better be prepared to relinquish everything they hold precious into the bottomless bubbling pot of a new American reality.

A considerably low-down deception liberals use is propping up their dead cohorts for one last fundraiser, promotional tour, attack on a hated conservative, or other slimy bit of zombie deception. This is one of their favorite maneuvers, and I will show readers how much liberals use what I call the "chapel cha-cha" to benefit their agenda. This dirty dealing done to the living using the dead is performed in two ways. As I discuss later in the book, in the chapter on the homosexual agenda, liberals like to co-opt great people like Martin Luther King to be showpieces they parade around for their own deviant causes. This is low-brow activity indeed, but the second way liberals use the dead is far worse. This is done directly after a death, while the American people are still emotionally weak, and the dearly departed (the "prop" in this deception) is barely off the embalmer's table. Liberals do two wrongs here, and no; two wrongs don't equal a right. First, liberals attempt, and in some cases succeed, to trick bereaved mourners who have gathered to pay honor to the dead into being unsuspecting participants in liberal political pep rallies. Second, liberals will report to the crowd that the dearly departed simply wanted to give their full support for one last liberal initiative as he or she was swept into the sweet by-and-by. There has got to be a special place in hell for this kind of manipulation. In this January 21, 2010, article I talked about the pilfering of the dead.

Pilfering the Dead: Barack Obama at the Pulpit of the Vermont Avenue Baptist Church

It has been said that death is a sweet release from the many struggles of this world. While this is most certainly true for most, it does not release some that have passed from here to the great beyond from being shaken down for their last remaining earthly valuables.

As my desire is to see America survive into the future, I speak at length about the great divide between conservatives and the modern day liberal. I talk about the destructive nature of Barack Obama's socialism when implemented within a free market capitalist society. People are starting to get that one. The issue of the socialist anti-American stance also becomes of paramount importance when the country must stand and not only rebuke our enemies, but defeat them with unquestionable force. Here again, the divide between how conservatives move forward with action to address those who would kill us versus the modern day liberal are clear, with the fruits of this administration's game plan to defend the homeland being truly dipped in American blood.

If America is to truly awaken from its apathetic malaise and self-imposed restraints of the national "choker chain" of political correctness, it will most likely take the most egregious of violations of decency to shock the needed numbers into action. With that in mind, let's look at how liberals pilfer the dead.

Because of the atheistic nature of liberalism, democrats make it common fare to politicize the most sacred events to gain advantage on issues they champion. Funerals have become prime real estate for picking up votes and pushing for socialist agendas and most often, this dirty work is done by asserting that the dead, who should be honored in their passing, are really anxious for one last chance to push a liberal agenda to the public.

We can see a consistent history of these detestable activities from liberal democrats. As if it were yesterday, one can recall from 2002 the untimely death of Minnesota Senator Paul Wellstone whose televised memorial turned into a

20,000-plus democrat rally for Walter Mondale to fill the seat by Wellstone's death. This debacle was filled with partisan booing by members of the political opposition and direct calls for republican politicians to support Wellstone's seat being filled by another democrat. The worst of the actions during this event was the clear assertion that to honor Paul Wellstone was to keep republicans out of his open seat. In flogging republicans in the name of Wellstone, liberals dishonored his name for personal gain in the same way one would by emptying the pockets of the dead for loose change. In a word, these actions were despicable.

In 2006, the repetitiously offensive Jimmy Carter would take the opportunity during funeral orations for Correta Scott King to viciously attack George W. Bush and the war on terror, making parallels between wiretapping done in the 1960's when Martin Luther King Jr. was fighting for civil rights and the current-day attempts to keep terrorists at bay by the Bush administration. "Liberals found Carter's denouncement of Bush (during funeral proceedings for Coretta Scott King) a bit of magical timing" when in fact, it was just another example of the unholy pat-down the left give the dead when they feel they have a bit of clout remaining to capitalize on.

When it comes to the yearly observance of the life of Martin Luther King Jr., Barack Obama is neither the first nor will he be the last liberal to rob for profit the name and beliefs of this fine man. However, the president has made arrogance and hypocrisy into a fine art, and once again seized the chance to pilfer the well-pilfered corpse of the civil rights activist, and to do it with unique Obama flare. In his memorial speech to Dr. King, Barack Obama managed to blame George W. Bush for the nation's current woes, urge the nation to support both of his socialistic initiatives in government healthcare and cap and trade, and then, as if challenging the rafters of the church to fall in on him, instructed the Christian assembly as well as the nation to promote the gay and lesbian lifestyle. Yep, he did it, but then again, who said grave robbers aren't bold?

Since leaving the Trinity United Church of Christ in Chicago, Obama has been reported to seldom attend church in Washington, as if after leaving the warm embrace of two decades of Jeremiah Wright, nowhere else just seems like home. Regardless of Obama's absence from a weekly spot in the church pews, he can more than carry his own weight when it comes to pick-pocketing the dearly departed to advance the agenda of liberalism.

I have mentioned that some of the liberal deceivers come right out of Hollywood. I should say from the start that not every Hollywood actor or singer is a Pinko-Commie-Latté-Drinking-America-Hater. But if I had a nickel for everyone that was, well, I would probably be living in Hollywood. The problem is that there are way too many. Also, we tend to want to love them all. I will give another example for people my age: Sean Penn, a liberal nut job who gives bear hugs to the communist Hugo Chavez and always has a whole lot of bad things to say about

America. I have no use for the man. However, for years, one of my favorite movie scenes came from Sean Penn's performance as Jeff Spicoli in *Fast Times at Ridgemont High*. This is one of those movies my mother would certainly not have approved of, but I am still overwhelmed with laughter when I watch the verbal exchanges between Sean Penn's character, Jeff Spicoli, and the extremely talented Ray Walston, who played the no-nonsense teacher Mr. Hand. It's Penn's best work by far. While we can appreciate their work at their day jobs, problems arise when actors become activists and show their true liberal side. The fond relationship between the actor and the public has to be severed in favor of authentic political commentary rather than the Hollywood dog-and-pony show. In March 25, 2010, I had to write about one of those breaks between myself and Tom Hanks and my refusal to accept his Anti-American propaganda war movie, *The Pacific*.

Hanks for the New Memories: A look at the Skewed Mentality of Hollywood

Some wonder how the Hollywood elite manage to make movies, build castles on prime real estate, fill their factory-sized garages with foreign sports cars, and still find the time to impress the great unwashed with their unequaled intelligence on political matters. As is often the case, sometimes it is best to stick with your day job.

With the release of the HBO military special *The Pacific*, Tom Hanks, while talking about his new film series, characterized World War II as a war of racism and terror and paralleled it with today's war on terror. These statements are unfortunate for two reasons. The first reason is that they create a negative wind around what may be another well-created Hanks/Spielberg production. Of course, even more heckling will come from the fact that while he is a masterful actor-producer in front of and behind the camera, Tom Hanks knows nothing of history. Worse yet, Hanks tries to create new memories for the public outside the cinematic screen of World War II, void of the most pivotal event that caused the United States to go to war with Japan, that being the Japanese attack on Pearl Harbor. Also, Hanks fails to grasp the dynamics of what is taking place in the current war on terror. The battle that is being waged by radical Islamic extremists against the United States and its allies today is not a war on race but a confrontation of ideologies. While Hanks earns only half a star, a "thumbs down," or a low box-office rating at the brain stem for his knowledge of history, he certainly does not stand alone.

When we look to Hollywood, there is an overwhelming tendency to find great actors that have a skewed mentality of the world. Through the politically correct dialogue of today, we are urged to describe these individuals as moderates, progressives, or whatever is the smallest imposition to everyone, especially those in question. For conservatives like myself, I find the need to pitch such deceptions as one would a faulty script and call these lurid, leering, latte-loving lunatics what they really are — the modern day liberal.

In defense of Hanks, he is simply one of a long line of Hollywood liberals who have uttered nonsensical statements that have been spread throughout mainstream media. In 1988, *Cheers* TV star Ted Danson stated that the oceans would be dead with the rest of humanity within the following 10 years. Obviously, Danson's words of oceanic wisdom were faulty, and when it comes to facing his detractors for this environmental doomsday prediction, Danson may be slow to go where everybody knows his name.

Additionally, in a sad conga line of silly statements and character-defining actions, Hollywood liberals Danny Glover, Harry Belafonte, and most notably Sean Penn found the public spotlight at the altar of communist dictator Hugo Chavez. Penn, who served as Chavez's most utilized puppet, was reported by the Associated Press in 2007 to be present with the Venezuelan dictator in Caracas as Chavez repeatedly attacked President George Bush and the war on terror. Chavez characterized Americans as a duped populace restricted from fomenting revolution only by their ignorance of the evils of the Bush administration.

It's always a toss-up as the envelope is opened but I think the "cake taker" of liberal wackiness is still held by movie star and former bully of *The View*, Rosie O'Donnell. O'Donnell decided to allow her hatred of the war on terror to cause her to defy common sense as she stated that 9/11 was the first time that fire had melted steel. Besides the fact that fire is how you melt steel, Popular Mechanics' 2006 book *Debunking 9/11 Myths* made short work of O'Donnell's conspiracy theories on Tower 7 with scientific data on the melting point of steel and the temperature at which steel loses its (structural) strength. Oh Rosie, Rosie, Rosie.

So what gives these Hollywood elitists such a skewed, anti-American view of the world? What makes them take time from their busy and lucrative careers to seek out the vilest communist dictators to help spread propaganda against their own countrymen? What it is not is a product of their money, houses, cars, facelifts, or fancy bling-bling. The foundation behind the skewed mentality of many in Hollywood is nothing more than an elaborate, sugar-filled version of the ideology of the modern day liberal found in every place in America. For regular folks, you just have to apply a little low-budget imagination to prove this true. Think of your neighbor with the Obama 2008 rainbow sticker on their Smart Car in the driveway and the "Ration Toilet Paper for Mother Earth" sign in the yard. Deposit 20 million dollars in his or her bank account and *Voila!* You're living next to Tom Hanks, Rosie O'Donnell, or the equivalent.

Whether this truth makes Tom Hanks and others a little more ordinary or your liberal neighbor a little more exotic is for you to decide, but decide quickly as liberals of all tax brackets would love for you to share their skewed mentality of the world. For me, it's "Hanks, but no Hanks!" Feel free to share that with your liberal neighbor next door.

I originally thought I would devote a full chapter to the Tea Party, because I write so much about their work in various grassroots groups across the country. However, when I started writing this book I found that the Tea Party has experienced so many different obstacles, challenges, and victories that it was better to discuss their influence throughout the book in all of the topic areas and in all the different arenas in which these patriots have dealt with and surpassed expectations.

An issue surrounding the Tea Party that had me reaching for the Tylenol bottle was a 2010 article written by David Frum entitled, "Tea Party is a turn-off for US Moderates." David Frum is a former speech writer for George W. Bush, which made his liberal propaganda more painful to read than if it had come from the usual blowhards. Ever have a family member steal money from you? It is much more painful than being the victim of a random theft. You feel violated in both cases, but, when betrayed by one of your own, it is like a knife through the heart. For the conservative movement, we must always be on the lookout for liberals operating in false conservative clothing. You've seen these folks, the disruptors in the conservative chat rooms who hide behind created names and profess to be as patriotic as George Washington, but want to argue with everyone and use Obama-like talking points. Or worse, liberals who hold their tongues in the chat rooms until opportune moments, when they nicely suggest strategies that are completely self-destructive to Republicans and conservatives. Have you come across these folks? Most likely you have, and when they are exposed they are usually termed "trolls." Well, trolls don't just operate on the computer. These trolls may run for school board, they may be teaching your child's 5th grade class, and they may infiltrate other places where you may presume traditional values will be represented. For a conservative movement to succeed, we need to build our numbers, and those numbers must be true believers in the cause. David Frum was a troll, a classic deceiver, but for some conservatives, he was also like family. This former Bush speech writer was advocating for more liberals, (which he called "moderates") in the Republican Party. In other words, Frum wanted Republicans to include more of the very people who have been killing the party from within. Frum's argument was an attempt to further liberalize the Republican Party, and to attack the conservative movement that has blossomed within the Tea Party. What was his plan? Frum's strategy was to widen the divisions that had been lingering between Republicans and the Tea Party going into the November 2010 mid-term election. The Tea Party groups, along with other conservatives around the country, carried the Republican Party into the winner's circle in the mid-term despite deceivers like David Frum.

Get Out of My Tent! Fruming over the Tea Party Movement

What does it mean to be a Republican? What does it mean to be a Democrat? Are they both the same? The answer is no they are not, well not completely. I was disheartened to read David Frum's article, "The Tea Party is a turn-off for US moderates," not simply because it misrepresents the Tea Party movement which is usually the activity of angry liberals, but it also once again muddies the waters as to why we have a two-party system.

Frum frames the Tea Party activists as radical and angry people which makes me believe that he most likely has never attended these events and never met the people who come to show their support for America. There is also a major disconnect in Frum's reality of the liberal media and this movement. Contrary to Frum's belief, the Tea Party has never been portrayed by the media as an unstoppable force. Actually, if anything, these gatherings that take place all over the country have been downplayed in every possible way. In his assessment of the Tea Parties, Frum sounded more like Keith Olbermann than a former speech writer for George W. Bush. He implies that liberalism within the Republican Party is a needed working part of its existence. Frum calls them the "moderate faction" of the Republican Party, and he indicates that it is they who are offended by these angry activists. He scoffs at the Republicans for rejecting Arlen Specter and thinks it would have been a good strategy to have kept this liberal under the Republican tent.

There is obviously a major disconnect here that needs addressing. I will do so now as someone who has attended many Tea Parties as a speaker, master of ceremonies and often just as a proud American concerned about the future of this country. Tea Party goers are not angry, misguided people. They are not radicals unless limited government, controlled spending, the Constitution and traditional American values are radical ideas. If these ideas are to be placed within the category of "radical" then let my name be placed there as well.

I believe that the Tea Party movement is due partly to the Republican Party's failure to be a true tent in which conservative values can be found. Too many donkey tails are sticking out from under the Republican tent. In this, Frum is inadvertently correct; the liberals who hide in the vague title of "moderate" do exist in the Republican Party, and they have all but destroyed it. Barack Obama is the direct byproduct of the political breakdown of the two-party system. The Tea Party movement is not a Republican movement, but it has served to pull the party further toward conservative values, and that is a positive thing. Why? Because the Republican Party can and should take back the mantle as the party of conservative values. They are the only viable option.

If we follow Frum's advice we simply keep stuffing more donkeys under the Republican tent. This is subsequently what liberals call rational thinking. This action might avoid the debate over the need for perfection in Tea-Party-supported candidates but it continues to feed the disease of liberalism that is destroying the country. Attend a Tea Party and you will see regular Americans that understand the effects of liberalism. If Frum is right then core values are negotiable and victories at the cost of the soul of this nation are events worthy of jubilation. If Frum is right then the so-called moderates of the Republican Party will silence the people of the Tea at the polls and they will be forever viewed as angry militants. But if he is wrong, let's say, as wrong as wrong has ever been, then the Tea Party movement may embody exactly what has to be done, and just in the nick of time. If this is true then the Frum mentality must be told, "Get out of my tent!"

"We can make you better than before, better, faster, stronger." These were the words said by Oscar Goldman as bionic implants were placed within the body of astronaut Steve Austin in the television series, *The Six Million Dollar Man*. In the 1970s television series, Steve Austin's body had been enhanced by the highly secretive governmental department called, the Office of Scientific Intelligence (OSI). Following Austin's bodily "improvements," he went around doing good and putting bad guys in their place. Well, there are a whole bunch of people right now that want to help Americans young and old improve their bodies and just be better people. They also come from the government, though not from a branch quite as secretive as the fictitious OSI. They come with smiling faces like that of San Francisco Mayor Gavin Newsome, New York Governor David Paterson, and the fashionista of "junk-trunk" exacerbating wardrobes, Michelle Obama. They all want to make you better by denying you dietary freedoms of choice that are "high in carbs." Rule of thumb to avoiding the liberal health-deceivers: just because an initiative is wrapped around the word "health" does not mean it is good for you. Always ask the question "Do I get something equal or greater than what I give up?" See if healthy options in those initiatives will be optional or forced. Why would they be forced? Because liberals most often find it's not in their best interest to give the American people an option when it comes to health initiatives. You see, in the eyes of liberals the average American just can't be trusted to do the "proper" thing. Lastly, see if those who are pushing the health initiatives are actually living by the same code they are trying to force on others. This can be very revealing, and is the only reason I would use the term "junk-trunk" and Michelle Obama in the same sentence. On July 23, 2010, I was investigating the standard rhetoric of liberal health deceivers, and you can bet that their good intentions mask the usual liberal expansion of government and limiting of personal freedom. I titled the article, "Obamaca: Reshaping Society Through Government Control." It's not about stopping education on health issues, it's the fact that free people should not be forced to fit the agenda of what a hand full of government elites feel is a better health plan for the nation.

Obamaca: Reshaping Society Through Government Control

In 1997, under the direction of Andrew Niccol, people viewed on their cinema screens a sterilized world of growing government perfection. The movie, "Gattaca," depicted a world where through genetic selection only children with their parents' desired hereditary traits were given societal acceptance. The children that were born naturally, void of the process called preimplantation genetic diagnosis, were labeled "in-valids" and were treated as societal junk and placed in menial labor jobs. To the elites of this futuristic world, this made for a more productive humanity. Like liberals today, the power wielders of this science fiction story wanted to make their version of a better, more productive and certainly healthier society, and to do that they needed the power of the government. Gattaca was a world of sterilized government control where the "haves" and the "have nots" of social class warfare could be identified with the technological speed of an eye scan, cheek swab or blood test.

It would be easy to leave these Orwellian-style cinematic depictions of worlds with governments running amuck at the doors of the theatre if it weren't for the disquieting reality that society seems to mirror these movies at an alarming rate. One has only to look to recent events to see that it is the modern liberal of today that works feverishly to build the Gattaca of tomorrow. Ed Morrissey of Hot Air reported on July 6, 2010 of New York Governor David Paterson's attempt to tax the fat out of people, with a high-profile levy on sugary drinks. The ultra-liberal, get-your-Gattaca-here Mayor Gavin Newsom achieved level one of calorie control in his sphere of influence by declaring Coke, Pepsi, and Fanta Orange as in-valid and thus rejecting them from city vending machines and exchanging them for soy and rice milk.

If you think that you can avoid having to choke down Newsom's rice milk by simply avoiding San Francisco, you are not seeing the bigger picture. Liberals wish to control every aspect of human life. This is a desire based not simply on their warped belief that they know better than average citizens how average citizens should live, but also on the less altruistic reality that liberals like to wield power through government control. Of these liberal builders of a bigger, better and much bolder government of tomorrow are the Obamas. As president, Barack Obama has expanded government control into the private industries, the banks, health care and soon the energy by which all of these entities operate. Michelle Obama, well she wants to build a better tomorrow by way of your children.

As reported in Politico, with Michelle Obama's outlet on LetsMove.gov, the first lady tries aggressively to move beyond simple nutrition education and into the world of liberal mandates when it comes to school food. Michelle Obama was quoted by Politico as saying, "Kids are malleable, and they're also open to learn. We're the ones that stand in the way." She further states, "We're going to have to step it up and make some changes on our own to get our kids where we want them to be." Within this same vein she spoke about her future plans to eliminate school desserts and push her agenda to the public forefront, at the level of attention given to the AIDS epidemic. In other words, move over Newsom, with you rice-milk-filled city vending machines, it's the Obamas who wish to draw up the master blueprints to a healthier world through government control. The effects in the schools are moving quickly. Alison Bologna of Fox News Boston reports that children are now being sent home with "fat reports." The school is reported to be required to calculate the body mass index (BMI) of children to decide what portions they are allowed to eat. The "valids" and "in-valids" at school will now be determined by the governmental BMI.

Is this assessment nothing more than fear mongering, an attempt to falsely portray a soon-coming world of "Obamaca" where only science fiction really exists? Some will say so even as Barack Obama expands the government into every part of the economy and Michelle Obama trots school desserts into the parking lot to be shot. I say that any time government mandates supersede education and free choice, we move further away from what America stands for, and what had made this blessed nation great. Freedom — it's as American as apple pie with all the glorious calories.

In the early summer of 2010, I had Jason Mattera, author of the book, *Obama Zombies* on my radio program, "Conscience of Kansas." Mattera is a very young man. He is full of energy and has a positive spirit, but equally as important, he sees the bigger picture about liberals and what they are doing to the country. He is also a valuable asset to our growing conservative movement from the perspective of tactics and strategies. I will keep stressing throughout this book that victory comes from winning the numbers game. In every endeavor the conservative movement undertakes, our numbers must be overwhelming. Mattera's book discusses, among many other things, how Obama's superior marketing campaign helped him win the presidency in 2008. In this article published on April 8, 2010, I make the case for true conservative values and also for a massive initiative using modern technology to represent and promote traditional values to the people of this country.

Techno-Politics: The War for Downloadable Supremacy

It used to be that the world was a place of "hands." Every important exchange came slowly and directly through face-to-face conversations sealed with a handshake or a newspaper placed in the palm and digested by the slow and deliberate hand turning of the page. Today's modern world offers a plethora of almost mindboggling opportunities to reach vast numbers of people with the mere extension of a fingertip. When it comes to the ideological battle continually being waged between political forces, there has never been a better opportunity for conservatives to dominate by shear majority of numbers than now, but that is not happening.

Most struggle to some degree to answer the question of why a nation with an overwhelming majority of conservatives finds itself with the most liberal congress in modern times and a socialist president who tells the American people in his primary campaign speeches that the most prosperous nation on earth is in need a "fundamental transformation," and he wins!

The most intelligent conservative thinkers usually surmise that the Republican losses in 2006 and 2008 were hinged on the following: fiscal irresponsibility, political correctness, poorly articulated values, and too many wishy-washy politicians under the Republican tent. The analysis usually starts and ends there. It's not a bad list as all are true, but it lacks one critical addition, which without acknowledgment makes future conservative victories doubtful. This lacking component, which plagued the 2008 election as badly as John McCain's inability to be the rock-solid conservative when one was needed, was the GOP's total failure to harness modern technology to disseminate their message.

Jason Mattera's book *Obama Zombies* lays out in a detailed fashion how the Barack Obama campaign machine used technology to not only lift a Democratic presidential candidate to a cult-like persona, but also to maximize social networks that got people to the polls in numbers, outworking and outperforming John McCain. Mattera's book is a remarkable read once you absorb the mental impact of *Facebook* and *Youtube* in electing a presidential candidate with no qualifications to govern and no vision for the future that cannot be referenced from Karl Marx's *Communist Manifesto* and Saul Alinsky's *Rules for Radicals*.

Mattera's book focuses on the youth and how Obama's campaign machine used social networks to bring in new voters and coordinate rallies and events like free rock concerts for the purpose of creating future Obama Zombies. They were more than successful in this endeavor, and the fundamental reality that elections have consequences has never been more forcefully shown to the American people.

So while Barack Obama and his surrogates in the Democratic Party continue to inflame the majority of this nation, don't count them out. Why? Because right now on some computer, somewhere, they are live streaming and excuse, they are downloading some spin, they are twittering a tantalizing tall tale of twisted half-truths or its equivalent without an adequate conservative challenge. Conservatives must engage in the war of techno-politics that is raging. Liberals today use their mastery and organization of technology and the "power of the download" to tell the young and old to hate and fear conservatives such as Sarah Palin for using the term "reload." The rebuttal to such attacks by the liberal left must be felt in endless volleys of terabytes that shake the world's information systems to their foundations. Any efforts less than this are the same as tossing messages in corked bottles into the ocean. For those of you with slow downloading capability, here it is one more time: America needs a president that adheres to traditional conservative values and can articulate that clear message to the American people, but if that message is not allowed to resonate fully through modern technologies, it's four more years of Barack Obama.

For the Tea Party movement in particular, the signing of Obama's socialist healthcare plan into law was a tremendous slap in the face of conservatives. The way the President responded to Tea Party opposition only added insult to injury. As anti-tax Tea Parties were taking place all over the nation on April 15, 2010, and the American people were showing their anger over high taxes and Obamacare, the President was incongruously looking for a pat on the back. On April 16, 2010, the Associate Press reported that President Obama was said to be amused by the anti-tax Tea Party protests which had been taking place around tax day. Obama told people at a fundraiser in Miami that he'd cut taxes, contrary to the claims of protesters. Specifically, in the face of widespread public opposition Obama said of protestors, "You would think they'd be saying thank you" (Real Clear Politics, 2010). This is part political deception from the President, but it also demonstrates his detachment from reality. In that moment, Barack Obama reminded me of a deranged King shouting edicts from a castle tower. You make the call.

Barack Obama: Another Grasp at the Crown?

We here in the United States have long since separated ourselves from our former position as a colony of England. In doing so it would seem that our people's direct interaction with a king as our designated sovereign would be forever over, but is it? It is painfully apparent that currently Barack Obama seems more accurately described as a king than a U.S. president.

First, and most painfully obvious, Barack Obama has recreated the "taxation without representation" scenario that led to the American Revolution as though he were rigidly following a historical script. Eliminating the Bush tax cuts, implementing a socialistic healthcare bill that will require higher taxes, and starting Cap & Tax in the wings have placed the colonial-style yoke of oppression on the American people. Equally as disheartening to the subjects of Obama, is that this president has the same royal disdain and mental detachment from the reality of the growing anger of his subjects as did King George III. From his perch within the walls of the White House, Barack Obama was reported to be "amused" by the millions of Americans protesting in Tea Parties around the country. His flippant attitude was much worse when he showed his complete break with reality by attacking Tea Party-goers saying that they should "thank him" for the dire economic situation in the country that the president has created.

Second, as was pondered during the times of the great Kings, Americans today argue amongst themselves as to whether our President is crazy, dangerously misguided, or just plain evil. Hereditary fits of insanity were shadows upon some of the royal bloodlines of the past. During the War of the Roses King Henry VI was periodically locked away with fits of insanity as was King George III while the colonists fought a revolution. Can we watch as our president drains the American coffers dry and then borrows from our competitors in China until the country is no longer economically viable, without asking where the sanity in this course of action is? Are we simply to smile politely as Obama tells the masses of unemployed that his reckless spending and government expansion can now be considered a historic success? In these dark days of American woe might we find it prudent to bring back bloodletting and exorcisms in the search of a cure for the mental disorder of liberalism that surely affects the king?

Third, what we do know is that Obama, like past Kings, has acted to amass power by bringing the competition (free market) under the royal tent. You can call it socialism, communism, or whatever term is still legal to utter within the realm, but they all include a powerful dictator with random arbitrary edicts flying left and right that benefit only those in power. They all include extended government control and loss of individual freedom. They all end in slavery, suffering, and death.

While the United States is quickly sinking under the weight of its growing debt, Obama is portrayed as a savior, not unlike the kings of the past that were seen as divine in nature. The Obama camp has simply replaced the term "divine" with "historical," but the same projection of mystical power is still modeled, and it remains an act of heresy to question the validity of this title.

Some in the country fear that the president will take one of the many momentous calamities that he has brought about and use it to seize permanent control of the country and avoid being removed from the throne in 2012. These ideas would seem far-fetched if it were not for the fact that we know kings actually do crazy things. The saving grace from our knowledge of the kings with their destructive nature and irresponsible ways is that they often underestimate their subjects. Americans have already shown one king that we will not be slaves, and it is time to show another

The Washington Post's deception of the American people was an interesting incident to cover. It centered on David Weigel, who was the Post's token conservative, who often covered Tea Party events and talked at length on conservative issues. He often smelled a little "lefty," if you know what I mean, but the Post defended him and their objectivity in having a "conservative" to balance out their liberal commentators and reporters. Then Weigel was exposed by Matt Drudge, who you may remember as the guy who broke the national story about Bill Clinton's DNA sample on Monica Lewinsky's dress. If you remember that little bit of White House drama, your prize for such a quick recollection is… A cigar! Moving on. David Weigel was exposed as a conservative-hating liberal. Remember our talk about trolls? In this article I lay the accountability for the deception on the Washington Post, which should have either vetted Weigel to get a real conservative, or explained to the American people that they really didn't want a balanced political lineup of writers. Beware of deceivers who cloak themselves in well established organizations and companies. Deception is deception, even if it comes with a corporate seal.

Burning Drudge, Burning Weigel: A Fiery View from the Washington Post

The forced resignation of David Weigel by the Washington Post will probably be forgotten by tomorrow, nothing more than a little blip on the radar of those submersed in the world of the Washington Post. Weigel's online communications were nabbed and made public to expose the writer as a liberal who thinks Matt Drudge should set himself on fire and that conservatives are inherently doing evil. If you are a conservative you might shake your head, grit your teeth, or even laugh at some of Weigel's private meanderings about the opposition. What you would not be is surprised. The Washington Post wants you to think that they are awe-struck and amazed, as if their writer were suddenly part of an E-True Hollywood story in which never-before-seen hidden details are suddenly being illuminated. Please.

Howard Klutz reported in the Washington Post that their Executive Editor Marcus Brauchli said, "We can't have any tolerance for the perception that people are conflicted or bring a bias to their work. . . . There's abundant room on our website for a wide range of viewpoints, and we should be transparent about everybody's viewpoint." This is a vague statement at best, more than a little silly at worst. The fact of the matter is that all writers, even the freest of thinkers, bring at least some bias to the table and editors know this. In fact, beyond their ability to creatively communicate with the public, writers, bloggers, you name it, are sought for their general political leanings. This is where things may have gone south for Weigel. It appears the Washington Post got caught with a "political lefty" writing as a "political righty." Who placed David Weigel writing the column titled "Right Now — Inside the conservative movement and Republican Party" That's right, the Washington Post.

So who is at fault here? If you say it's the Rush-Limbaugh-hating, Tea-Party-hating, Matt-Drudge-wanna-see-ya-burn liberal Weigel, you're wrong. The fault lies directly with the Washington Post for failing to screen the people they hire, or worse, for purposely deceiving the public. If you want to critique a liberal for his or her wacky statements, that's fine, we can make a day of it, but don't think its transparency of viewpoint that the Washington Post is protecting; it's their gluteus maximus. Bloggers are not insidious double agents, or at least never effective ones, and Weigel is no exception. To think so gives the Washington Post political cover they have not earned. In fact, I think they have earned the need for some additional scrutiny.

So, in the aftermath of the private e-mails made public, David Weigel's career at the Washington Post will be burned away, and for what, being a closet liberal? Howard Kurtz of the Washington Post reports that in 2006 Weigel referred to gay marriage opposers as "anti-gay marriage bigots" on his Twitter page. Think we might be dealing with a liberal here? This was obviously not a red flag to the Washington Post. Brauchli blamed it on the budget and said, "We don't have the resources or ability to do Supreme Court justice-type investigations into people's backgrounds. We will have to be more careful in the future." Does that explanation fly with you? I think it is not a far cry to assume that the Washington Post was more than comfortable with their writing arrangement with Weigel until their employee's point of view became overtly known to the public. Then it was transparency time. A time for purity and as the witch hunters say, nothing purifies like fire, or a good firing. Hopefully when the smoke clears there will be some interest left in finding accountability for the Washington Post.

Beware of deceivers who will hold out Big Bird, Ernie, or Bert as a quasi-human shield in one hand and slice you up with the liberal sword in the other. That is the way public tax funded organizations such as NPR and the Public Broadcasting Service do business. National Public Radio may have programming which is enjoyable and even educational to the public; however, should everyone in America pay through taxes to fund their operation? The answer is no. Why? Because, NPR is not any more neutral than Rush Limbaugh when it comes to political and social rhetoric. I personally think the "Maharushi" provides a public service to the country, but liberals would never accept having their taxes go to funding his projects and ideology, and they should not have to. That is why we have a free market where popular content that is well-created and sought after can flourish. If you don't like a certain kind of free market content on the radio or television you can turn your back on it. Millions of radio listeners do that very thing to conservatives like Rush Limbaugh every day. Fortunately for Limbaugh, millions of radio listeners also decide to tune in and follow his program. We are told by its political supporters that the public gets many positive things from NPR and PBS. The question is this—if they're so successful and valuable, why can't they thrive on private funds rather than taxpayer dollars? Groups like PBS and NPR deceive America by arguing that they use so little public funds that it should not matter, but then fight like wild dogs to keep that strong-armed cash coming. Why do they act this way? It is because NPR and PBS are overtly liberal organizations. NPR ruthlessly fired Juan Williams (Marsh, 2011), a highly capable liberal pundit in their employ when he appeared to have positions that might mirror conservative thought on Muslims and air travel. Reported by Marsh (2011) for Reuters, the House successfully voted on March 17, 2011, to defund NPR by a vote of 228-192. The vote came in the aftermath of the James O'Keefe sting operation that yielded video and audio footage of a chief NPR fundraiser openly attacking members of the Tea Party and the Republican Party. Liberals in the Senate will fight this effort to defund public radio and it will take the power and influence of a strong conservative movement to make groups like NPR and PBS sink or swim with the quality and popularity of their programming content. Liberals are dusting off and playing old footage of Mr. Rogers giving congressional testimony on the need for taxpayer cash for shows such as "Mr. Roger's

Neighborhood." At the time of the Rogers testimony, Richard Nixon was contemplating cutting public funding for PBS to fight the war in Vietnam. Could Mr. Rogers have afforded to be "your neighbor" if the government had not forced the entire neighborhood (taxpayers) to partially fund his show? We need a little honesty from the government and these pick-pocket-public-broadcasting-people. Let me just say, in the most beautiful way, "Won't you please, won't you please, please won't you be, truthful." On October 30, 2010, I wrote an article entitled, "National Public Radio and the Skinny Fat Man" to highlight name change deceptions taking place with organizations that just must have your tax dollars.

National Public Radio and the Skinny Fat Man

I once knew a guy who was about 50 pounds overweight. Any time a friend or family member would address him on the issue of cutting out the sweets, he would get indignant and quickly inform inquiring souls that he was completely fit in all areas except his midriff, which he would address in his own good time. We might surmise that from this gentleman's thinking he thought his body was nothing short of a series of physical quadrants of which he had worked to address all but a final set of coordinates: his stomach. More than likely, the man was just fat and did not like being told so.

Brian Montopoli of CBS News tells us that National Public Radio no longer goes by that name; it's NPR now. Well, I mean, the legal name is still National Public Radio as it has been for the last 40 years but they now request their brand name "NPR" be the title spoken on air. Why? Like a fat man demanding that he be called "Speedo-challenged" instead of simply overweight, National Public Radio is trying to run the fat-man scam on Americans. Montopoli talks about conservative pundits like Sarah Palin who call for cutting off public funding to National Public Radio and he insinuates that Palin is misguided as the federal funds the non-profit organization receives are considered by him as minimal. While the overall percentage may be less than 10 percent of their total budget, NPR receives millions of public tax dollars yearly. The case Montopoli forwards is as compelling an argument as when our gentleman friend with the mild protuberance tells us he has reduced his daily cupcake intake from twelve to nine of the tasty treats. Of course, the point is that he should not eat any, especially if we the American people have to flip the bill for the indulgence.

The public funding issue with National Public Radio comes to the forefront because of the firing of NPR contributor Juan Williams. Williams, who had been employed by NPR for a decade, was fired for saying that he gets nervous when he sees passengers in Muslim clothing on a plane. Not only was Williams fired by phone without an option to talk to upper-level NPR staff, a simple courtesy to a journalist of his standing, he was described as psychologically impaired. NPR CEO Vivian Schiller said that Williams' beliefs should stay between him and "his psychiatrist or his publicist." The issue here goes beyond the viciousness of the Juan Williams' job slaying. It goes beyond the fascist nature of NPR and the hypocrisy of such liberal organizations who lament their support for diversity as long as that diversity stays off Fox News. The issue goes as far as asking if Americans should have to fund a liberal radio station such as NPR.

NPR should be allowed to be as liberal as they wish, as fascist as the law will allow — if their product is viable within the free market. It's a free country, but they should not be allowed to push their liberal agenda on the American people's dime. Not on one single taxpayer's dime. That is the issue at hand. That is what exacerbates the Williams tragedy. Montopoli alludes to the idea that despite NPR's vicious attack against a liberal on its own payroll, all is well because Williams has just signed a new contract with Fox News. Of course, this is a diversion from the extended "belly" of the problem. The problem is that National Public Radio, (NPR, if that sounds more private market to you) continues to be fattened with tax dollars they do not deserve. They should be forced to sink or swim in the private market — you know, the real private market. If NPR can flourish within its liberal scheme without a government handout taken from both liberals and conservatives in the country, the opposition has no choice but to accept its existence and engage it in the private market. However, if NPR flies solo within the free market and the wind beneath its wings lifts it only as high as "Air America," then we will know it should have never have been around in the first place. The free market has a way of taking care of dead weight. Now, the American people have the opportunity to address this issue. To do anything less is simply to keep loading the plate of the skinny fat man.

Oh, they are so funny! Meet the liberal deceivers of the comedic world of late night comedy shows. We know they are liberals, and we know that what they say is really crapola because we catch little pieces of conservative bashing within their funny schticks night after night. However, we have a tendency to come back for more laughs and general good-natured political punishment. I am the last person who will attempt to limit a person's joy in life and the positive power of laughter. In fact, I imbue my writing and radio work with humor because conservatives are happy people by nature, much more happy than liberals hands down. What I would say is that liberal humor is at best often tinged with anger and resentment, and the public should be a little more discerning about what they listen to. There is a lot of "funny" out there in the world and conservatives have enough selection to bypass some of the liberal comedians who mix political deception with comedy to make it go down easier. A good laugh should never end in depression. Trust me. You will laugh longer in life that way. In my November 11, 2010 article, Stewart and Colbert: Laughing with the Left Until It Hurts, I take on the not always so funny world of liberal humor.

Stewart and Colbert: Laughing with the Left Until It Hurts

There is just something about humor that makes it inviting in almost every situation. We love to have our funny bone tickled in so many ways, and it is both the joke and its creative delivery that keeps us coming back for more. Good comedy has the power to transcend many a strong grievance and many a harsh battleground. Take politics for instance. There is seldom found a more divisive subject that can be broached between two individuals. Politics has the power to set lifelong friends to physical blows at a high school reunion, or deacons to highly charged whispers of anger while passing the collection plate in church. I think you know what I am saying, and I bet you have been there before. If you haven't, you will be, as assuredly as death and taxes, but there I go talking politics again.

The point is that humor serves as a "pressure relief valve" that allows us all to laugh at ourselves as well as those on the other side of the aisle. Being able to do both is important. Knowing when to do it is a step toward the divine. Everyone seems to have the ability to laugh at their adversaries; however, many do it in ways that demean themselves and the comedic process. When liberals laugh in a red-eyed, frothing frenzy during Michael Moore films they are not paying homage to comedic flair, but instead are simply wallowing in the filth of partisan anger. This is because Michael Moore films are not funny, but are sad in that "I just ran over your puppy and I think I will blame it on your neighbor because he is a successful capitalist" kind of way. To applaud poor comedic attempts, or just plain acts of political sniping, is attacking one's own sense of where true comedy resides.

Then there are true comedians that test our ability to discern funny from mean. Seth MacFarlane is such a comedic talent. Despite being your typical over-the-top liberal activist, he is truly talented. MacFarlane has collaborated in many very funny and creative television shows such as Johnny Bravo, Cow and Chicken and Dexter's Laboratory. MacFarlane's outspoken support for gay rights, atheism, and the legalization of marijuana do not affect his ability to make us laugh when he creates something that is actually funny. Even his adult comedies Family Guy and American Dad are creative and humorous at many turns. Yes I said it, he is funny here too. Unfortunately, MacFarlane brings justified public anger upon himself in the political arena, when he does things such as attacking Sarah Palin's child with Down syndrome.

In this case it is not that conservatives don't have a sense of humor, as many from the right can and do laugh while watching "American Dad," with MacFarlane's indirect joke-poking at former president George W. Bush. What MacFarlane failed to comprehend was that attacking Down syndrome children would not be funny no matter which side of the political aisle you are on. The point is that when it comes to humor, Macfarlane often succeeds and should be acknowledge as funny despite being a liberal. Conversely, when he steps away from creating humor, and is consumed by his liberal nature and becomes mean, he should be acknowledged as a loser.

Thus enter Jon Stewart and Stephen Colbert and "Team Sanity." The liberal comedic duo of over-the-top Colbert with his "ultra-conservative" funnyman shtick and Stewart with his subconscious tendency to be an "angry little man" are running around the country to locations such as the National Mall with their "Rally to Restore Sanity and/or Fear" campaign. Many parts were really funny. There I said it once again. Liberals can be funny and most often it is when they are not being mean. While the event had the feel of comedy, even though it was liberal comedy, John Stewart still found a way of taking a person's smile and turning it upside down with a liberal diatribe about how there is no true division in the country and that negative affairs within the United States are being overblown. This, like Michael Moore and the nasty shades of MacFarlane, kills the event for comedy-seeking conservatives, the same conservatives that may at times flip to Comedy Central and have at least a momentary chuckle. Stewart failed at the National Mall, not just for being wrong about the world in which he lives — we can forgive him that, after all, he is a modern-day liberal. However, we cannot forgive him for not being funny about it.

The point of importance is that political persuasion should not be the gauge by which we decide where humor is found. If it is funny, we should laugh, even if we are at times laughing at ourselves. If it is not funny, to treat it as such, despite the political direction in which the failed attempt is directed, is to purposely demean oneself. It is laughing to the point of hurting one's dignity.

I don't believe it! One of the best ways to deceive people is to do things that are so unbelievable that no one will give your claims any credibility. When I was a young police officer, I was once sitting in an interview room with a local rabble-rouser. This person was being interviwed by a police veteran. The well known troublemaker was attempting to impress the officers present with his jailhouse legal knowledge, especially how at any moment, he could bring the city to its financial knees based on charges of police brutality. His vast array of evidence of police brutality ranged from evil stares to bitter department coffee. At one point during the interview, the police veteran, having become tired of the litany of litigious threats, said to man, "If we wanted to hurt you, we would close that door, and all us cops would get naked and beat you with rubber hoses while sounding off like chickens. Now you just try and get a jury to believe that happened." The troublemaker never mentioned frivolus lawsuits for the remainder of the interview. I promise the reading public that I was never a participant in a naked rubber hose chicken-sounding beat-down during my police career. But that unique situation taught me to think about the value of credibility. When I talk about Barack Obama, I tell people that for the most part, he has said he will do everything he has done while in office. That does not mean that the President has not been the beneficiary of being shielded from scrutiny by the outrageous nature of his life and policies. Almost everything with Barack Obama is so over the top, so outrageous, that it is hard to believe that it can be true. When faced with the hard truth of Obama's policies, liberals simply check out by chanting about "hope and change," and consoling themselves that Obama is "historic." Conservatives tend to freak out when friends and associates are unable to mentally grasp just how much worse off the country is now than it was before

Obama took the reins of office. Over time, the outrageousness of what Obama is doing to this country threatens to force everyone to mentally check out, to give up and just go fishing. Either way, Obama wins. This book hopes to bring readers, by way of the issues discussed, back to the reality that the country is on the edge of collaspe. People have to be made to face the harsh realities of this country's current situation. From that reality, we can work to fix this mess and make a better future.

The Barack Obama Presidency: When Being Unbelievable is the Best Defense

As we step into a new year I take a moment to reflect on what has been attempted and what has been accomplished in the struggle to preserve traditional conservative values in this country. This is a struggle to which I have committed myself for the long haul. Through my radio program "Conscience of Kansas" I have had the opportunity to bring to the radio-listening public some of the country's most renowned conservative minds. The topic they have all addressed in their own unique fashion is sections of Barack Obama's life and his effect on the country in his position as President of the United States.

Speaking about their books, articles and lectures, these individuals boldly stepped to the radio microphone to share their investigations of Barack Obama and their concerns for the future of the United States. Jerome Corsi submitted the question that has still today to be answered on the absence of candidate vetting in the years preceding the 2008 election that would place into power a politician that could not or would not proffer simple qualifying documents such as a long-form birth certificate. David Freddoso outlined the hypocrisy and arrogance of Obama before the country would see it full-blown from the White House steps. Tim Carney, with his sharp mind and energetic zeal, walked listeners through the economic disasters that would befall the country under the Obama agenda. Brad O'Leary gave credence to the attack on Christianity that has become part of the administration's operating procedure. David Limbaugh, when talking with me about the totality of the damage inflicted on the country to date in combination with Obama's nonchalant indifference to voices of opposition, showed his frustration with a strength of emotion that cannot be questioned. The concern that came to mind when listening to Limbaugh as well as these other voices of reason is, "will people believe them?"

I perceive that the problem for believability in cases like these are not based on a lack of factual evidence; on the contrary, the evidence brought against Barack Obama comes with endless pages of easily traceable source material which validate the arguments being forwarded. Since this is the case, it would be reasonable at first glance to assume that Obama would be politically doomed. To say this, however, is to underestimate the psychological advantage that sets in Obama's favor when being faced with the facts of his catastrophic administration. What advantage is that, you ask? The advantage is that the true story of Barack Obama's life and policies in practice, when grouped together, defy belief.

In fact, Barack Obama's life and presidency would be un-publishable as a work of fiction because in its totality, it lacks the realistic foundations that even the most fantastic works of fiction require. To put it plainly, the actions of Barack Obama are so historically over-the-top, so mindboggling in their destructive audacity, that on an average citizen's case-by-case analysis alone they appear to be pure fiction. When the actions of this President are presented in a chronological series, most people suffer a mental overload and simply disengage from attempting to place so many unbelievable pieces of information under their mental "fact" category.

Some of the most creative fiction writers have paralleled limited portions of the Obama history with success. Let's take a look. A fresh politician gains political ascension while being controlled by sinister powerful forces (*The Manchurian Candidate*, 1962). A death-panel-conducive healthcare system that combines utopian ideals with compulsory participation (*Logan's Run*, 1976), or the systematic denegation of society that sees people being completely dependent on government while that same government feeds upon the populace (*Soylent Green*, 1973). How about a government so totalitarian in nature that its citizens are instructed to turn in (flag) their neighbors when they challenge aspects of the government's agenda (*Nineteen Eighty-Four*, 1949) or one that turns its back on the biblical foundations of childbirth to embrace an atheistic, eugenic vision of the future (*Brave New World*, 1932; *Gattaca*, 1997)? Even individuals like Obama who appear to have the uncanny ability to draw vermin and other pestilence to their proximity have been documented into fictional works (*Amityville Horror*, 1977). The most compelling piece of fiction that Barack Obama has put into motion is the "all is well" scenario as seen in his "Summer of Recovery" tour while unemployment continued to hang near 10 percent (The Matrix, 1999).

If you tried to publish even a limited grouping of Obama parallels from reality to fiction, your piece would be rejected and you would be told it was too overwhelming, too grisly and too unbelievable. Publishers would tell you to tone it down, make it more like real life. This is what political writers face when attempting to counter the Obama agenda. To expose Obama, the opposition must expose the truth and in doing so readers are taken to the edge of their sanity. The President has, to a greater extent, been able to hide behind the outrageousness of his decisions. Still the battle for the acknowledgement of reality must continue. Personally, if the American people fail to take hold of the reins of government, I fear the future of America will fall somewhere among the realities of *Red Dawn* (1984), *Mad Max* (1979) and *Planet of the Apes* (1968).

Beware deceivers who use tragic violent events as pretenses to beat down their political opponents. That is the opposite of grieving together as a nation when catastrophes take place. Here is an example of how a tragedy once brought people together. When the Space Shuttle *Challenger* disaster occurred on Tuesday, January 28, 1986, the country was in a state of shock. We mourned collectively and gave respect and honor to those brave astronauts that had tragically died. No one was naïve about the fact that down the road there would be investigations, blame and much finger pointing, but for the immediate time following the tragedy, we simply came together and mourned. This was not the case in the tragic Arizona shooting of Gabrielle Giffords and other patrons who were present at an Arizona grocery store in January of 2011. This terrible situation should have been a time of national sorrow; instead, it became a liberal excuse for a propaganda festival attacking the Tea Party, Sarah Palin, the Republican Party, and conservatives in general. It was another example of liberals attempting to manipulate the people when the nation's emotions were on edge.

The Do's and Don'ts of Sheriff Dupnik: Another Ploy to Silence Conservatives

The recent shooting in Tucson, Arizona, that critically injured Democratic Representative Gabrielle Giffords as well as killing six other innocent citizens brings the nation again to attempting to find reasons where they are least likely to be found. At this time authorities are still discovering many of the details; however, it has been reported that the shooter in the incident, Jared Lee Loughner, was a mentally unstable individual.

In almost all cases that involve the taking of an innocent life, the quest to find the answers as to why such atrocities take place is never adequately found. This comes in part because there is no answer for loved ones being prematurely taken from this earth that can ease the pain for those that remain. We all know and have grudgingly come to accept the nature cycle of life and the shooting in Arizona violates all that we hold acceptable when it comes to death. Unfortunately, the case of the Arizona shootings is at risk of being misdirected from honoring the dead and helping to heal the injured to promoting political agendas based on a false premise.

When I heard Pima County Sheriff Clarence Dupnik start a political speech at the press briefing following the shooting, I could see the writing on the wall, "Conservatives need to shut up." Having spoken to the media about criminal matters as a former law enforcement officer, I perceive Dupnik's personal attack on those in radio and television as nothing short of bizarre. The links he drew between bigotry, national vitriol and this particular incident appeared politically motivated and makes him sound like a liberal no matter where his true affiliations stand. He is right about one thing: free speech does have consequences, but not the consequences the sheriff was trying to convey. The founding fathers supported free speech because they knew that through standing up and saying, "I don't agree," and "this is not right," and other words often spoken with great passion, that this country might break free from its shackles. The need for such free debate with all its emotion is still needed today if we hope to deny those that wish totalitarian rule back into this country.

The problem Sheriff Dupnik suffers from at best is that he has confused peaceful, passionate opposition with violence. He has failed to separate the actions of a nut with a gun from those of peaceful Americans that are fed up with the government and want to take back the reins. The American people are not acting like bigots, criminals or killers when they demand that the government exercise the people's will with the power voters have temporarily given it. From Dupnik's lips to the computer keyboards of the radical left, the demands for conservatives to be silent have begun.

In my morning e-mail inbox the usual daily assortment of angry liberal messages had distinct focus this week thanks to Sheriff Dupnik. The demands that I stop talking and writing about political issues included a laundry list of forbidden topics as is always the case, but this week they were unified in that my silence would now "stop the hate as seen in Arizona," and "save lives." Please. I was quick to give a physical address of where they could send their requests. Hint: it's a place warmer than Arizona.

Violence like what took place in this shooting incident is unacceptable, period. However, attempting to silence groups because of a single individual who might be associated, or is fictitiously associated, as a fringe member is the sorriest of Saul-Alinsky-style political maneuvers. Do Christians stop teaching the word of God because there is a rogue in Westboro Baptist Church running around preaching hate? Of course not, and nor should they. Ann Coulter brilliantly documented that it has been a liberal behind all the assassinations of our American presidents throughout history. Does this mean that all liberals are guilty of mixing vitriol and violence, including murder, in their quests for political victory? Even more importantly, should all liberals just shut up for fear that someone nuttier then them may grab a gun and start shooting people? The answer is no to both questions. I say this with full knowledge that in time the Arizona shooter Jared Lee Loughner is just as apt to be found a liberal as he is to be found a Tea Party attendee.

When it comes to Arizona's problems such as an unsecured border and the catastrophic financial burden illegal aliens place on the state and nation, much can and should be discussed in the future. The thing in this case is that the border, illegal aliens, gun ownership, the Tea Party, politically zealous sheriffs, and Sarah Palin are not the real issue. The relevant issue is that a mentally deranged person killed innocent people and there is now tremendous pain and suffering in Tucson, Arizona and the entire nation. The country's "do's and don'ts" list must be constructed with more thought than that of Sheriff Dupnik. The biggest tragedy now would be to focus on imaginary foes and minimize what has truly been lost.

The last deception to be discussed in this chapter is far too common. You've see it many times and I suspect like me, you have become frustrated with the repetitious way these actors orchestrate this trickery, and the dupes who seem to fall for it time and time again. We can call this one the "who's your buddy" deception. Liberals have this ruse down pat. When liberals in the Democrat Party have the power and political advantage, they are ruthless. They don't need to know or care what the other political party has to say. Their concern for bipartisanship is the same concern a steam roller gives to a snail on the highway. However, if their political fates should change, as they did after the 2010 midterm election, when Democrats lost their political majority, then it's time for bygones to be bygones. Liberals wish to play the political game on their terms no matter what their level of political power. The really sad part is that Republicans more often than not play right into this deception. Following the conservative victories in the 2010 midterm election, I wrote a January 21, 2011, article which highlighted my concern that Republicans would be duped into losing their political momentum. I think to some extent I was correct, and this highlights a common inability of the GOP to avoid very overt deceptions.

Democrats Look to Dupe GOP at State of the Union Address

The Democratic Party, if anything, is consistent with their actions. They took advantage of an ideologically weak Republican Party that failed to rein in spending in 2006. Democrats managed to place one of their most liberal politicians into the office of president in 2008 and then proceeded to pass bill after bill that would expand government control by monumental leaps in the hopes of fundamentally transforming the nation.

If we are honest with ourselves, even in this current environment of Obama-buyer's-remorse, in a best-case scenario only a fraction of the damage this administration has brought upon the country will be nullified. Unfortunately, that is the sunny account at best. Why? Because the Republican Party has become notorious for failing to consistently frame the political landscape that all are asked to play on. Equally as detrimental to the country, when an agenda does exist, Republicans have lacked true convictions that motivate others to join the cause.

Compared to the modern-day Republican Party, Democrats work with great efficiency. Foremost has been their ability to frame the political landscape. Consistently through his administration Obama has used a majority vote to ram his agenda through. Democrats have initiated the most socialistic national restructuring program in American history and claim it is emergency help for the middle class. While pushing their liberal agenda, they have framed Republicans as being the heartless party of "No." When Democrats have found one of two liberal Republicans to vote their way the story is framed as a Democrat victory with strong bi-partisan support. The recent past has been a repetition of Democrats initiating and Republicans reacting.

Even the current environment with its potential for a sweeping shift in political power has not been the product of the Republican Party pulling Americans toward the Constitution's call of freedom and conservative values. Far from it — the first round of victories against the Obama machine were made by regular Americans who formed their own meeting tents under which to congregate and strategize for the future of their country. Republicans have been painfully slow to embrace what are for all intents and purposes their base supporters. Groups like the Tea Party and their equivalents defeated Democrats in historical numbers in the last mid-term and literally dragged the Republican Party into the winner's circle. This is not acceptable nor is it repeatable.

There is hope for the GOP; in fact, major victories are more than attainable if they will simply consolidate the party as the place where true conservative values are found. Oh yes, they will also need to have a backbone in conjunction with a well-developed and disseminated message. As important, they will have to avoid allowing Democrats to set the tone for the new Congress and in the ensuing days to the next election. Democrats can see the writing on the wall and they will most certainly attempt to control a Republican surge toward 2012. The next framing of the political landscape will most likely push off with the upcoming State of the Union address. The message from Obama will be for compassion and cooperation with the subtle implication that groups like the Tea Party and other constitutionalists are promoting hate and violence. The Arizona shooting incident, ironically framed in its aftermath by another liberal in Sheriff Clarence Dupnik, will be marked as recent proof of how dangerous life can be when we do not all get along (translation: to be more liberal is to be more reasonable).

David Jackson from USA Today reports that Democrat Charles Schumer of New York and Republican Tom Coburn of Oklahoma say that they will sit together during Obama's annual address in the hopes that congressional colleagues will follow suit. This call for unity is not done because love is in the air. It is a ploy by Democrats to set the stage for the political future because they are losing ground on all fronts. So, while it was full steam ahead with their political agenda when Democrats had a majority vote, now that they can be blocked in the House and potentially routed in 2012, it's time for us all to come together and put the partisan, if not deadly, vitriol as spun by Sheriff Dupnik, away for a more harmonious liberal reality. Once again Democrats wish to frame the political landscape and they hope that Republicans will be foolish enough to go along with it.

This trickery is but one of many schemes that will be spun over the coming months. The GOP will again fall prey to being reactionary pawns in a democratic game unless they set the stage for the future themselves and force Democrats to play by their rules. The truth screams to be told by the GOP if they have the backbone and the vision to see it through to its fruition. The country needs to be brought back to its constitutional foundations and the current tentacles of socialism must be shrugged away with the national disdain it deserves. The restoration of the country requires fiscal responsibility that is quantifiable, not simple lip service.

A true merging of the Tea Party and the Republican Party will be pivotal to achieving voting power in 2012. Instead of adapting to liberal agendas, the GOP must force Democrats to vote against the people's will and thus expose themselves to future elimination at the polls. Republicans should spend their time, such as that during the State of the Union address, to more clearly define themselves as the party of conservative values, and reject falling for another bi-partisan illusion that in the end, simply furthers the liberal Obama agenda.

Chapter 3
Taking Responsibility

Conservatives are naturally drawn to taking responsibility for their actions. This is not vanity, nor an assertion of perfection, it's the truth. People who believe in traditional values make their share of mistakes, and we saw several examples of that in the last chapter. Despite being just as human as everybody else, conservatives are far more likely to admit when they are wrong and to take their lumps for it. The future of this country must be controlled by those who will be responsible for what they do. We need a conservative movement that has the power to affect society for the long-term, to enter and control all facets of government. Only those who are strong enough to take responsibility for their actions and the problems that face this country will be able to meet the challenges ahead of us. This chapter will look at the issue of responsibility from the perspective of government, the individual, and culture.

Let's begin with government at the level of foreign policy. America has to take responsibility for the friendships we make. This does not mean that countries which fall apart internally and become controlled by leaders who hate us have to remain our allies. What it does mean is that countries which ally with us and share our beliefs should be able to depend on America to have their back. That's a responsibility which is incumbent on us. Being a staunch friend of America must mean something in the world if we, as a nation, are to mean something around the world. The responsibility of backing allies has mammoth consequences from a governmental perspective. Again, that's on us as a nation. Liberals have a tendency to think like socialists, and in doing so their friendships tend to be generated by a collective mentality instead of one of mutual reciprocity. You have probably heard some lefties talk about being "citizens of the world." Well, if you are a citizen of the world, America's importance becomes very insignificant. That's probably fine if you are a Martian, but if you are an American and you think this way, there are some negative effects. This kind of thinking makes NGOs like the United Nations have more importance than they should, more importance than what they are worth.

One of the fundamental flaws of the United Nations is not the theoretical intentions of the organization; it is how it performs when the chips are down. The United Nations was constructed with the idea of protecting the world from rogue aggressors. The organization was intended to be a forum where nations could arbitrate their problems through peaceful consensus and reduce the need for armed conflict. It was hoped that NATO would enforce international law and ensure global peace. These were all noble goals. However, the United Nations has been more of a failure than a success. The reasons why the United Nations is a failure go beyond mere corruption. The fundamental reason the United Nations fails to accomplish their main mission of maintaining peace in the world is that they refuse to follow through on their responsibilities. To put it simply, the United Nations is overtly spineless. While liberals lay the responsibility for the war in Iraq on George W. Bush, I lay the lion's share of blame on the United Nation's inability to be anything but a passive enabler of dictators like Saddam Hussein. Just as President George W. Bush took responsibility for the safety of America against Saddam Hussein, Barack Obama should be taking responsibility to protect Israel, one of our best allies. There is no subtlety in Obama's cold relationship with Israel; the President simply does not support this longtime ally. Once again, the President's strange relationship with the Muslim countries of the world appears to push him further from our country's responsibility to stand by our friends and allies. On January 30, 2010, I wrote about the White House's betrayal of Israel, and called for action to actively support our longtime friend.

America and Israel: You Got a Friend in Me?

What is the meaning of friendship? What makes the bonds that we call a true friendship mean something? We have all heard of the fair-weather friend and most likely we have all had one or two of them. The fair-weather friend stays by your side as long as all the conditions of life are optimum. Unfortunately, we often need our friends most when times are bad, and that is when the fair-weather friend often disappears, and in some cases, sides with the forces we are struggling against. "Thanks a lot!" Those may very well be the parting words that pass our lips when we come to the painful realization that not all that play "buddy-buddy" are actually in our corner.

Conversely, a true friend is a powerful force in that it allows for the extension of values and beliefs into places that one might not be able to tread alone. America has had a long history of creating lasting friendships with countries, and those bonds have created economic prosperity and security in many places. For the most part, this country has shown the proper discernment in selecting who will be our business associates in the global economy and who will be allies when the world gets tumultuous. Despite those who like to denigrate this great country, one of America's strongest selling points is that within the global community, this country has been known to come through with what it says it is going to do. With that said, we would be wise to remember that while American exception to remember that while American exceptionalism exists, it does so in conjunction with our ability to make and maintain true friends across the planet.

America's true friends (versus casual business associates) and many of our enemies with which we have politically correct states of "ceasefire" are not hard to identify. True friends share our values and beliefs. Unfortunately, and in conflict with Barack Obama's "olive branch" tactics in many parts of the world, we will never qualify under our belief system as true friends with some on this planet. In fact, because of our beliefs and values, which include our Christian faith, democracy, a belief in freedom and equality, and many others, some will always want to destroy us. Coming back full circle, that is why it is good to have friends.

At the most practical level of thinking, the defense of our true friends is nothing short of a defense of ourselves. Beyond allowing us the ability to create coalitions to protect American interests when the need arises, protecting our friends preserves a common set of beliefs. What would be the ramifications to this country and the beliefs we hold dear if Great Britain or Australia, to name just two, were to be suddenly torn asunder? I would submit that the loss of mutually embraced values and beliefs would be as impacting as the military firepower they offer. In reality, beliefs and defense are tied together for as the direction of the heart goes, so will the militaries go that are wielded by those hearts. In short, "We need friends like friends need us."

Despite the necessity for friends, America is only worthy of having friends to which we are true. This brings us to the matter of Israel. The tiny State of Israel has flourished despite having enemies that surround its borders. It has defended itself time and time again, often with tepid support from America and other "free" countries of the world. America has on many occasions joined other countries in placing the global stopwatch on Israel when driving its enemies from its borders, and in encouraging its leaders to make deals that are not in its best interest. Often the strongest support America gives Israel, our friend, is neutral statements of the desire for peace and negotiation. Remember the fair-weather friend? If we are to be honest we must say that for Israel, the weather is seldom fair.

2010 will be a year in which America's friendship to Israel will be tested to its limits. The growing threat to Israel from Iran, if not the entire world, will most certainly come to a head. In America's action or inaction, we will show the world what kind of country we are, and what value can be placed on being a true friend of this country. In return, we will reap what we sow, and America would be wise to remember that defending our true friends in the world is a defense of ourselves and our mutual beliefs.

In addition to defending our cultural and ideological allies overseas, we should not forget to defend our culture and beliefs at home. There is a lot of useless dribble in American culture today. From kids wearing their pants below their bottoms to the rise of Lady Gaga, we have it all here in America. It is partly a product of our extensive freedom, which must naturally be protected. I am the last person who wants to curb the freedoms that we have, even the freedom to be callow and shallow. But even free societies like America must balance freedom with responsibility. Is it culturally responsible to promote useless reality shows in which young people see how drunk, violent, and sexually promiscuous they can be in a 24 hour period? We have a font of verbal and visual vulgarity spouting through our televisions at all hours, suggesting a radical decline in popular culture in just a few decades. Worse yet, popular culture seems to celebrate the lowest elements of human behavior. This is not something whispered in dark backrooms; we see it on the nightly news, primetime television, the newspapers, and in movie theaters. I am not asking for a perfect world, some unattainable utopia, but for a return to civility and propriety, and for our children to grow up in a country where doing the right thing is applauded and doing wrong is shunned. On July 16, 2010, I wrote about the Barefoot Bandit, and why we as a society need to take the responsibility not to romanticize deviance.

The "Barefoot" Culture and the Promotion of Deviance

CNN reports that police authorities in the Bahamas have captured 19-year-old Colton Harris-Moore, known by the media as the "Barefoot Bandit." This 19-year-old boy has been on the run from the law for more than two years for stealing cars, boats and even airplanes. Even his arrest ended in a dramatic fashion with a high-speed boat chase in the waters of Harbor Island. To some, the Barefoot Bandit is surely the stuff that great stories are made of. The question is whether or not this is a story worth repeating.

It is within the framing of stories such as the Barefoot Bandit that we see the moral condition of the country. Like the genetic makeup of any living being, it is from within that one can see the true nature of what is visible on the outside. Every society has the option to frame its heroes and villains, and what do our societal standards dictate when it comes to teenage felons like Harris-Moore? Juan McCartney and Mike Melia of the Associated Press say that Harris-Moore has built his reputation as a 21st-century folk hero. Of course thieves don't "build" as they have no time for such labors. They are too busy stealing what others have built. Even with the factual terminology in place, one cannot say that Harris-Moore even managed steal a reputation as a 21st-century folk hero. No, to be factual it must be said that this young man's celebrity status was a gift from the media, paid for by modern society. Unfortunately, even after the Barefoot Bandit's arrest, the debauchery over deviant behavior is just beginning.

Even now, legal defense funds are being constructed for high-profile lawyers to drain in what will be no doubt another circus trial, and all the while the dangerous criminal activities of a teenage boy will be lifted up in a Jesse James-like fashion. Do you smell TV and movie rights? If not, then your sniffer has gone bad. The fact that Harris-Moore most likely placed many innocent lives in danger with his crime spree had no effect on his over 60,000 Facebook fans, many of which appear to be cheering on his continued victimization of all who crossed his path.

The romanticizing of deviancy comes with a heavy price. The obvious outward signs of society's inner moral decay come with the copycat offenders that will emulate this barefoot buffoon to be the next Barefoot Bandit. Long after the media's exalted villain is forgotten, the aftershocks of rewarding deviant behavior are felt by society. I tell you this as a former police officer who went on countless copycat calls following the sensationalized media framing of the Columbine massacre, the effects of which have arguably not been mitigated by time.

If justice were to be served to humanity, then Colton Harris-Moore and his deviant ilk would be noted by the news only for the simple purposes of capture and containment. This would be as one would note a rabid animal on a city street where the fanfare is nothing more than the sound of the gathering of nets. When the capture had been completed, deviants of this nature would be catapulted into the vacuum of obscurity, a literal world of silent shame. Who would be rushing in line to be the next shunned nothing, the next punk nobody hears of or cares about? Probably not a lot of Facebook pages for that position. Instead of silent rejection of the deviant, the worst among us, or at least the ones that can catch the attention of the media by being bad for a long as possible, get to be barefoot folk heroes. With this societal mentality we guarantee more of the same activity.

Americans also need to take the responsibility to stand up against so-called progressives (how hastening the decline and degradation of the American civilization constitutes "progress" is a mystery to me) who want to ban the government from supporting acknowledgement that people need to talk to God on a daily basis. The main obstacle to the expansion of governmental authorities beyond natural law is God. We should be thankful for that. If the men and women in America have an authority higher than those of earthly leaders like the Barack Obamas of the world, then government will always be limited by Godly people when its directives are in opposition to God's word. Think about it: Americans may render unto Caesar what is Caesar's, but those who value the original values of our Founding Fathers will refuse to give a secular leader everything. Secular progressives (liberals) know that they cannot successfully push their agenda unless they separate mainstream America from God. They seek to break the Christian opposition to the liberal agenda by trying to get believers to stop talking to their biggest opponent: God. As has been mentioned at length in this book, liberals seldom attack from the front but instead, chip away at conservative values over time, piece by piece. When necessary, liberal activist judges use their power to push the left's agenda along. Eliminating liberal judges from the bench is paramount to taking back the country.

The National Day of Prayer: The Value of Offending

A federal judge in Wisconsin has ruled that the National Day of Prayer is unconstitutional as it is reported to violate the first amendment against the government's establishment of religion. No, the lawsuit was not filed by the anti-Christian ACLU, but by an organization known as the Freedom from Religion Foundation. The Freedom from Religion Foundation, an organization of overbearing agnostics and atheists, has decided, as liberals often do, that it would be in the best interest of their minority to require the majority within America to live as they do, Godlessly.

However, in the larger scheme of things, the National Day of Prayer has been under attack by many forces besides the "No God Here" group from Madison, Wisconsin. President Barack Obama was already scaling back the National Day of Prayer before the court ruling took place. Harry Truman created the National Day of Prayer back when one could use the concept of prayer and the Democratic Party in the same sentence without receiving strange looks. George W. Bush made the National Day of Prayer a very public event where religious leaders would come to the White House and offer prayers. The overarching theme of such gatherings and of the event itself was not focused on a specific religion, but on the idea that America is a country where prayer has value and worth. President Barack Obama reduced the public White House event to a memo in his first year in office.

So what should Americans do in the face of those who attempt to strip God from all aspects of American life starting with prayer? Those who attempt to change history to make it read as if our founding fathers did not believe in the paramount importance of faith when it came to the grand experiment that is America? Those that have an agenda that is nothing short of an attack on religion itself? I believe that mainstream America should be offensively straightforward on what we believe and what we stand for as one nation under God. Be it annoying the agnostics, aggravating the atheists, or simply making the liberals livid, we must stand tall for the necessity of kneeling in prayer. We must acknowledge the forces that are at work to separate America from God. This attempt is seen in the deceptive nature of the Day of Prayer observation argument. To deny the simple acknowledgement of the value of communication with a higher power is nothing short of poisoning the seedlings from which organized religion grows. No matter how it is presented, the arguments forwarded by groups such as the Freedom from Religion Foundation are nothing more than the usual vomitous verbal spray of liberal propagandists who try to sell Godlessness as the freethinker's utopia.

Well, freethinkers, think freely on this: the battle for the soul of this nation will end with a winner and a loser. Communication with the divine is the lifeline of America's survival and prosperity. It is more valuable to the body of this country than air is to the lungs. Without it we are doomed, and will die as a nation gasping in the dark. This being true, the voices of opposition become of little importance to a national recognition of the value of prayer. Would we feel regret or concern if animosity were heaped upon us for simply breathing? Of course not. Our answer to such challenges would be, quickly and without hesitation, "too bad, it's what I do; it's how I survive."

The National Day of Prayer is a symbol of the nation's undeniable need to communicate with God, to breathe in the unmistakable life-giving bounty of the Almighty. Offending the "No God Here" crowd has merit as a public display that we Americans, as individuals and as a country, have not completely lost our way. That we, like the founding fathers, still believe in talking to God, still believe in the power of prayer.

The religious roots of our country and its role in our prosperity as a nation led to our substantial freedoms, and it is a terrible irony that the suppression of religion in public discourse is on the rise thanks to the liberal agenda. Let's not forget how this country got where it is. The freedoms we have as a nation come in part due to our prosperity. Face it; poor countries always have lower standards of living and less freedom than those with stronger economies. America has prospered under free-market capitalism. Everything you and I have, we owe to free-market capitalism. Your house, car, job (or at least the job you had before Obama), and all the gadgets and gizmos that make your life easier are a product of the capitalistic free market system. Free market competition is what makes manufacturers work harder to get you a better product, faster, and at a cheaper cost. Competition is the key. Liberals hate the free market system and they will tell anyone who will listen sad stories about the death of the "Mom and Pop Shop" and the dispassionate, greedy, corporate fat cats that make too much money at the cost of the poor. That's a really sad story; thankfully, it is more fabrication than truth. True, CEOs and other top managers of highly successful corporations make huge wages, but they earn them. Liberals don't want to give you the details of the positive, cascade effect of effective corporate leadership. The top managers in business today are required to create profits which will provide jobs and benefits for thousands of employees. Additionally, successful businesses have succeeded in determining how to make the best quality products for the most competitive price. Successful companies and corporations back their products with service guarantees and stand by those guarantees across the world. Successful CEOs must accomplish all of this, as well as making a profit for the stockholders who invested the capital that allows the business to grow and stay competitive within the market. Liberals tell you to hate the top managers in business because they resent the fact that their success is proof of the free-market system's superiority. That makes liberals sad, and then angry. For liberals, the idea of becoming successful through innovation, to compete your way to the top of the business world through hard work, to prosper through successfully handling a complex market and huge business decisions is seldom contemplated. Instead, liberals push to reduce the pay of CEOs because in doing so, they feel a little better about themselves. When negative outcomes come from following the mentality that free-market success is evil, and under liberal administrations they generally do, a creative blame game ensues.

Liberals like to romanticize Mom and Pop shops of the past, when in actuality these businesses themselves were once in fierce competition with cart vendors and other small specialized businesses and tradesmen. In reality, the successful Mom and Pop shop ran their fair share of competition out of business as they rose to the top of the market food chain. Now there is a larger, healthier, stronger competitor in the mix and it is Mom and Pop's time to be left behind by market evolution. That may not be romantic, because it makes larger businesses like Wal-Mart seem less like the devil and more like a simple reflection of the natural dynamics of the free market system at the base of American prosperity. In my January 31, 2011, article entitled, "The Pet Rock versus Obamacare," I compare the positive impact of the successful fad "Pet Rock" with Obama's health care program. Which one represents the greater economic success?

The Pet Rock versus Obamacare

In 1975 advertising executive Gary Dahl had one of the simplest and most rewarding marketing ideas of the decade. He placed a shiny little rock in a box decorated as an animal carrier and offered it to consumers to buy and keep as a "pet."

Dahl marketed this (unique) product by reminding consumers of the unwanted expense, time and effort that conventional pets take compared to his lovable and low-maintenance "pet rock." Within a six-month period, the Pet Rock received national fad appeal and Dahl made millions of dollars before market saturation and copycat competitors, in combination with the next line of fanciful fad products greatly diminished the short-lived pet rock craze.

If you asked me if the pet rock changed the world I would say no. However, if you asked me if the Pet Rock, when compared with the colossal Obama health care system that now looms over the country, will be seen as having more of a positive impact over time, I would say absolutely. Liberals will jump out of their skin at such a statement because Obamacare, with all its countless socialistic tentacles, is advertised as a cure-all for so many issues that the list of its potential good deeds is still being written. With all that said, I still pick the rock. Why? While both the Pet Rock and Obamacare fall within the category of goods and services, we have to look deeper to see what they really represent if we really wish to see their impact on the country.

The thing of importance that separates the two products from one another is the ideological foundations by which both are presented. Both the Pet Rock and Obamacare become relevant when we look at the issue of equality, though they are evaluated differently. Nobel Prize-winning economist Milton Friedman called these two competing ideologies on the perspective of equality, "equality of opportunity and equality of outcome."

Gary Dahl's pet rock is easily an example of the freedom of opportunity. Anyone could have created and marketed the idea of the Pet Rock, but it was Dahl who conceived the product and took the leap of faith with a possibility of succeeding or failing. What is of importance is that Dahl was not restricted from attempting to achieve wealth beyond people with less innovation in the marketplace. We can safely assume that at some point Dahl was more than likely approached by someone that spoke against selling a rock in a box as a pet. The point of significance here is that no one, most importantly not the government, tried to stop Dahl from attempting to move ahead of the pack. That's America for you, or at least America in the 1970s.

Equality of opportunity, as Friedman aptly shows, is reflected within the Declaration of Independence with, "We hold these truths to be self-evident, that all men are created equal, that they are endowed by their Creator with certain unalienable Rights that among these are Life, Liberty, and the Pursuit of Happiness." This equality is greatly enhanced when all are allowed the freedom of opportunity to win and lose in the marketplace, to choose their own destiny as individuals. As important is the freedom of opportunity to try again when first attempts fail within the marketplace.

When applying equality of opportunity, we can easily replace Gary Dahl's humble pet rock with Henry Ford's Model T automobile or Bill Gates' software magic at Microsoft, and the equation remains the same. Equality of opportunity does not guarantee riches or happiness but it opens the door for the pursuit thereof.

Conversely, Obamacare is openly advertised as an equality of outcome proposition. The problem is not a lack of compassion or good intentions here; the problem is innate within the mechanism by which this product is rendered to the people within the free market. To start with, Obamacare subverts the free market by requiring that all participate. The freedom to choose your participation level within the system is taken away under the guise that all will be guaranteed admittance.

As Friedman shows, the push for equality of outcome can only create an environment in which freedom is reduced and innovation is subsequently limited. Forced participation, reduced freedom of choice, skyrocketing costs and reduced quality of service are not simply potential dangers of the ideology of equality of outcome, they are inevitable realities. The divide between the intent for equality found within the Declaration of Independence and the reality of the implementation of equality of outcome is massive and fraught with negative consequences.

One of these consequences is that implementing equality of outcome from which Obamacare is birthed within the free markets of America threatens to create a rancid enveloping fog of mentality that government-managed mediocrity is acceptable as the status quo. This is a dangerously contagious kind of thinking that will most certainly expand its way beyond this monstrous health care bill for years to come. Yes, when compared to the huge promotional campaigns of the glories of the new health care program, the pet rock may be seen as inconsequential; however, when both products are compared ideologically, the freedom of opportunity that made Dahl's rock in the box a short-lived sensation had a more positive impact on the country than will Obamacare.

On November 30, 2010, I wrote an article entitled, "Taxes and Punishment: Why Attacking Achievement Hurts Everyone." This was another free-market article which focused attention on taxation. You already know that liberals want to take your hard-earned income away from you and transfer it to someone else. This article focused on a push by liberals wanting to cut the Bush-era tax cuts. Liberals lost this argument and later claimed they only wanted the money of those no-good filthy rich people. In this article, I made the argument to give ALL Americans a tax break, as history has repeatedly proven that the more money every citizen keeps in their own pockets, the better it is for the future economy.

Taxes and Punishment: Why Attacking Achievement Hurts Everyone

The political wrangling over what to do with the Bush-era tax cuts that are set to expire has created another opportunity to observe the ideological difference in perspectives between liberals and conservatives on the issue of taxes. Most importantly, it highlights differences that go beyond differing blueprints for the economic future of the country and more to the contrasting viewpoints in how taxes should be used in modern America.

Out of the gate, liberals in the Democratic Party were resistant to extending the tax cuts in general. After the first rounds of debate it appeared that Democrats were willing to appease Americans with tax cut extensions for all but the wickedly rich. The problem with that plan was that the wickedly rich, which were deemed by the Obama administration as those with an income exceeding $250,000 also included arguably as much as half of all small-business owners. Despite the extensive political quibbling over what percent of small businesses will be negatively affected with higher taxes in a weak economy, there is an equally important question which is seldom addressed: What about the rich?

While many conservatives bring forth consumption tax proposals, these ideas receive quick and absolute rejection from the Democratic Party. Yes, liberals love the current system and pursue leveling taxes on the living and the dead with equal vigor. However, the left places their taxation efforts most forcefully on those who have achieved the highest economic levels in the nation. Why? If you listen to liberals such as Barack Obama, you will hear the argument that the rich can simply absorb additional taxes without any adverse effects. Under the surface of these arguments is a not-so-subtle hostility towards the rich. It is as if high income earners have dodged doing their fair bit in the tax department and liberals are just balancing the scales a little more in these hard times. Are they right? Are the rich deserving of a little less cash? Can the government do a few more wonderful things with a little bit more of their money? Let's look at the economic facts.

In 2007 economist Stephen Moore addressed the same general set of questions and found that the top 1 percent of income earners pay 37 percent of the income taxes collected by the government. The top 10 percent of wage earners — that's the filthy rich if you are wondering — pay almost 70% of total income taxes. The bottom 50 percent of wage earners pay only 3 percent of the taxes. Yes, in case the point has been overlooked, the rich pay the lion's share of taxes in America and in doing so, received more money back from the Bush tax cuts than middle-class Americans who paid less in taxes, and the poor who don't pay taxes at all. What is not talked about is what Moore observed as the final outcome of tax cuts regarding the rich. That is, when the wealthy got tax breaks they hired more employees as they expanded their businesses and in the end, they paid more taxes. More taxes to the tune of $100 billion recorded by the IRS in 2005. The number of tax filers who made a taxable income of more than $1 million went up from 180,000 in 2003 to over 300,000 in 2005. Yes, you guessed it, more people improving their financial income led to an increase in tax collections.

So, if tax cuts throughout history have created economic prosperity when enacted by presidents from John F. Kennedy to Ronald Reagan to George W. Bush, why do liberals still oppose them with all their might? The answer most likely has some complexity. It may be in part that liberals do not grasp the unintended consequences of economically strangling high wage earners that employ hundreds, if not thousands. It may be that liberals are inflicted with a form of economic nearsightedness that denies them the vision to see that in attempting to help the less fortunate at the expense of the wealthy, they are prolonging the economic misfortune for those that wish to find jobs in this country. Remember, a poor man or woman has never given anybody a job.

Unfortunately, with these possible explanations we must also entertain the conclusion that much of the aversion to tax cuts for high wage earners in America stems from a liberal hatred of economic achievement, the achievement our capitalistic society is founded on. Why else would liberals block programs that in the end would bring in more taxes? With economic prosperity come additional freedoms to buy what you want, to live as you wish, and to steadily turn away from a reliance of government intervention. This is not the Democratic way; in fact, it appears that they see taxes as a way to punish success, a billy club to beat down those that they see as having too much of the American dream. Small-business owners making over $250,000 a year may find themselves to be collateral damage as liberals attempt to attack the achievement of higher income earners. In the end, we all suffer.

How is your checkbook doing? If you are like most people, you have been hit hard by the economic downturn. Many people are working two jobs at lower hourly wages, or have been out of work because of layoffs. People are watching their money, and spending less because they have less. Regular people have to be responsible with their money. That is how it works in the real world. Our current government does not live in the real world. Our current government is spending this country into oblivion. Obama thinks like a socialist and spends like a socialist too: he will spend until he runs out of other people's money and the wheels fall off our economy. So, what happens when the wheels fall off an economy? You become a slave to the more economically sound governments which bail you out. On May 14, 2010, I laid out some painful truths about debt and denial after the bankruptcy of socialist Greece. Our country is not far from having to face our own national bankruptcy. Can you say "Brother, can you spare a dime" in Chinese?

America and Greece: Beware the Path of the Black Cat

In you live in America, Europe, or many other places on the planet, then you probably have heard the tales of bad fortune that befalls unprepared souls who allow a black cat to cross their paths. In this realm of superstition the most capable and blessed black cat path-crossers find themselves with bad fortune, and heaps of it. In an ironic twist of fate, it is said that even the unluckiest people who test this taboo find out that their low lot in life can and will get lower. That's sad.

Some would question the strolling power of the black cat even in the face of undoubtedly real catastrophes that take place among people who believe they have triggered this unstoppable bad luck. Could it be that when Mr. Whiskers crosses a person's path people act in ways that increase their risk of misfortune? Possibly they may believe, at least subconsciously, that with bad fortune on the horizon, who needs to worry about well-thought out decisions? The skeptic in me sees the black cat as the perfect scapegoat. A matter of fact a person doesn't have to face the real cause of their misfortune when it can be laid at the furry dark paws of the bad luck giver.

When it comes to tangible misfortune, Greece has the current spotlight with the country's bankruptcy and the $146 billion IMF bailout, which most likely will be only the beginning of the loans that the country will require for survival. Despite the limited impact of Greece on the European markets, they have a powerful story regarding what awaits America if we continue to follow the socialistic blueprint of limiting the free market and expanding governmental control.

For Greece, the conversion from the drachma to the euro was the only excuse needed to engage in unlimited spending that went to the unions, social programs, and government double-dealing, which are always part of the quest for the socialistic utopia. Sound like America? More than you know. America has followed Greece's fast track to ruin by electing a socialist president who barely screamed above the fanfare his intentions to fundamentally transform the nation and begin redistributing wealth. It is easy to see what America is allowing to cross its path.

America is poised to assist with the Greek bailout through donations to the IMF. I would say that we are paying for the right to compare America's and Greece's fates, and we should not waste the opportunity. First socialism failed in Greece, and other countries will soon fail in Europe from the same system. Second, and comparable to America, Greece will soon learn that without the capitalistic free market, no amount of borrowing will fix their financial problems. Lastly, the deaths in Greece at the hands of union protesters and others should be a wake-up call to all Americans of the consequences of the mentality that goes with government entitlement, as well as the dangers that come with attempting to remove those entitlements.

There will be more violence and turmoil in Greece as they are pushed by the IMF to face their poor decisions as a country and what has brought them to the brink of economic destruction. Will they embrace the truth that it was socialism that brought their bad fortune, or will they blame it on the winds of fate? Possibly a black cat passing their country's path?

In the end, countries must break free from the excuses found in convenient myths and superstitions like the kinds that make certain colored kitties so unpopular. All of us must stand on the truth that our fate is the product of the decisions we make, and the decisions we allow our governments to make on our behalf.

As a nation, we should hold people who do extraordinary things in challenging times in high esteem, and give them praise. Even within Hollywood, a place which is often the target of my strongest criticisms, praise can be given. Actors, producers, writers, and others within the entertainment industry offer Americans entertainment and creative ways to escape the rigors of everyday life. Americans watch attentively for the next movie or book that will appear for the public's consideration. I love Hollywood as a capitalist. I love it as a movie and book enthusiast. It is a wonderful part of Americana. What we must remember as we gladly pay to enjoy the work of these talented members of Hollywood is that they should also be held accountable for observing the same laws, rules, and regulations as "ordinary people." Some Americans might say that I am wrong, and that these people with their names on billboards and faces in the magazines, living in extravagant homes in places most of us can't fathom, are truly not accountable as regular citizens. Conferring aristocratic status on mere Hollywood celebrities is a clear betrayal of the American principle of social equality. That mentality is a national problem, and it is up to conservatives to depose this new "royalty" and demand that all Americans have to be accountable to the law, regardless of celebrity. Unfortunately, right now Hollywood elites often get preferential treatment. Self-destructing actors like Lindsey Lohan and other Hollywood types are treated by the courts and the criminal justice system as if they are "too fragile" to do a few days in jail, or send them home rather than pay the cost of extra security to manage the influx of media and the institutionally disruptive impact of housing a famous inmate. Take Paris Hilton, this starlit was quickly sent home with an electronic device on her ankle instead of doing her 45 day jail stint as ordered by a judge. Nicole Ritchie spent only 82 minutes of her four day jail sentence for her second DUI. It has become commonplace for movie stars to be treated as though they do not have to be accountable for their crimes. Worse yet, we are so used to this that we are collectively shocked when a member of Hollywood actually does "the time for the crime." This has got to change. Sometimes the crimes are so egregious, and the voice of Hollywood so aggressive in minimizing personal responsibility, that it warrants a huge public outcry. On May 23, 2010, I wrote about international authorities who had the filmmaker Roman Polanski detained pending a potential transfer back to the United States for criminal sentencing. Polanski, a convicted sex offender who had been on the run from U.S. authorities for decades, was being glorified by the Hollywood elite as an unfairly persecuted artist, despite the fact that his confessed crime was the forcible sodomy and rape of a 13 year old girl. I have dealt with rapists as a law enforcement officer and rape is always motivated by the desire to have power. Most rapists feel that going to jail for a rape conviction is more than just a temporary loss of freedom; it is a transfer of power from their hands back to their victims. Rapists are power hungry narcissists, and they very often reoffend. Roman Polanski should be viewed worldwide as a pariah and an outcast in mainstream America, Hollywood, and the whole planet. His victim deserves that much.

Roman Polanski, Pay Your Debt to Society

From the frills of the 2010 Cannes Film Festival, liberal elites from around the world stand in defense of convicted sex offender Roman Polanski. Polanski was charged and convicted in the late 1970s of having sexual intercourse with a 13-year-old girl and then fled the U.S. before his sentencing. Living as a fugitive from justice in the non-extraditing country of France, Polanski has continued with his filmmaking career until recently traveling to receive movie awards in Switzerland, where he was held on house arrest pending a potential transfer back to the U.S. for sentencing on his 1970s sex crime. As additional allegations of sexual misconduct are being leveled at the filmmaker, just what should be the emphasis of the Polanski story?

Unfortunately, this story is not about criminals that take the innocence from children and the triumphs and failures of the criminal justice system in penalizing such activities. In reality, the Polanski story is about the continual battle for supremacy between the liberal and conservative ideologies in the modern world. The United States, being framed with conservative values, has a criminal justice system, even with all its imperfections, that is constructed on the concept of personal accountability. Within our ideological system, Roman Polanski had not paid his debt to society when he fled to felon-friendly France. It is as simple as that.

However, to the liberal mind, personal accountability is much more negotiable, and some find more than enough "wiggle room" when it comes to what truly is punishment for Polanski's crimes. The Associated Press reports that actor Woody Allen told a French radio station, "It's something that happened many years ago... He has suffered.... He has paid his due." Allen further stated, "He's an artist, he's a nice person, he did something wrong and he paid for it. They (his critics) are not happy unless he pays the rest of his life." Woody Allen's words are painful to hear for more reasons than the obvious fact that this actor's life has had more immoral outgrowths than a soiled Petri dish left out in the summer sun. Allen's defense of Polanski marks the total disconnect that modern liberals have from accountability.

It should be stated that Hollywood and European liberals alike follow the same mindset as Woody Allen that Polanski is more victim than criminal. To these disconnected liberals, prima-facie evidence of Polanski's suffering is apparent to them because in hiding from his sentence in the U.S., he has been denied total freedom to travel. I guess it is true that the filmmaker has been denied the penthouses and fancy cars of America and has been reduced to merely basking in the penthouses and fancy cars of other countries. Allen highlights the liberal mentality that Polanski's time-evading justice mitigates the crime itself as well as the fact that this felon is a nice guy who has a talent for making movies. When it comes to the court's sentencing for sex crimes with a 13-year-old girl versus the filmmaker's continued freedom, liberals judge the debt to society as being paid in full. This is shameful.

If you share this moral relativistic view you are not alone, but make no mistake, you would be a liberal. Personal accountability dictates that Polanski must pay his debt to society as would any other non-award winner. You can pity the downfall of a talented soul. I do, as Polanski's film "Rosemary's Baby" is still one of my classic favorites. I recommend this fine film to as many eager eyes as possible. Who knows, maybe they still have a movie night in prison and the filmmaker can share a few special insights with fellow inmates as he squares his debt with society.

If you are going to be part of the growing conservative movement which aims to win the culture war and make a difference in the lives of all Americans, you had better have very thick skin. Liberals have been running wild with the reins of this country for some time now, and they will not freely or easily return control to traditional Americans. They will attack you personally, they will find ways to diminish you, and to demonize and divide you from your allies. Here is the worst part: sometimes they will win. As members of a conservative movement, we must be as good at getting up out of the mud as we are at taking victory laps. I tell readers this from experience. I have had many victories, and I am encouraged by the possibility that together we are going to take this country back, but prepare yourselves for some cuts and bruises along the way. Many of the knocks that conservatives will take from the left will truly be "low blows." In 2010, I was run out of the liberal university newspaper, "The Collegian," at Kansas State University. What was my transgression? I was one of the most popular columnists the college paper had, and my articles were all centered on conservative values. To this liberal college newspaper, I was a major threat to their agenda. For them it was not about giving readers what they wanted, or enabling free and civil discussion on the topics of the day. For this college paper, it was about forwarding a regular stream of controlled liberal propaganda. Writing for the college paper was a paying gig and no one likes to have money pulled from their fingers because of ideological conflict, especially since political speech is supposed to be protected from such abuses. I share my story of liberal bias and the price I had to pay as a conservative because other conservatives will most likely have to face something similar in their own jobs or personal lives at some point. My experience is one battle in a larger war that we must wage together, back to back. When (and it is not "if", it is "when") you get the shaft because you stick to your beliefs, never go down quietly, do as I did, and let the world know what liberals do and why they do it. Never give an inch in silence, even if you are called, as I was, too dangerous to print.

Too Dangerous to Print: Liberal University Bias

Thomas Paine once said, "He that would make his own liberty secure, must guard even his enemy from opposition; for if he violates this duty he establishes a precedent that will reach himself." How true these words are. One of the most fundamental reflections of liberty is the freedom to question, challenge and debate the world around us. This freedom does not exist everywhere in the United States and certainly not at the university level.

As a lifelong Kansan, it would be much less painful to talk about liberal bias in places like Berkeley or Columbia University, but unfortunately my example comes from the least likely of places expected for liberal bias, Kansas State University. It was here that I was hired to write a political opinion column for the college newspaper. I was not naïve to the Collegian's historically antagonistic relationship with conservative writers. In my 2009 book, "Feeding Lions: Sharing The Conservative Philosophy in a Politically Hostile World," I had documented the firing of fellow conservative writer Chuck Armstrong, who was sent packing by the Collegian after writing an article about radical Islam. Armstrong's article, based on his radio interview with scholar Robert Spencer, was labeled as racist and the Collegian threw Paine's words out the window.

When it appeared that I would be given the free speech go-ahead by the Collegian, I submitted months of my political writings to make sure they had full knowledge of my writing style and content. Collegian editorial staff told me that I was a superb writer and that they were happy to have me aboard. Despite what I had seen in the past, I forwarded my opinion column in the hopes of creating civil discourse on what I felt were important subjects. All the articles I wrote for the university newspaper were listed in the "Most Popular" category on the Collegian's Web site. Reader comments were abundant and, might I add, heavily in the favor of my arguments—so far so good.

I wrote an insightful article in which I argued that Republicans have done more for minorities throughout history than Democrats. Within the article I had a small misstatement in which I said that Clarence Thomas, instead of Thurgood

Marshall, was the first African-American appointed to the Supreme Court. Instead of simply correcting the misstatement as had been done in the past and moving on, I was sacrificed on the altar of liberalism. Collegian staff openly accused me of inventing facts and it was quickly apparent that forces were marshaling against me.

Communicated through e-mail and later a copy-and-paste version in the college paper, the Collegian said I was in error in my article and their support for such a charge was stated as, "George W. Bush was not the first president to fill two Cabinet posts with minority candidates. Bill Clinton appointed six minority secretaries: Jesse Brown and Togo West, Jr. to Veterans Affairs; Federico Peña to Transportation and Energy; Henry Cisneros to Housing and Urban Development; Ronald H. Brown to Commerce; and Alexis Herman to Labor." The problem here is that I never made any statement to this effect. I wrote, "George W. Bush was the first to extensively fill influential Cabinet positions with minorities including Colin Powell, Condoleezza Rice and Alberto Gonzales." I explained to a very angry Collegian staff that Condoleezza Rice was the first African-American woman appointed as Secretary of State, Alberto Gonzales the first Hispanic appointed to the highest law enforcer position in the country as Attorney General, and Colin Powell also appointed as Secretary of State and the first African-American male to fill that position. I used the term "influential" and used it properly as these positions are the top spots in the president's Cabinet. My explanation was nonchalantly shrugged off and I was called a liar.

By this time the Collegian was making a fool of itself but they went even further to purge their ranks of a conservative voice. I was told that I had lied when I said the following, "The Democratic Party, on the other hand, opposed the 1964 Civil Rights Act, which outlawed school segregation and inequality in voter registration. Democrats led an excruciatingly long filibuster to deny civil rights to blacks, which was eventually defeated." When I asked Collegian staff to legitimate this charge of lying, I was told that yes, Democrats had opposed the 1964 Civil Rights Act, but not all of them, and so I was a liar.

The Kansas State University Collegian gave me my walking papers, showed me the door and said my services were no longer needed. I was told that I was too dangerous to print. In fact, it was affirmed that I was so dangerous that there was true fear that I would bring down the entire university paper through litigation if I was allowed to continue to put pen to paper. If you think this sounds preposterous, you would be understating the situation. I wrote thought-provoking opinion articles that struck a chord with readers and ruffled the feathers of university liberals. Liquidating Ibbetson opinion articles in the Kansas State University Collegian avoided months of university liberals being brought to anger by inflammatory issues such as the Constitution, liberty, freedom and of course, God.

I wish to end this column with the same straightforward articulations I bring to all my writings. The Kansas State University Collegian has the right to hire whomever they want to write opinion articles, and I respect that right. However, I wish the staff would have been honest enough to say there was no place for strong conservative writers at their paper. While affirming the true existence of university liberal bias, they would have prevented a bunch of problems, and the necessity for this article. In the end we are brought back to the wise words of Thomas Paine—"He that would make his own liberty secure, must guard even his enemy from opposition; for if he violates this duty he establishes a precedent that will reach himself." The Kansas State University Collegian may rue the day they reap what they sow.

As this book was being written, Donald Trump was relentlessly calling for Barack Obama to submit his long form birth certificate. On March 28, 2011, "the Donald" presented to the world his own long form birth certificate and again challenged the president to do the same. Such challenges were nothing new. Heck, I had even challenged the President on my radio show to swap long-form birth certificates for public inspection. While it was fun to watch Donald Trump make whoopee over Obama's refusal to provide a long-term birth certificate, his media antics are a little like watching professional wrestling. It may be a fun distraction, but nothing real ever comes from it. Donald Trump is rich enough to play like he might run for president, and while we all know he is a sharp business mind, we know now that nothing is going to come from the birth certificate issue. After years of withholding his long form birth certificate from the world, President Barack Obama finally made public his long form birth certificate on April 27, 2011 (Beck, 2011). Obama, with his chin elevated in arrogance (a pose the president seems to save for special occasions) tried to use this long awaited moment of disclosure to attack "birthers" for being off base in their many accusations about his presidential illegibility. Barack Obama should not be applauded for this long form birth certificate disclosure but held responsible for purposely causing needless mystery as to his nationality. The issue of Obama's birth certificate has been monstrously distractive to the nation. The "birthers" only existed because of the President's pointless refusal to provide documentation of his nationality, documentation that any candidate with a non-American parent who spent so much of his childhood in other countries would certainly be required to provide. Barack Obama created the "birther" conspiracy by failing to take this reasonable request seriously earlier, and he should be held accountable for it. Obama's chimerical position on this subject is a quintessential example of what I've called "classic monster politics."

Classic Monster Politics

What do Bela Lugosi, Boris Karloff, Lon Chaney and Lon Chaney Jr. have in common? They are forever known as the faces of the classic monsters Dracula, Frankenstein's monster, Phantom of the Opera, and the Wolf Man. Whether you were frightened by these classic representations or the continual evolutionary adaptations that have followed, we all know these monsters when we see them and we all do the same thing when they are thrust into our faces: we take a big step back.

As interesting as the creatures themselves is the construction in how they are perceived. With this in mind, no relevant "monster talk" would be complete without addressing the most prevalent but least identified monsters of today. This identification is made if we are smart enough to expand our minds to enlightened ways of thinking and bold enough to shine our torches into the deepest, dankest recesses in which these illusive modern ghouls take refuge. The problem in the end is that when we finally take a bold look, we are more likely to find a beast with a three-piece suit and briefcase than a creature in rags and chains. In place of ravenous, blood-sucking fangs, we are likely to find smiling faces, stacks of ambiguous laws and a well-manicure hand that can whip out a signature in total darkness. Who are these new slithering, sinister surrogates of evil? Without a doubt it is the modern-day politician.

This is not an indictment of all those who go into this field of public service, rather the recognition of a framing process that takes place where some politicians seem to shine while others are deformed by the monster politician persona. The term "monster politics" serves to describe an environment beyond normal debate

72

and division that highlights the power of the psychological to supersede the theatrical. It is the process by which a politician embraces political circumstances in a way that generates a negative persona, alienating the politician from his or her constituents and creating a dangerous air of unpredictability that is not conducive to future political service. We can appropriately call this the "terminal term," or the building of the non-re-electable politician. While this is not the inevitable ending point for all who serve in public office, it seems to be the unfolding story of Barack Obama.

For perspective we should understand that all politicians come into office with a certain population that will always oppose them. Equally assured, all presidents through the course of their term have historically made pressing decisions that inflame segments of their own base constituency. Additionally, all presidents fall prey to the occasional faux pas, but monster politics is not evoked from these actions. Like the theatrical characters from which our perception of the monster arises, it is the actions after the critical incident — the bite, curse or lightening-induced creation itself — that frames the individual as the monster we know. It is the same with the president and it is here that Barack Obama, through his own actions, pushes the polls' numbers of public sentiment toward the dark, dank depths of monstrous non-re-electability.

CNN's August 4, 2010 poll shows that 27 percent of Americans have doubts that Barack Obama is an American citizen. Also, the most recent Pew Research Poll shows that 18 percent of Americans believe the president is a Muslim. This is a 7 percent increase from 2009 poll results. From Democracy Corps' July 2010 polling results, 55 percent of Americans think Obama is a socialist and 56 percent think he is too liberal. Arguably, both charges may be one in the same. For Obama supporters it is not just the existence of poll classifications such as these that should be disheartening, but also the fact that Obama's numbers are increasing in these areas over time.

It is the Obama administration's inability to deflect, and often its overt actions, which perpetuate these negative attributes that have emboldened the classic monster politics scenario that now surround the president. Is the president a Muslim? Doubtful, but like an overactive Dr. Frankenstein, Obama has created his own monster persona through his own book quotes, Middle East apology tour, anti-Israel stance, and forceful, non-solicited statements such as those recently heard on the issue of the mega mosque fiasco near ground zero in New York. Like the fear and hatred generated by our classic monsters, the motivating force is the same in monster politics. It is the grouping of calamitous actions with alienation and unwanted mysteriousness, the latter two points exacerbating the first, which bring about such negative outcomes.

That is, in simple terms, the monster truly does bad things, but that is not enough to bring about its bad reputation. It must be in combination with personal characteristics that are in opposition with, or simply alien to the general populace, as well as a mysterious nature that creates an environment of unpredictability. Welcome to the world of Barack Obama. With this knowledge there is little wonder why Obama's two decades of attendance at a radically socialistic church under the tutelage of Reverend Jeremiah Wright fails to give him public identification as a Christian with a growing number of Americans. It is in part a lack of personal Christian identification, if not hostility toward Christian conservatives in America, which has prompted more and more people to speculate Obama as having alternative religious affiliations.

Is Obama an American-born citizen? Probably, but like a vampire that refuses to stand in front of the mirror to be justified, Obama's secretive, if not deceptive, actions on this important issue breed the mistrust from which caskets are torn open, castles are stormed, moors are patrolled, and approval numbers plunge into the abyss. Is Obama a socialist? The president has done nothing here but reinforce the affirmative by his actions and rhetoric, but even many of the socialists of today have avoided being caught up in the career-ending calamites of monster politics. If the president continues to separate himself from the American people by attitude, rhetoric and policy, he will do more than open the door to more grim conjectures about his future policies and personal character; he will have created his own forever-told horror story of the one-term president from the depths of monster politics.

Two-faced positions on social issues are a common feature not only in politicians, but in the garden-variety liberal as well. Smug liberals will tell you that they drive a Prius (or similar) while cheerfully ignoring the fact that fossil fuels still are required to make the electricity that hybrids use. They will proclaim themselves sinless vegetarians while neglecting to consider the source of their leather goods, much less the glue that binds their books together. They hold the richly nourishing proteins that the rest of the world views as a luxurious reward and blessing in contempt. There is little chance that I will ever get an appreciation plaque from PETA with this attitude. I seem to have an issue with telling them too often that they are crazy anti-human socialistic nut jobs. I also really like meat. I debate the PETA folks on a regular basis and I am proud to say I have never lost a go-around with these folks who would put as much energy into saving a snail as they would use to save a human. These are really strange people. I did show restraint in 2010 when a pro-gun organization that I will not name offered me a 12 course all-meat meal if I would eat it all during a scheduled phone interview with a member of PETA. I pride myself on being professional, and I passed on the offer despite a rumble of opposition from my stomach. I use the analogy of food in this article published on September 11, 2010, in which I talked about the president's responsibility to defend our fighting military men and women and the political fallout for failing to do so.

Just Relax Your Throat: Liberals and Their Need to Force-Feed America

Are you hungry, America? Got a rumble in the tummy telling you it's time to eat? If we are honest about it, Americans have a really big appetite for almost everything. I will admit that to self-loathing liberals, who bemoan this country at every turn, that this is a characteristic requiring praise, not apology. Hunger to excel, achieve, compete and succeed has been an individually engrained American quality for our entire history. While it is very anti-PETA to say it, America doesn't seek the lettuce of prosperity; we want the big, thick, juicy meat of victory and success in everything we do. I get hungry even thinking about it.

It's not the case today that liberals from Barack Obama to the ACLU are trying to cut in line and get the best portions of what America has to offer for their own plates; that would be too straightforward, too capitalistic. Instead, liberals want Americans to consume an ideology counter to our appetite, and to take up policies detrimental to our well-being. This is why as a nation we must be discerning in what we consume. Chew on that.

If danger and stupidity were foods, liberals would be an all-you-can-eat buffet with endless foreign dishes proffered with the constant mantra that you must always fill your plate. Man-made global warming, downsizing the military, raising taxes, socializing the nation, rewriting the constitution, rejecting traditional values and the utter attack on our Judeo-Christian foundations are just a few of the daily specials that are cooked in the modern liberal kitchen. What makes these offerings most noticeable is that you are not allowed the free-market choice to pass on any of these courses.

"All-you-can-eat" takes on a new meaning within liberal government as "all-you-*must*-eat." Take ObamaCare; if you were against it, you were not just in the majority; you were in the overwhelming majority. Public opposition to this bill that was not in the country's best interest didn't slow America's communistic connoisseurs from whipping it up and jamming it down the people's throats. We were told to "eat it!" and that we would acquire a taste for it over time. Contrary to this country's free-market appetite, liberals won't stop force-feeding us their liberal utopian policies. Restraint seems to be beyond their nature and each morning seems to bring a new dastardly dish without the decency of even a shout of warning, "with forks and spoons here come the loons!" With a tone of arrogance, liberals think we should be gracious because they offer us periodical trips to vomit between force-feedings.

Here is another bitter dish. The line of economists that will tell you the stimulus package lengthens, not limits, America's economic struggle to rebound keeps getting longer and longer, but liberals served it up with zeal, despite its funny smell and terrible taste. The country is still ill from this economic E. coli and yet liberals continue to shout, "just relax your throat, you can hold a little more." Notice how I refrained from mentioning the gay marriage push with the last statement, even though you get the thrust of what liberals are pushing in the country's face on that issue. This is one more example of the social salmonella that degrades the health of the country. Even though the U.S. military has been receiving rancid dishes from liberals since the war on terror began, Obama made sure to serve them fresh pitiful plates of poor platitudes as the turndown in Iraq begins.

Barack Obama's flaccid and lackluster acknowledgement of the U.S. military's success in Iraq following the surge that he and other Democrats opposed was noticeable to everyone. Obama supporters try to say that the president is showing signs of job fatigue, but it is more likely that he is just not used to eating crow when it comes to the U.S. military. Bon appétit.

So don't be fooled into thinking that America's woes are based solely on our healthy appetite; it's what we are eating that is doing us in. Burp if you agree. We have a mess on our hands and it is a mess that only we, the American people, can fix. To do so, we are going to have to step away from the schmuck's smorgasbord, the buffoon's buffet, and throw down the utensils of apathy. We need to get our hands dirty in the kitchen and do some cooking of our own and create some dishes for both this country and the liberal opposition. The former being nutritious, the latter being something best served cold.

Being responsible for what we consume—ideologically, fiscally, and culturally—is a value that we can share with each other, and with people of other nations. When we see the destructive nature of socialism and communism in other countries, it does not mean we have to invade every nation across the world, but we should at least take the responsibility as individual citizens, when the chance arises, to tell the people of communist countries their nations will never get any better. That communism always fails. That ignorance is not bliss, it's just ignorance. On October 1, 2010, I wrote about the futility of communism in Venezuela and how the dictator, Hugo Chavez, will never turn over power without force. I have shared my views on this issue with both politicians and everyday citizens of that country. I encourage readers to do the same with family or friends in places like Cuba and other socialist and communist countries. Regular Americans are better representatives of American values than the White House at this point in history, and will therefore ultimately have more of an impact fighting dictators around the world by spreading grassroots democracy. Frankly, I trust the American people to do a better job to spread freedom than any initiative right now coming from the White House. Conservatives must take on the responsibility to encourage the average citizens of countries still stuck in the rut of communism to fight for the freedoms that we enjoy in our own country. Once this happens in Latin America, it will have the secondary benefit of radically reducing illegal immigration by people who would risk their lives to come to live in our country. We should honor their courage and sincerity in wanting to live in a democracy; those who would risk much to come to America should instead be empowered at all levels and by all Americans—from the most powerful to the least—to create democracies in their own countries. The elections in Venezuela illustrate how difficult and necessary this process will be.

Mid-term Elections in Venezuela: Did Revolution Make it on the Ballot?

As reported by the Christian Science Monitor, Venezuela's communist dictator Hugo Chavez faces his biggest challenge to retain his political voting monopoly since ascending to power almost twelve years ago. Citizens of Venezuela are building in dissatisfaction with the country's growing crime rate and poor economy. As Steven Bodzin of the Monitor reports, the token opposition parties that currently exist under the totalitarian reign of Hugo Chavez will attempt to use any mid-term election successes as a springboard to actually defeating the president in 2012. Good luck.

While it seems cold to highlight the futility of using the electoral process to improve the lot of individuals anywhere within a communist dictatorship, truth is still the best medicine. What is the truth in the face of a growing population of Venezuelan people who want more money, less crime and in the end, more freedom to make it happen? The truth is that it will never transpire under a communistic regime run by a dictator like Hugo Chavez.

Since Hugo Chavez has occupied the "throne" in Venezuela, he has done what dictators always do. That is, Chavez has brought to his country pain, punishment and repression, and has laid the groundwork for the country's future peril. How so? Following the communist blueprint, Chavez has worked tirelessly to shut down all opposing dissent. He has done this not only by creating a voting monopoly, but also by simply shutting down almost all non-state-run media. In 2009, Chavez made a major push to shut down radio stations that dared to report news opposing his totalitarian-style government. As reported by Reuters, Chavez justified his actions by saying, "We haven't closed any radio stations, we've applied the law." Putting the communistic stamp of approval on his censorship, Chavez said, "We've recovered a bunch of stations that were outside the law, that now belong to the people and not the bourgeoisie." Through the iron grip of Chavez's hold on media outlets, the people are now privy to impromptu, marathon-style rants from the president at any and all hours of the day. As far back as 2007, the Guardian reported that Chavez was asserted to have set the record for the longest state-run television speech, which ran all of eight hours. During the government-controlled broadcast, Hugo Chavez was reported to have sung songs, delivered jokes, broken into angry rants and discussed breasts implants — all things one can do with absolute power and no accountability.

It is not with great shock that we see that in 2008 Hugo Chavez forced through a referendum to end presidential term limits. There is little doubt that Chavez has no intention of ever stepping down as president. In all honesty, the people of Venezuela need to face the cruel reality that despite polling results, Chavez will never allow any opposing party to supersede his political will. Therein lies the futility of the mid-term. Venezuelan elections are a sham designed simply for public consumption, with the end results pre-destined by the totalitarian ideology of the puppet master at the country's helm: Hugo Chavez.

Last, like giant evil magnets seeking to lock together, the communist dictator of Venezuela is drawn to other dirty birds in anti-capitalist, anti-freedom and anti-American dictators like Iranian President Mahmoud Ahmadinejad. As America is pulled toward a potential future conflict with Iran, Chavez's own chosen alliances with such radicals place his country in an unneeded tenuous position for the future.

It is always difficult to fully grasp the pulse of the people of nations under communistic control because of the lack of factual information flow. Venezuela may follow Cuba in resigning itself to having a poor economy and for all intents and purposes, a life-long dictator. On the other hand, if a majority decides to rid the country of Chavez and his lackeys, they will only do it by way of revolution; nothing short of that will have any true effect. Whether the people of Venezuela know it or not, their elections will remain nothing more than a futile public exercise until revolution is placed on the ballot and the majority of the people vote for it.

Another benefit of democratizing Latin America (in addition to helping to radically reduce the motivation to illegally immigrate to America) is the reduction of government-sponsored or enabled drug cartels. The impact of drug addiction on American society is fueled by foreign and domestic enemies of this country. When I joined the Montgomery County Drug Task Force in the late 1990s, I entered the strange world of the drug addict and learned a great many things about denial. Having grown up in the heartland of Kansas I was unaccustomed to the drug culture and the people that moved in and out of that bizarre world. This is not to say that Kansas is drug-free. There were drug users in my high school, and in the communities in which I lived. However, I was raised to avoid those people, and those activities, and I lived free of those influences. As a drug enforcer, I had a lot to learn. I studied the training films on the different kinds of drugs and how drug users would physically degenerate over time. These were like horror films. I studied magazines such as "High Times" to see what the dope culture was about. It was interesting reading "High Times." It was like entering a culture that legally advertises how to live as a criminal. Unsurprisingly, drug culture magazines such as these were also very educational for understanding liberalism. The authors that wrote articles in these pro-dope publications focused most of their writing on teaching people how to grow marijuana, avoid the police, and minimize criminal liability when you eventually get caught. There was endless paraphernalia for sale, and wrapped around it all was the ideological snuggie blanket of rhetoric justifying being a pothead. This self-justification of self-destruction is common ground for the modern day liberal and the brain challenged cannabis smoker. Magazines such as "High Times" claim that drugs such as marijuana are harmless, certainly harmless compared to "the Man," or the criminal justice system that wanted to throw poor harmless hippies into prison. This is identical to the standard liberal operating procedure we have already discussed: minimizing the detrimental activities that liberals do by contrasting it to a villainized perception of what conservatives believe in and support on this issue. These magazines offered benign reasons to keep "hemp" around for products ranging from shirts to soap. In general, these magazines were nothing more than glossy propaganda pamphlets of talking points for drug-addled liberals to push a dangerous agenda on America. I can tell you from extensive experience of watching the destructive nature of drugs on good peoples' lives that there is no utopia in the druggie's la-la land. There is no happy-go-lucky "Cheech and Chong" world out there to be lived by using marijuana, methamphetamines, heroin, or LSD. I have seen smart, decent people of all ages fall prey to the liberal mollycoddling that teaches drug users that society, rather than the users themselves, are responsible for the destruction they cause on these drugs. It is no surprise that predominately liberal states such as California are more prone to the fallacy that addictive, mind altering drugs are somehow the answer to life's problems. On October 23, 2010, I addressed California's continuing problem with being a gateway drug state.

California: The Gateway Drug State

When California legalized medical marijuana in 1996 with Proposition 215 to address their citizens' headaches and shoulder pains, I along with many others saw this as the beginning of a push for wider legalization of the drug. This concern has now been validated with Proposition 19 that is on California's November 2 ballot. If passed, California's new pot law will allow individuals 21 years or older to legally possess one ounce of marijuana as well as to create "pot gardens" for recreational use. Legal pot will have transcended the need of any ailment to be consumed openly by Californians. Of course, the federal government may still throw you in jail, and that is an issue that might keep those secret marijuana-growing rooms secret.

As reported by the Christian Science Monitor, when California legalized medical marijuana the law was not picked up by the entire country. In fact, only 13 other states decided that the drug would become part of their healing regiment. Why? Because the federal government continued to enforce the drug laws prohibiting the drug's possession and use. Both the administrations of Bill Clinton and George W. Bush prosecuted users and sellers after proposition 215 passed in California. The authority to enforce the federal drug laws on divergent states like California was affirmed by the U.S. Supreme Court. That revelation is probably enough to make a California herb enthusiast drop his or her handcrafted water bong in slow-motion shock. Barack Obama's "hope and change" in part brought change to how the federal government would treat medical marijuana states. Currently the White House's stance is no prosecution for medical marijuana states.

Despite medical marijuana's gateway legalization and protection from federal prosecution brought forth by the Obama administration, the White House has decided to at least give lip service to the idea of enforcing federal law on "marijuana for fun." From the Christian Science Monitor we see that Attorney General Eric Holder, after receiving a letter signed by nine former DEA administrators, now says that he will enforce federal drug laws no matter what the outcome of Proposition 19. I don't think the cannabis connoisseurs of California have much to worry about either way. For one, except for when facing off with conservatives, Holder's spine tends toward a consistency of linguini. Secondly, despite Holder's vow to make marijuana prosecutions a "core priority" of the Justice Department, the lion's share of arrests will still be made at the state and local levels.

As is often the case, the most important issues transcend the immediate topic. The issue of legalizing "marijuana for fun" is simply another symptom of the growing liberalization of the country. There is little doubt that liberals in California have played a major part in the liberalization of the country, being banner carriers for leftist causes from gay marriage to the gateway legalization of marijuana. However, on the marijuana issue, much of the country has stood by in befuddled apathy listening to the equivalent of back-alley drug dealers tell Americans the economic benefits of mainstreaming the drug in California to save the state's economic woes. The success of this progression is present for all who wish to see it. Medical marijuana for the dangerously ill led to marijuana for ankle sprains, all in the name of healing and all in direct violation of federal law. This led to the progressive thought: "why should people fuss with the doctor's note when California can make an ounce of personal marijuana legal and collect some needed taxes to boot?"

Of course, if marijuana is not to be framed from the standpoint of pot promoters as a "healing herb" and now can be seen as a product of taxable income, would it not be more efficient and profitable to collect taxable income on this drug by the pound instead of by the ounce? Of course it would, and if proposition 19 passes on November 2, watch for increases in pot possession amounts, soon to follow. You can bet on it, or more aptly, you can bank on it. Moral relativism has been the catalyst to propel much of California's "gateway" thinking, and don't think that issues such as gay marriage and marijuana are the lowest points of this pitiful, progressive pit. Heaven forbid when California liberals discover the taxable potential in crack cocaine or kiddy porn. I will equally dread watching Eric Holder and the Obama administration try to show some spine on those issues, considering they are cut from the same clay as those they will have to oppose. Those who can't see the direction the country is going through initiatives like Proposition 19 may not just be stupid, they may be high.

Democrats deserved the butt-whooping they took in the 2010 midterm elections. They turned their backs on the American people after kicking dirt in their faces. Regular everyday citizens made a statement at the polls, and liberals were sent home in historic numbers. Now mainstream America must take the responsibility to cull out the rest of the liberal politicians who will be up for re-election in 2012. It's not just Obama who has to go. It's not just Democrats who have to go. Republicans who are not true conservatives must also get the boot. 2012 needs to be known as the year of the "Great Culling." It needs to be another strong step toward bringing our nation back to the core values that made it a success. It will require an even greater number of dedicated conservatives in the voting booths. For that to happen, more and more people must be educated about the politicians who are vying for their support. Republicans and Democrats will be asking for a job, or asking to keep their jobs, and some on both sides need to be sent packing. On December 23, 2010, I discussed the need for the Republican Party to move into a position of political power in the next election if we are to save this country. We, the American people, must make one unflinching requirement: the GOP must present candidates worthy of the task.

Love, Hate, and a Dry-Eyed look at the Future of the Country

One reality of the 2010 midterm election is that voters have rejected the current agenda of President Barack Obama. Uncontrolled government spending with its repetitious forays into the private market has not settled well with the American people. The president's promise of decreased unemployment after huge government spending did not come to fruition as promised, and as expected, people began to grumble. For those that are fighting the liberal agenda of the Obama administration, between demented Democrats in denial on one hand and weeping Republicans on the other, it is hard to keep the full reality of what is taking place in perspective. However, since the last couple of years have brought home the truth that elections have consequences, we should be very accurate about the recent midterm election and what it means and what it does not mean for the future of the political parties and this country.

The historical rejection of Democrats can be seen as more than a product of liberal politicians' unwavering support of such plans as Obama's compulsory healthcare program, apocalyptic government spending, or even his backward mentality on national security issues. Yes, the American people opposed Democrats because their policies were bad for the country. However, they came out in droves and voted them out of office in historic numbers because of the Democrats' hostile stance toward anyone who questioned what they were attempting to do. As Barack Obama's policies moved further and further away from the traditional economic and moral blueprint of this country, the voice of the American people rose in opposition. It was then that Democrats decided to forcefully turn their backs on voters to push the liberal agenda of the Obama administration through.

Democrats guaranteed their midterm losses by modeling an appearance of arrogance and disdain toward voters. They projected a belief that the administration's policies were so perfectly constructed that they were beyond question, above scrutiny. The elitism that exuded from the democratic leadership heading up to the 2010 midterm may very well be historic from the perspective that it superseded the usual reflections politicians give to their own political survivability. In the end, Democrats lined up in mass numbers and fell on their swords for the ideological belief system they shared with Barack Obama. The question now is has anything changed? Is anything going to change, or will the country continue moving in the direction of the Obama agenda? Here in reality we have to take a really hard look at the Republican Party.

While it is only fair to allow the House of Representatives with its new Republican majority to settle in before they are judged on what part they will play in correcting the destructive misadventures the country has experienced since 2008, the psychological ramifications of the election are in the forefront and are worthy of evaluation. The first reality that Republicans must acknowledge and model through their direct actions following the aftermath of the midterm is that voters simply rejected Democrats, they did not embrace Republicans. The Republican Party has been blessed with an opportunity to get back into the political game. Opportunities come and go and thus are fleeting in duration. If the Republican Party wishes to gain back its former prominence and the presidency in 2012, they will have to model and articulate a fiscally and socially conservative message for the future. For the Republican Party, this has been much easier said than done.

The GOP needs to put their nose to the grindstone and get back to thinking like free-marketers, constitutionalists, and God-fearing Americans. They must get back to being the innovators and creators of positive ideas. They have a constituency, from the Tea Party to Americans across the country that eagerly wait for their votes to take on meaning. Some would say the GOP is doing that now. I would say if they are, then their marketing stinks. The components of political success for the Republican Party are to have a political vision that is superior to that of their opponents. Republicans have this won even on a bad day, but vision alone will not save the country. To gain political success, the Party must articulate a message more clearly and more effectively than their opposition. Important political success is found with those who can balance the strength of their convictions with the ability to listen to others.

Here the Republican Party has great strides to make. Not only must Republicans come out of the gate in the new Congress with bold initiatives to cut spending, reduce government control and safeguard the Constitution from liberal attack, they must also show a purity of spirit and strength of will as they bring these issues to the forefront. Changing the Obama agenda will be an epic battle not for the faint of heart. In this instance, the success of the GOP and the country itself are tied together. The Obama administration will attempt to use the Republican majority in the House to their advantage and House leader John Boehner as well as the Republican leadership will be called upon to stand for conservative values in stopping more bad legislation from getting through Congress. Love it or hate it, this will not be a battleground of tears, but a dogged fight for the viability of the Republican Party and the future of the country.

Chapter 4

Why The Ron Paulies Hate Me

This book asserts that conservatives must take back the country if we are to save it from moral and economic destruction. If liberals can't or won't join us in bringing the country back from the brink, then conservatives, the majority of the nation, will inevitably have to do it by ourselves. With so much at stake, the conservative movement must be wise in its political strategy. While conservatives currently hold a majority in America, it is important to understand that there are a number of ways for a majority to lose its power to affect change. One fundamental way for this to happen is to have internal conflicts that distort or cause contradictions within the central messages of a movement. Ron Paul brings such contradictions to the conservative movement.

Let me say that I do not hate every facet of the Ron Paul philosophy or the man personally. In fact, at a cursory glance, it would seem that a Republican politician who advocates for the Constitution, limited government, and the free market would not only be the ideological conservative's dream, but also a needed ally. Unfortunately, this is not the case with Ron Paul. When people ask me why supporters of Ron Paul hate me so much, (and I have the hate mail to prove it) I try to be very straightforward with my answer. Just as I do with all politicians, I hold Ron Paul accountable for what he says, and what he says has troubling implications for the conservative movement. In these historic times, the American people must face the truth on a lot of tough problems. We cannot afford to delude ourselves as a nation or to be self-destructive. The painful truth is that saving this nation will not be done with the assistance of the liberals in this country. It will be done for the most part against their stringent opposition. How will a conservative movement save the country when faced with almost complete opposition from the left? We will save the country by defeating liberals at the ballot box, by defeating liberals with our purchasing dollars within the free market, and with superior conservative ideas disseminated and modeled within American culture. Americans who wish to see traditional values win the day must focus constant attention not just on winning, but utterly dominating the ballot box on these ideological issues. We must outnumber the liberal opposition at every turn, and on every issue of importance. With conservative unity so necessary for our ultimate victory, this makes taking a sober look at what Ron Paul stands for, and his impact on the conservative movement of the upmost importance. Splitting and splintering the conservative vote is something that we cannot afford. In the interest of saving the country, I will now ruffle every feather in the Ron Paul flock. Let's get some of the preliminary questions out of the way. So what is wrong with Ron Paul? What is the big deal? There are those that will say, "He can't be as bad as Nancy Pelosi and Barack Obama, or any other example of the myriad of modern day liberals who frustrate conservative America." Right? Readers deserve a straightforward, but also a comprehensive answer to these questions. A fundamental problem with Ron Paul is that he is in the wrong political party. Ron Paul truly is a libertarian and not a Republican. What does this mean? It means that while he is conservative on fiscal and economic matters, he is a liberal on almost all social issues. When it comes to things such as drug use, Paul takes the familiar moral relativist position of the modern day liberal. When we look at the principles of conservatism: 1. God, 2. Family, 3. Country, libertarians find themselves in conflict ideologically with conservatives about half of the time. Those are better odds than you have of getting along with a liberal, but in the long term, important issues such as abortion, big government, environmentalism, the death penalty, and others often become contentious topics for libertarians and conservatives. On April 25, 2011, on the Fox network, Sean Hannity interviewed Ron Paul about libertarianism versus conservatism. Paul framed the founders of the country as "libertarian conservatives" – as if the two can be blended without issue. Not only is Ron Paul's assessment of the Founding Fathers' ideological leanings inaccurate, the congressman is incorrect to assume a cohesive relationship between libertarians and conservatives. As I highlighted above, the ideological conflicts, especially on social issues, are too great for this to happen. The next question readers may ask is "Can libertarians be useful to the conservative movement at all? Can we find middle ground on the issues or political candidates that the country needs today?" The answer is yes, but the way these two groups join forces is crucial. Conservatives must bring forth candidates who are attractive to libertarians on conservative grounds, and are compelling enough that the Libertarian voting bloc will settle for them instead of the liberal alternative. The word "settle" needs a bit of qualification here. Of course all parties settle on political candidates and political initiatives that are not ideologically perfect. Compromise is always present to some degree, and that is to be expected. However, if we as a nation have learned anything over the years, it is that when it comes to core conservative values, we have to take a firm stand. We are in our current mess as a nation because we have given ground on too many important core issues. Conservatives have drifted from the right to become more liberal to appeal to voting blocs among Democrats and Libertarians, and this has to stop. While the battle to save this country through conservative values is not limited to members of a single political party, the Republican Party has historically been the political tent in which conservative values will most likely be found. It is the only party that has the ability to defeat Barack Obama in 2012. The Republican Party tent has the ability to be wide and diverse and that is a good thing. However, there must always be a clear and uncompromising conservative ideological anchor, or the movement loses focus and loses meaning. With that said, libertarians can join forces with conservatives and be a positive force at the voting booth when the occasions arise, but they cannot be allowed to control the Republican Party any more than the party can allow liberals to control the helm. In fact, if we examine our heart we can see that the pejorative term RINO (Republican In Name Only), is as applicable to libertarians as it is for the Arlen Specters of the nation. Ron Paul is a RINO magnet, but he also draws in other negative and destructive groups. We will discuss them at this time.

The internal conflicts that Ron Paul brings to the conservative movement and the Republican Party with his libertarianism are perpetuated by the people who carry his banner. These individuals fall into four main categories: the kamikazes, the conspiracy nuts, the communists/anti-Americans, and the fence straddlers. Kamikaze voters constitute a considerable percentage of Ron Paul supporters. These are the fanatics, the suicide constituency, who wish, consciously or subconsciously, to be political martyrs. They understand that Ron Paul will never be president and cannot be elected, but still desire to go down with the Ron Paul presidential campaign ship every four years. These folks find a certain masochistic pleasure in losing elections with what they perceived as the perfect presidential candidate. The Ron Paul kamikazes can be identified quickly by their fanatical zeal and destructive intolerance. Here are a few fan quotes taken from posts at the dailypaul.com, a well frequented Ron Paul fan site.

"Ron Paul, the **only** honest politician who has the ability to resurrect the USA back to freedom and away from being a banana republic!"

"Ron Paul is a **modern day Founder**."

"He's the **only** true conservative in congress."

"Ron Paul. He is the **truest** conservative in politics."

"I turn 18 in 2011, and I will cast my first vote in support of the Constitution, i.e. Ron Paul.

"The American public **are not worthy** of a Ron Paul presidency."

"If **Ron Paul doesn't run** I do think we are looking very seriously at an imminent collapse and breakup of the United States. **I don't want to live** under a "good" dictator or a "bad" dictator."

In case the point has not been brought home yet, here are some quotes from Ron Paul supporters that left responses at my YouTube channel (http://www.youtube.com/watch?v=-X7ifVf_QHQ) when I challenged Ron Paul's viability as a serious presidential candidate. Hide the children.

"You are an idiot Ibbetson. **I have never heard Ron Paul say anything that I disagree with, everything he says has reason.** You on the other hand are high!! You are the idiot who has been educated in the demoncratic edumakation system! You are saying the things left wingers say on every issue, and now it's time to call you as I see you...AN OBOSO LOVING LIBTARD!!!! You don't care about issues, you can't discuss issues, you make attacks on Ron Paul based on libtard points. EAT %&#@ AND DIE YOU IDIOT LIBTARD!"

"I don't know anything about Ron Paul's view of the 9/11 conspiracy theory, but I do know that **when I hear this man speak it is music to my ears. I have never heard anyone speak for the American citizen the way Ron Paul does.** His views sound strange because they are what our country was founded upon, and we have all been taken for a ride away from the Constitution by both left wing and right."

"Ron Paul stands for America becoming a Republic again like it was intended. **What his supporters worship is his message** that he has never wavered from his entire career and that this country once followed.)

Most of the Ron Paul crowd places all their political eggs in one basket while simultaneously showing the world that they are few eggs short of a full omelet. This is abnormal behavior for either liberals or conservatives. For instance, Hillary Clinton supporters staunchly advocated for her 2008 presidential campaign, but when it became apparent that she would not win the nomination, most transitioned to their nearest ideological candidate, Barack Obama. Ron Paul supporters refuse to transition to a more viable conservative candidate. It's Ron Paul or nothing. Ron Paul supporters hate Sarah Palin with venom that makes liberals seem like staunch supporters. The Paulies don't support Jim Demint, Allen West, Michele Bachman, Marco Rubio, Newt Gingrich, Mitt Romney, Tim Pawlenty, or Mike Huckabee as secondary choices for presidential candidates, as each falls short of the political purity of Ron Paul in their eyes. This is not the making of a conservative movement; this is the making of a cult.

The second cohort in the Ron Paul cabal is the conspiracy nuts. If you had an aluminum foil hat factory, you could make a fine living off these over-the-shoulder-lookers who continually circle around the Ron Paul camp. Ron Paul is not alone when he pushes the conspiracy theory agenda often found in his political rhetoric. More often than not it is a tag team act with other well-known conspiracy vendors such as Alex Jones and Jesse Ventura. Alex Jones operates the website infowars.com. This website covers the entire spectrum of government cover-ups, all things big, small, and totally imagined. Jones has been known to paint himself up as the "joker" from the movie "Batman" and go on long incoherent tirades about secret organizations and infamous backroom plots that he alone has discovered and brought to the public's attention. This fear merchant has made a living selling paranoia to the American people but, for those who wish to live in the real world, hanging with Jones comes with a price that is higher than many of his advertised products. To live in this world of constant conspiracies, nothing in life can be as it seems or taken at face value. Simply put, for Alex Jones and his faithful followers, if they wake up in the morning and it is raining, it's a conspiracy. If you question their sanity, it's simply proof that you're in on the conspiracy too. It is not a question of whether or not a conspiracy is being hatched somewhere on the planet, the question is whether everything in life is a conspiracy. The answer is, of course, no. Life is not a never ending cycle of secret plots. The actions of most bad guys are highly predictable and many bad things in life just happen by themselves without the assistance of masterminds in smoke filled backrooms.

The 9/11 Truthers, (those folks that have the tendency to think George Bush and Dick Cheney blew up the Twin Towers for who knows what reason) fit nicely into the Ron Paul and Alex Jones crowd. The philosophical match present between the 9/11 Truthers and the followers of Ron Paul's 2008 presidential bid were so closely tied together that some supporters taped together "Ron Paul 2008" and "9/11 was an Inside Job" signs during the campaign. Former Minnesota Governor Jesse Ventura, host of the conspiracy show, *Conspiracy theory with Jesse Ventura*, is a slightly more accomplished name than Alex Jones when it comes to selling "crazy" to the public. Oh, for the days when Jesse Ventura was wrestling or simply a bit actor in Arnold Schwarzenegger movies. Now Ventura can be seen actively working the Ron Paul moonbat circuit. Ventura has toured with Ron Paul, and they share the same conspiratorial view of government organizations such as the FBI and CIA. The website RonPaul.com ran a poll asking readers to select up to 7 candidates to join a potential Ron Paul presidential candidacy in 2012. The poll attracted 10,660 voters. Jesse Ventura came in a strong second place with 27% of the vote (up from 22% in Aug. 2010).

So Ron Paul has a few paranoid supporters, how does that hurt the GOP and the conservative movement? Conspiracy theorists cause a massive collective I.Q. drop in any group they join. The nature of their busy lives full of attempts to legitimize a world of secret agents involved in world plots run by nefarious organizations precludes an ability to function or succeed in normal society. Don't believe me? Take a quick visit to Alex Jones' website at infowars.com, and you will see an assembly line of the overly strange and less than believable scenarios being sold by the boatload. Conspiracies are a never ending, time consuming adventure for these folks. In the end, the conspiracy theorist is either too busy role-playing life or is too deeply seated in the Alex Jones/Ron Paul/Jesse Ventura conspiracy version of real events to be useful in effecting positive change.

When the conspiracy theorists attempted to fit George Bush into the Dr. Evil category for the events of September 11, 2001, they looked crazy. When they tried the same conspiratorial framing of Barack Obama, they still looked stupid. Think about it. There is no conspiracy taking place in the Barack Obama administration. Obama was very clear that his intentions were to "fundamentally transform this country," and his Marxist ties were well documented before the election. What the President is doing to the nation is not a shock; he said he would do it. The shocker is that the American people voted him into office and gave him the opportunity to bring his promises to fruition. No conspiracy theories are needed when Barack Obama's presidency is analyzed. His socialist policies and their implementation is by no means a secret plot. When the 9/11 Truther conspiracy for the Twin Towers was laid to rest in the Popular Mechanics

Debunking The 9-11 Myths series, the anger expressed by conspiracy theorists was not so much focused on the answers presented in the magazine; it was directed against the destruction of their whole multi-layered, grandiosely devised worldview. The notion that certain mysteries are completely void of villainous elements was a direct affront to conspiracy advocates. To the conspiracy theorists, the conspiracy of 9/11 must go on at all costs. The 9/11 Truthers still troll Tea Parties today, still link themselves to the Ron Paul crowd like magnets, and public visibility thanks to sound bites from the liberal media who know that the Ron Paul/9/11Truther union can only reduce the legitimacy of the conservative Tea Party movement and the GOP.

Conspiracy theorists marinate in a perpetual soup of negativity. Show me a happy, positive minded conspiracy theorist if you can! These groups live in a world of continual victimization in which forces beyond their control, usually in the form of corrupt government, are forever keeping them down, limiting their life chances, and doing them wrong. When they whine, the conspiracy kooks sound just like liberals, and are just as annoying. What makes these whiners bad for the conservative movement is that negativity is highly communicable. The "woe is me" attitude has a natural way of spreading if not kept in check. Not only does this type of mindset cause depression and malaise within the ranks of a movement, it can cause panic, finger pointing, and backbiting. Conservatives have the statistical majority in this country; we have no reason to project anything but positivity. It is only reasonable to believe that people will not join a conservative cause if it means joining a bunch of angry paranoid crybabies. Conservatism's greatest attraction is that it is a positive movement. Being responsible for yourself, your money, and your life should bring a smile to a person's face. The conspiracy theory crowd can't bring these positive emotions to the table. One of my more dogged articles on Ron Paul is entitled "Ron Paul and the 'Cujo' Effect." This article got a rabid response from the Ron Paul crowd as it forced them to take a long hard look at the Texas congressman.

Ron Paul and the "Cujo" Effect

In the early 1980's Stephen King made all dogs a little more suspect with the horror novel *Cujo*. The story hinged around a more-than-loveable St. Bernard that contracted rabies while chasing a rabbit and became an unpredictable, crazed killing machine. A large portion of the novel and its well-created movie equivalent was centered on a mother and child as they fought to stay alive against the continuous attacks of the transformed-rabid dog. Among the thrills and chills of this story, one can pick out many sad parts to this tale. I have long thought that among the many losers of this story the dog Cujo got the worst end of the stick.

You see, Cujo, while depicted as evil and deadly, was not so; he simply had a "little crazy" in him. Unfortunately, that "little crazy," in the form of rabies, permeated his character and affected all the actions of the dog until his demise became the only reasonable solution. Heck, by mid-way through the story we were all praying that Cujo would die, and die quickly! In the end, unfortunately, a "little crazy" goes a long way and on that note, we transition easily to Ron Paul.

Ron Paul, the failed presidential candidate of 2008, has become the Cujo of the Republican Party, but not for many of the reasons you may think. Just like the loveable St. Bernard of Stephen King's creative mind, there is an often unobserved duality to the Texas congressman. Like Cujo, Ron Paul is far from being "all bad." Many of his long-standing beliefs in the constitution, limited government, and the free market are not only conservative beliefs but also bedrock examples of what has made this country great. As well, Paul's military service to this country is exemplary and worthy of emulation.

Unfortunately, Ron Paul's positive points are outweighed by his radical views on many important issues. While many rail against the tax system we currently have, Ron Paul advocates eliminating the Federal Reserve and the IRS with no feasible replacement system. When Paul gets to slashing government entities, he includes the FBI and CIA, saying they should also go the way of the dodo bird. It is here that the inflammation of a skewed viral way of thinking begins to be seen in the Paul mentality. This is not something new for the Texas congressman. During the 1980's Paul was attacking Ronald Reagan on the use of the CIA along with his "eye rolling" support for the legalization of drugs. Today, Ron Paul's modern day conspiracy theory stances and "blame America first" positions have garnered him the 9/11 truth crowds and the paranoia-pill pushers such as Alex Jones and Jesse Ventura. In reality, this is a dog that has been hunting for a long time. It is the added benefit of perspective that shows Ron Paul and Cujo to be on similar ground. Both are not inherently bad, they both just have a "little crazy" in them.

The rabidly rough ramifications of Ron Paul are that despite his libertarian foundations, he is one more unneeded albatross around the neck of the Republican

Party who has enough problems already. Paul's straw poll victory at CPAC is more than a little reminder that non-scientific polls have drawbacks; it is a reflection that the Republican Party can still be easily made to look foolish. Of course, Ron Paul will be no more electable in 2012 than he was in 1988 or 2008 and those who believe otherwise should be quarantined and observed. What he does achieve is creating more-than-adequate fodder for those that wish to link Republicans, Tea Party goers, town hall meeting attendees and the mainstream majority of this country with a few radical elements of this nation. As for those who wish to defeat Barack Obama and the big government socialists currently at the helm of this country, they must separate themselves from the frothing fans of Ron Paul. Yes, a "little crazy" also goes a long way in killing credibility for political parties, and this nation cannot afford another loss by default in 2012.

As in the case of Cujo, the presidential aspirations, and more importantly the political impacts of Ron Paul, must be "euthanized" in the country before more damage can be done.

The next major category of Ron Paul supporter is the "America Hater." Ron Paul gathers these supporters through his anti-Semitic stance against Israel and his blame-America-first stance on almost all foreign policy issues. In 2009, while on the Larry King Show on CNN, Ben Stein called Ron Paul anti-Semitic after Paul's infamous statement that the terrorists "attacked us because we are over there," Rudy Giuliani took Ron Paul to task during the 2008 presidential debates for similar, blame-America-first statements. When it comes to issues of terrorism, we can find Ron Paul consistently siding with terrorist organizations such as Hamas and al-Qaeda and blaming America for terrorist events instead of the terrorists themselves. Ron Paul supported the Mega Mosque at ground zero, a project which many Americans viewed as a symbolic slap in the face to the families of victims of 9/11. Blame is often rightly assigned to Barack Obama for being weak in the war on terror, but the president did sign the kill or capture order for Osama bin Laden. In comparison, Ron Paul disparaged Obama for circumventing Pakistan and taking out the number one terrorist in the world (Summers, 2011). The crypto-communists found in organizations such as Code Pink find the Ron Paul philosophy very appealing. In my article, "Ron Paul, Whose Side Are You On?" I called Congressman Paul out for his anti-Israel and anti-American statements and drew a line in the sand. You can decide which side you want to be on.

Ron Paul, Whose Side Are You On?

Everybody takes sides. When the chips are down on important issues, everybody can eventually be found on a side of their choosing. Those that claim to be neutral on the important issues of life are either ignorant of the reality of where they truly stand or are attempting to deceive someone. Percentages are higher on the latter, which is unfortunate because it creates a disingenuous world where people carry false banners of affiliation and advertise ideological beliefs that contradict the way they really think and act.

Texas Congressman Ron Paul's interview with Don Imus over the Israeli embargo of the Gaza Strip raises a number of disturbing questions about where this self-proclaimed Republican stands on a number of important questions. Ron Paul, a longtime isolationist, shocked many when he not only admonished Israel's lawful blockage of the Gaza Strip, but also said that Israel's action were nothing short of an act of war. When Imus mentioned that Israel was not attempting to stop humanitarian aid in the region, rather weapons being smuggled to the terrorist organization Hamas, Ron Paul released a tirade of unbelievable statements.

Paul legitimated the terrorist organization Hamas and attacked both Israel's and America's attempts to restrain terrorist organizations using boycotts and embargos. Specifically, Paul denounced actions taken against known terrorists and enablers in Palestine, Iran and Iraq under Saddam Hussein. According to Ron Paul's thinking, the terrorist organizations and the countries that harbor them have been victims of Israel and America's inability to continue to reach out in friendly dialogue. Ron Paul told Imus, "America should tell Israel they are on their own." Paul's assertion that we should abandon our ally Israel is shocking but it is only the tip of the iceberg of the congressman's misguided thinking. If we are to question Ron Paul's anti-Israel stance, should we not also question his overt anti-America stance?

Ron Paul's interview with Don Imus is riddled with "blame America first" rhetoric. Paul starts like a modern day liberal by minimizing radical Islamic terrorism and placing the terrorists as victims and America as an imperialistic aggressor. The congressman also shows how naive he is regarding the differences between past aggressors of the world and the modern terrorist. Highlighting this point, Ron Paul casually says of Hamas, "Yeah, they're probably not the best people in the world, but you know, didn't we talk to the Soviets...?" This disconnect from the realities of terrorism combined with a "blame Israel and America first" mentality does not represent the Republican Party and is not in the same universe as conservative values. Ron Paul not only sounded like a Democrat when talking to Don Imus, but his rhetoric embraced the worst of the beliefs and values of the modern liberal. Ron Paul's own words demand that he be asked, "Whose side are you on?"

The assertion that because America supports elections in the world we must also support and lift up terrorist organizations such as Hamas is more than simply wrong, it's repulsive. If Ron Paul really believes that, then his long-term view of the world can be measured in inches. Americans have the sense, the ability and the right to reject terrorist organizations no matter how they come to power. America doesn't abandon its allies for its enemies. Israel is being attacked by Hamas daily and it is here that war has been declared, not in the country's attempt to safeguard itself through embargos.

We all take sides and we are all accountable to which camp that places us in. Ron Paul does not have to adhere to conservative values or even to the Republican Party. He is not required to be a friend of Israel or even to have positive American sentiment, but he needs to be clear about where he stands, which camp he really calls home. Ron Paul, whose side are you on?

Lastly, we have the fence stragglers. These are the people I call the reasonable Ron Paul supporters. Yes, they are out there. These individuals like the fiscally conservative side of the Ron Paul rhetoric but don't agree with his anti-Semitic stances. They also shun the blame-America-first mindset that Ron Paul promotes. These people want a politician who will follow the Constitution and free market ideas and they are torn between what they like about Ron Paul and his distasteful side. It is to these people, people who can calmly discuss this politician without physical violence or e-mailed death threats, that I forward a calm but stern call to action. To the fence stragglers I say: leave the sinking ship that is Ron Paul. Time has asked and answered the question as to the political viability of Ron Paul ever winning a presidential campaign. The answer is absolutely no, no way, no chance, never. While this candidate can only pull 2-5% in a losing effort, those votes could be the difference in defeating Barack Obama in 2012. This chapter was written well before Ron Paul made his official decision to run for

President in 2012. Some people have asked me why I would invest the time to write about this guy. The answer is that a discussion of this nature has been a long time coming and for reasons that supersede this individual politician. The conservative majority in this nation has been so browbeaten through political correctness that making value judgments about anything is treated like an act of violence. If we are not careful, we will to lose our country in total silence. This has to stop now, and I am going to do my part. In doing so, I am going to make some people angry. In my 2009 book, *Feeding Lions: Sharing The Conservative Philosophy in a Politically Hostile World*, I made the case that the fight for this country is not against people, but against ideologies. This is the relevant point to take from this chapter, there will always be a need for conservatives to avoid internal decay, loss of focus, and mixed messages which conflict with a movement's core values. In short, the conservative movement will always have some sort of Ron Paul type dilemma at its doorstep. We must be ready to deal with it. The majority of Americans in this nation are just now waking up to the fact that liberals have been running roughshod over this country for years. As much as we need to face this fact, we must also understand that as a nation with a conservative majority, the reason we do not consistently dominate policymaking is because we have welcomed a number of self-destructive elements into the GOP and more importantly, the conservative movement. We must be ever vigilant to maximize our potential to win through superior numbers, and that will happen through a clear, concise, and optimistic presentation of conservative values.

Chapter 5

The Homosexual Agenda

There is an aggressive and pervasive homosexual agenda active in America today. If it were not of the utmost importance for the conservative movement to deal with this issue, many people (including myself) would avoid it due to the intense emotions that are evoked when traditional and homosexual ideologies collide. However, several important things must be stated about the homosexual's position within America. The battle being fought to maintain America's traditional conservatives values is ideological. When it is applied to the homosexual agenda, nothing changes. Individuals who embrace the gay lifestyle are not separated from humanity, simply separated by a differing ideological belief system. Most people within the gay community are intelligent, kind, and giving individuals. They are Americans who often invest themselves into the culture just like everyone else. These individuals have the right to advocate for their ideological beliefs within society. They deserve the same freedoms of speech and protection from abuse as others in this country enjoy. My position is that conservative Christians also have a right to advocate for their beliefs within the public square. Conservatives have the right to openly oppose the ideological deficits of the homosexual agenda. Without conservative opposition, those who wish to redefine the moral compass of America will do so, and with detrimental results. This ideological battle has been brought to the door step of conservatives and not vice versa. It is my position that as with other issues in America, liberals have been advancing the homosexual agenda with little opposition. The conservative movement must understand and deal with this problem. Let's get to understanding what we are dealing with and how it works. The advocates of the homosexual agenda undertsand that to be successful they must degrade traditional American culture in small, incremental stages. Conservatives must be wary of how gays and lesbians will attempt to minimize their encroachment on traditional culture. These inviduals also work to maximize obstructions preventing conservatives from defending some of the foundational pillars of society. To which pillars am I referring? In this chapter I will talk about the homosexual attacks on traditional marriage, military service, and employment and public accomodation.

Members of the gay community minimize their public accountability by framing the changes they wish to make to society as separate from the issue of sexual conduct. Those who advocate changing traditional marriage say that the gay marriage controversy is only an issue surrounding legal bonds between two loving individuals and their recognized status in society. Those wishing to fundamentally change society's perception of gays in the military most often will avoid saying they wish to invade all aspects of American culture or that they wish to force America to validate their sexual practices. In reality, deviant sexual conduct cannot be separated from homosexual issues because it is a pivotal factor that separates the homosexual from the heterosexual. However, for gay activists to change the culture successfully, the public focus on sexual conduct is all but eliminated and emphasis is placed on more benign debates such as civil rights. If these issues are addressed honestly, gays will lose their attempts to change America's values. To win their battles, supporters of the gay agenda have augmented the meaning of certain words and phrases to attack those who might offer up opposition. Here are a few examples. The term "homophobic," which traditionally has referred to an individual who is afraid of homosexuals, has been augmented today to mean anyone that challenges anything that homosexuals do or say. In fact, the term "homophobe" is currently framed by many within the gay community as referring to an individual who is not only fearful and angry, but also potentially violent against gays. The term "tolerant," which traditionally means allowing deviation from the standard, has been hijacked by the homosexual community and reframed as meaning complete capitulation to the gay agenda. In other words, if a person offers no opposition to gay-ifying America, he or she is tolerant. Conversely, anyone who wishes to debate topics of morality when it comes to these issues is considered intolerant. To be intolerant is to have the homophobic qualities of being fearful, angry and violent. The term "discriminate" has also been transformed into a tool to beat down Christians in the public square. The term "discriminate" means to distinguish or differentiate. If one observes the homosexual agenda with naiveté, one might come away thinking that to "discriminate" means to beat people to death, or make people fear for their lives. That is not the case. That is what happens when propagandists get a dictionary and start playing with the definitions. In reality, discrimination is a very good thing. If your friend is about to offer you either a hamburger or a rattlesnake, it's time to discriminate. If two jobs are offered in the newspaper-- one is managing a department store and the other is a carnival job catching knives thrown by the "Amazing Drinks-a-Lot" with your teeth--only fools will fail to discriminate between the two job offers. For Christians, discrimination is much more serious business and again, comes back to the principles of conservatism. Remember : 1. God, 2. Family, 3. Country. Christians are commanded to take personal responsibility for their lives, and that requires that they live at a higher standard than simply "going with the flow." If we get down to the simple truth, the homosexual community is simply another faction of the familiar liberal cohort, and they share a similar rejection of God. But even these liberals have to face the reality that America was not designed to be receptive to their lifestyle, and to get what they want, they attempt trickery and deception to get the majority to get out of the way. A conservative movement must reestablish conservative Americans as the deciders in this nation when it comes to important moral issues. Abraham Lincoln said in the Gettysburg Address that we have a government system that is "of the people, by the people, and for the people." The traditional value of marriage has been a bedrock that has been supported by the collective will of the American people. Gay advocacy groups know that if they are to be successful in changing American culture on this topic, they must take this important issue out of the American people's hands and place major cultural decisions in the hands of special interest groups and liberal politicians. When the Defense of Marriage Act was being debated to be placed on the ballot, gay special interest groups and liberal politicians did everything possible to keep it from the American voter. In my home state of Kansas, liberals pushed the idea that a new era of progressivism was upon us and that there was no need to place the issue of marriage on the ballot. Hundreds of priests, pastors, and preachers from across the state converged on the state capitol in Topeka, Kansas, and through prayer and public pressure fought liberal politicians to allow Kansans to vote on the issue. When the dust settled, in 2005, 70% of registered Kansans voted for traditional marriage. Twenty six other states also adopted the Defense of Marriage Act. Here are the states and the percentages of voters who voted for marriage to be between a man and a woman. States that created bans of same sex marriage are as follows: Alaska (1998- 68%), Nevada (2000-69.9%), Mississippi (2004-86%), Missouri (2004-72%), Montana (2004-67%), Oregon (2004-57%), Colorado (2006-56%). Hawaii (1998-69%) passed an amendment granting legislative authority to ban same sex marriage. The following states passed amendments that banned same-sex marriage and civil unions but not other contracts: Nebraska (2000-70%), Alabama (2004-81%), Arkansas (2004-75%), Georgia (2004-76%), Kentucky (2004-75%), Louisiana (2004-78%), Michigan (2004-59%), North Dakota (2004-73%), Ohio (2004-62%), Oklahoma (2004-76%),

Utah (2004-66%), Kansas (2005-70%), Texas (2005-76%), Idaho (2006-63%), South Carolina (2006-78%), South Dakota (2006-52%), Wisconsin (2006-59%). Banning same-sex marriage, civil unions, and other contracts: Virginia (2006-57%) (Doma Watch, 2011).

I have previously said that liberals will never give up attempting to achieve their agenda. A conservative movement is needed because we have been losing ground on important issues, and nations suffer when core traditional values are destroyed. We are not just playing catch-up here, we have to think of the future. Conservatives must have the numbers to vote in conservative judges, politicians, teachers, and individuals in every elected position that affects daily life. Remember, liberals will take the majority's voice away if they can. On August 15, 2010, I wrote about the citizens of California and how their voice had been taken away on the issue of traditional marriage by a gay activist judge. This is a salient example of the battle that is before the American people.

Gay Marriage: Court Decisions from Sodom and Gomorrah

In a recent court decision, California's Proposition 8 initiative, which stated that marriage was to be between a man and a woman, has been struck down as unconstitutional. As reported by Fox News, the decision that overruled the voters of California was made by openly gay U.S. District Judge Vaughn Walker. Walker, one of three openly gay federal judges in the country, said that the people's choice in California for traditional marriage was unconstitutional because "Proposition 8 fails to advance any rational basis in singling out gay men and lesbians for denial of a marriage license. Indeed, the evidence shows Proposition 8 does nothing more than enshrine in the California Constitution the notion that opposite-sex couples are superior to same-sex couples." Of course, homosexuals around the country dance in glee at the new court decision amidst the flutter of rainbow flags, while appeals and other court battles over the gay marriage question prepare to begin.

Today, to oppose the destruction of traditional values is to violate the less-than-silent-but-always-growing edict of political correctness. So in the spirit of being overly fair to gay marriage proponents, let us revisit Judge Walker's rationale for overturning the country's long-standing tradition of marriage. Judge Walker states on the issue of marriage that opposite-sex couples must not be seen as superior to same-sex couples. The word "superior" is commonly defined as having a higher importance, above the average in merit, or being of higher quality, to name a few. So using Judge Walker's argument on couples, is traditional marriage of higher importance than gay marriage? From the standpoint of Californians, it most certainly is. In one of the most liberal states in the country the people rose up to defend traditional marriage in November 2008. The importance of this issue was so strong that the people took action to correct the decisions of their liberal courts within five months of the state Supreme Court's legalization of gay marriage. They did this legally through the voting process, and traditional marriage won because of its importance to the voters of California.

Is opposite-sex marriage higher in merit than same-sex marriage? Turning to our Judeo-Christian foundations, the answer is swift and absolute. Homosexuality is stated clearly within the Bible as an act of sin and an abomination to God (Leviticus 18:22). Furthermore, Romans 1:26-27 observes the shameful, unnatural indecency of the homosexual union. If merit, the claim to respect and praise, is still in question, 1 Corinthians 6:9 leaves no doubt that homosexuality is unrighteous, and those who engage in this activity will be rejected from the kingdom of heaven. Far beyond damning what Judge Walker wishes to lift up in gay marriage, the Bible, from its opening pages (Genesis 2:24) throughout (1 Corinthians 7:2-16, Ephesians 5:23-33), clearly states that marriage is between a man and a woman.

Lastly, is opposite-sex marriage of higher quality than same-sex marriage? Since Judge Walker has rejected the will of the people of California to decide this issue, and he undoubtedly would wish to avoid addressing the biblical ramifications of his court decision, we are left with the matter of the constitutionality of gay-ifying the institution of marriage in America. Unfortunately for Judge Walker's position, like a remote island filled with only gays or lesbians, in time you are left with nothing but the truth. The truth is that Judge Walker's constitutionality argument is brought around again to face the findings from points one and two.

Despite the attempts of liberal activist judges to recreate the Constitution as a morally relativistic reed that blows wildly in the direction of their personal agendas and deviant desires, the law remains steadfast as a document of the American people infused with our culturally engrained Judeo-Christian values from its inception. It is from these values that the Constitution is unique. It is from these values that we as a nation have been blessed so fully. Most importantly, it is from these values that the people fight today to maintain the fundamental viability of American culture through the observance of traditional marriage.

The court decision from U.S. District Judge Vaughn Walker is far worse than an improper reading of the Constitution, it is an over attack on American culture, which the Constitution was meant to safeguard. This attack on traditional marriage is nothing short of more legislation from the court benches of Sodom and Gomorrah. So, while gays and lesbians exalt Judge Walker's court ruling in all its glitter-covered, spandexed glory, the judge's own words are revisited, and a conclusion can be extracted. Yes, Proposition 8 did "enshrine in the California Constitution the notion that opposite-sex couples are superior to same-sex couples" on the matter of marriage. It does so factually, reasonably, biblically, and constitutionally. Meanwhile, the majority of Americans have to decide either to take on a long, nasty battle to keep marriage traditional, or to stand silently as pillars of salt while America quickly becomes something radically other than America.

America is a Christian nation. Not kind of a Christian nation, but an country that overwhelmingly self-designates as Christian. According to the American Religious Identity Survey from 2001, 76.5% of Americans identify themselves as Christians, compared to 13.3% who identify as non-religious. These numbers help to explain why conservatives greatly outnumber liberals in this country. It's not just a recent phenomenon. The Christian majority in America and its rejection of homosexuality is a testament to who we are as a country. 50 of the 55 framers of the Constitution were Christians. Liberals like to focus on Thomas Jefferson and call him a Deist. They especially like to take his private letters written to the Danbury Baptist Church and somehow get the world to believe that there is a "separation of church and state" clause found in the First Amendment of the Constitution. For the record, that is not the case, and it has never been. You can find a "separation of church and state clause" in the old Soviet Union's Constitution, but not in America's. We can see that the founders had no inclination to separate Christian values from government; rather, they wanted to safeguard the people from having the government designate one church, as they had seen with the Church of England becoming government endorsed. Those who wish to run to Thomas Jefferson to validate a mild stance on homosexuality will be very disappointed. Jefferson advocated dismemberment (castration) as the proper punishment for homosexuality in his home state of Virginia. According to Miller (2011), the founding fathers would have been incredulous, incensed, and outraged with the modern-day homosexual agenda. In fact, the common thought on homosexuality during the time of the founders concerning the crime of sodomy was described by renown British attorney, jurist, law professor, and political philosopher, Sir William Blackstone—In Blackstone's Commentaries on the Law of England, in the fifteenth chapter of volume IV, "Offences Against The Persons Of Individuals," this pre-eminent legal scholar said the following:

> HAVING in the preceding chapter considered the principal crime, or public wrong, that can be committed against a private subject namely, by destroying his life; I proceed now to enquire into such other crimes and misdemesnors [*sic*], as more peculiarly affect the security of his person, while living.
>
> OF these some are felonious, and in their nature capital; others are simple misdemesnors [*sic*], and punishable with a lighter animadversion. Of the felonies the first is that of *mayhem*.

I. MAYHEM, *mahemium*, was in part considered in the preceding volume, as a civil injury: but it is also looked upon in a criminal light by the law; being an atrocious breach of the king's peace, and an offence tending to deprive him of the aid and assistance of his subjects. For mayhem is properly defined to be, as we may remember, the violently depriving another of the use of such of his members, as may render him the less able in fighting, either to defend himself, or to annoy his adversary. . . . [Book IV, Ch. 15, p. 205]

II. THE second offence, more immediately affecting the personal security of individuals, relates to the female part of his majesty's subjects; being that of their *forcible abduction* and <MARRIAGE< i>; which is vulgarly called < an>. . . . [p. 208]

III. A THIRD offence, against the female part also of his majesty's subjects, but attended with greater aggravations than that of forcible marriage, is the crime of *rape, raptus mulierum*, or the carnal knowledge of a woman forcibly and against her will. . . .

The civil law punishes the crime of ravishment with death and confiscation of goods . . . [p. 210]

. . . And by statute 18 Eliz. c. 7. it is made felony without benefit of clergy: as is also the abominable wickedness of carnally knowing or abusing any woman child under the age of ten years; in which case the consent or non-consent is immaterial, as by reason of her tender years she is incapable of judgment or discretion. Sir Matthew Hale is indeed of opinion, that such profligate actions committed on an infant under the age of *twelve* years, the age of female discretion b common law, either with or without consent, amount to rape and felony; as well since as before the statute of Elizabeth: but the law has in general been held only to extend to infants under *ten*.

A MALE infant, under the age of fourteen years, is presumed by law incapable to commit rape, and therefore it seems cannot be found guilty of it. For though in other felonies *malitia supplet aetatem*, as has in some cases been shewn; yet, as to this particular species of felony, the law supposes an imbecility of body as well as mind. [p. 212]

IT is true, says this learned judge [Matthew Hale], that rape is a most detestable crime, and therefore ought severely and impartially to be punished with death; but it must be remembered, that it is an accusation easy to be made, hard to be proved, but harder to be defended by the party accused, though innocent." He then relates two very extraordinary cases of malicious prosecutions for this crime, that had happened within his own observation; and concludes thus: "I mention these instances, that we may be the more cautious upon trials of offences of this nature, wherein the court and jury may with so much ease be imposed upon, without great care and vigilance; the heinousness of the offence many times transporting the judge and jury with so much indignation, that they are over hastily carried to the conviction of the person accused thereof, by the confident testimony of sometimes false and malicious witnesses."

IV. WHAT has been here observed, especially with regard to the manner of proof, which ought to be the more clear in proportion **as the crime is the more detestable, may be applied to another offence, of a still deeper malignity; the infamous *crime against nature*, committed either with man or beast. A crime, which ought to be strictly and impartially proved, and then as strictly and impartially punished. But it is an offence of so dark a nature, so easily charged, and the negative so difficult to be proved, that the accusation should be clearly made out: for, if false, it deserves a punishment inferior only to that of the crime itself.**

I WILL not act so disagreeable part, to my readers as well as myself, as to dwell any longer upon a subject, the very mention of which is a disgrace to human nature. It will be more eligible to imitate in this respect the delicacy of our English law, which [p. 215] treats it, in it's [*sic*] very indictments, as a crime not fit to be named.

THIS the voice of nature and of reason, and the express law of God, determine to be capital. Of which we have a signal instance, long before the Jewish dispensation, by the destruction of two cities by fire from heaven: so that this is an universal, not merely a provincial, precept. And our antient law in some degree imitated this punishment, by commanding such miscreants to be burnt to death; though Fleta says they should be buried alive: either of which punishments was indifferently used for this crime among the antient Goths. But now the general punishment of all felonies is the same, namely, by hanging: and this offence(being in the times of popery only subject to ecclesiastical censures) was made single felony by the statute 25 Hen. VIII. c. 6. and felony without benefit of clergy by statute 5 Eliz. c. 17. And the rule of law herein is, that, if both are arrived at years of discretion, *agentes et consentientes pari poena plectantus* [i.e., both the active and the passive partner are equally subject to the same punishment]

THESE are all the felonious offences, more immediately against the personal security of the subject. The inferior offences, or misdemesnors [*sic*], that fall under this head, are *assaults, batteries, wounding, false imprisonment*, and *kidnapping*.

V, VI, VII. WITH regard to the nature of the three first of these offences in general, I have nothing farther to add to what has already been observed in the preceding book of these [p. 216] commentaries; when we considered them as private wrongs, or civil injuries, for which a satisfaction or remedy is given to the party aggrieved. But, taken in a public light, as a breach of the king's peace, an affront to his government, and a damage done to his subjects, they are also indictable and punishable with fine and imprisonment; or with other ignominious corporal penalties, where they are committed with any very atrocious design. As in case of an assault with an intent to murder, or with an intent to commit either of the crimes last spoken of; for which intentional assaults, in the two last cases, indictments are much more usual, than for the absolute perpetration of the facts themselves, on account of the difficulty of proof: and herein, besides heavy fine and imprisonment, it is usual to award judgment of the pillory (Blackstone, 1769; Miller, 2011).

What we can see from the Blackstone commentaries is that when it came to describing punishments for serious crimes involving the body, the legal scholar appeared to find addressing the issue of homosexuality more distasteful than issues of murder and rape. The point here is not that homosexuality is a higher defilement of the body than murder or rape, but that there is historical consistency in the rejection of homosexuality within American culture. The original 13 states all had laws forbidding same-sex relationships when the Bill of Rights was ratified. All 50 states in the Union outlawed sodomy until 1970. The fact that America's people have traditionally rejected homosexuality based on Christian values is undeniable. We have been blessed as a nation for following God's commandments, yet liberals continue to chip away at the moral cornerstones of American culture. One of the homosexual movement's focus points in recent decades has been the military. Where once the military's stance was clear--no homosexuals allowed--in 1993, liberal democrat Bill Clinton opened the door to homosexuals with a law that allowed gays to serve as long as they stayed silent about their deviant lifestyle. The members of the homosexual community weren't satisfied, they wanted more. Barack Obama would be their enabler to push the homosexual agenda further into the ranks of the U.S. military.

If a person understands the risks those in the military take at home and abroad for our safety, it seems impossible not to have a feeling of affection for them. If we analyze fully how all of the fruits of America--its freedom, innovation, wealth, charitableness, and values--are a direct product of its security, we understand that the actual debt U.S. citizens owe their military is immeasurable. We should love those in the military, and we should respect them. This makes the homosexual assault on the military a much more personal affront--an attack not just on the soldiers of today, but on all those who have fought and died for the values of America. George Washington said, "Of all the disposition and habits which lead to political prosperity, religion and morality are indispensable supports." On December 31, 2010, I wrote with great frustration and a heavy heart on Barack Obama's decision to choose the gay agenda over American values on the issue of service in the U.S. military.

The Repeal of DADT: To March or to Sashay Into The Future?

On December 22, 2010, President Barack Obama signed a law that repeals the "don't ask, don't tell" policy for gays wishing to serve in the military. DADT was enacted by President Bill Clinton in 1993 and was a considered by many liberals a compassionate turn from the military's previous ban on gays' serving in the military. In a somewhat ironic turn of fate, in order to move the homosexual agenda forward Barack Obama would have to classify the social engineering escapades of Bill Clinton to be barbaric. At the repeal signing President Obama said that the new law would strengthen the country's national security and upholds the values that the military fights to defend. He also spoke about the new law allowing skilled homosexuals who were previously turned away from the military to now join the American fighting forces and increase the ranks of our national defense.

To the case that Barack Obama makes for radically altering the standard of operations for military service, the President stands in complete opposition to the belief system of the founding fathers and the traditional standards of this country. How far is the gap between the value system that guides the current President on the issue of homosexuality in the military than that of the founding fathers?

Cliff Kincaid of Accuracy in Media writes of George Washington's opposition to homosexuals in the military. In 1778 a soldier was court-martialed for attempted sodomy. The official record of the trial verdict and punishment makes clear Washington's disgust with homosexual activity within the military's ranks. The record of soldier Enslin's attempted sodomy court-martial was discovered in a discussion by David Barton of Wall Builders on homosexuals in the military and was collected from the writings of George Washington from the General Orders at Valley Forge. It reads as follows: "At a General Court Martial where of Colo. Tupper was President (10th March 1778), Lieutt. Enslin of Colo. Malcom's Regiment [was] tried for attempting to commit sodomy, with John Monhort a soldier; Secondly, For Perjury in swearing to false accounts, [he was] found guilty of the charges exhibited against him, being breaches of 5th. Article 18th. Section of the Articles of War and [we] do sentence him to be dismiss'd [from] the service with infamy. His Excellency the Commander in Chief approves the sentence and with abhorrence and detestation of such infamous crimes orders Lieutt. Enslin to be drummed out of camp tomorrow morning by all the drummers and fifers in the Army never to return."

So while the Continental army was in the fight of its life and the projection of victory was unsure at best, George Washington found it of utmost importance to place high value on personal conduct within the military ranks. To maintain the dignity and the cohesion of the fighting force, Washington went beyond forbidding homosexuality within the ranks; he aggressively punished it. The reasoning behind Washington's strong opposition to sodomy and other homosexual acts in the military was based in part to biblical values that repetitiously and without the slightest bit of ambiguity state that homosexuality is a sin and an abomination to God. Additionally, Washington, as well as other military leaders, understood the disruptive and demoralizing effects of promoting the homosexual lifestyle within the close confines of military duty. In other words, Washington had a very different vision from Obama's on the ideals that the military fight to defend.

The biblical issue of morality is a message that finds only deaf ears today from the liberal left. The idea of God's law when it comes into opposition of the homosexual agenda is framed with words such as "homophobia." For the advocates that would follow the radical reframing of American values on military service created by Barack Obama, it is easier to say heterosexuals fear homosexuals than to say that God is right.

Even the mentality surrounding future military participation added by overt homosexuals that may wish to join a more gay-friendly armed forces, something that Obama touts as a bolstering factor to the country's future national security, is full of warped inconsistencies. Many military experts have voiced concerns that existing U.S. soldiers will not want to share showers and other intimate living arrangements with overt homosexuals. My interview with retired Lt. Col. Robert Patterson, author of the book, "Conduct Unbecoming," who was responsible for the Nuclear Football under President Bill Clinton, highlights one such voice of opposition. On my radio show Conscience of Kansas, Patterson stated his opposition to the repeal of DADT saying it would lead to lawsuits and a lowering of military morale. According to Patterson's conversations with military personnel, he estimated that up to 25 percent of serving forces would leave, or consider leaving the military due to the repeal of DADT. A mass exodus of traditional soldiers would most likely outweigh any national security increase brought forth by overt gays entering the military.

In other words, from a national security standpoint, Barack Obama's repeal of DADT will most likely make the country less safe, less secure. From a moralistic perspective, Barack Obama is doing far more damage than simply asking the military to march to a different cultural tune; he is demanding that they sashay into moral debauchery as defenders of the free world. The repeal of DADT is truly proof that America has come a long way; the problem is that we have come a long way all in the wrong direction.

I have spent the last 10 years of my life in academia surrounded by liberals. One of the many areas in which I have found conflicts with these ivory tower masters of the Marxist reading rooms concerns how much information regular people should be given by the academic elites. I have always placed my trust in the average American citizen over the academic elitist, and I still believe this to be the right decision. Real people who work for a living tend to be more grounded in the real world and there is no doubt that a successful, growing conservative movement will find its strength in the heart and soul of America: the regular working man and woman.

It has already been made apparent that liberals will flat-out deny citizens a vote if that vote will get in the way of their plans. This also applies to the homosexual agenda. In reality, liberals will do much more than deprive you of your vote. The activists politicians and special interest groups who want to make America more morally gay-compliant have no problem taking your cash, shutting down your business, and destroying your good name. They wish to do this by making Lesbians, Gays, Bi-sexuals, and Transgender people a protected class. I addressed this issue as it was presented in my hometown of Manhattan, Kansas; however, groups such as LGBT are nation-wide, and they are pushing their agenda in every state in the country. Most readers can immediately identify an instance where they have read or seen an example of homosexuals demanding, or through back room deals forcing citizens to comply with, or worse, to endorse the gay lifestyle. I refuse to do so. This article, entitled "LGBT: Kansas, You're Not in Kansas Anymore," was published on December 12, 2010. I wrote the article documenting my opposition to the aggressive homosexual agenda that was being forced against citizen consent on the people of Kansas.

LGBT: Kansas, You're Not in Kansas Anymore

"Toto, I've a feeling we're not in Kansas anymore." Those were the troubled words of Dorothy Gale as she found herself in a foreign world in the movie The Wizard of Oz. Many have used that sentence over the years for different reasons but in general it highlights a feeling of being somewhere that is so alien to our sense of normality that we cannot fully articulate where we are, only where we are not. As a lifelong Kansan I have felt that my state, as well as its location within the heartland, is a special place where traditional American values tend to be unbending to the onslaught of the political left. When I hear liberals scream words like, "gun toter" and "bible clinger" as they fail to advance their agenda in the heartland I have to say it puts a spring in my step. However, today as the sun shines down on the plains of Kansas, a liberal storm of great consequence is brewing.

Government officials in the city of Manhattan, Kansas are about to pass a modification of an existing anti-discrimination ordinance that will create the most intrusive pro-homosexual ordinance in the country. A gay advocacy group called LGBT (Lesbian, Gay, Bi-Sexual, Transgender) that enjoys an office at Kansas State University has been part of a five-year movement to pressure city officials to create a radical alteration to the city's existing anti-discrimination ordinance.

So, what will these changes look like and how will it affect Kansans within its jurisdiction? I interviewed Dr. Paul Barkey, a Kansas pastor who has been researching the potential ordinance change on my radio program Conscience of Kansas and we covered the issue in detail. You'll need to sit down.

If the revamped anti-discrimination ordinance is passed as it currently stands, lesbians, gays, bisexuals and transgender people will be made into a protected class. This would come into effect even though there have never been any documented cases of discrimination in the city involving this group or their members. Despite this fact, after becoming a protected class these individuals would be able to bring forth allegations of discrimination against citizens and businesses. This newly designated protected class can start proceedings against average citizens simply if they feel they are "about to be discriminated against." Let that sink in for a moment. The ordinance is stated as dealing with all matters surrounding housing, accommodation and the work environment — in short, most everything in life. So pervasive is the ordinance that it is said by some to take authority over state and federal entities within the city of Manhattan. This smells more than a little fishy from a legal perspective, but let's keeps moving.

Under this ordinance, if a person is charged with discrimination they will be made to come in front of a three-person tribunal for judgment and sentencing. Out of compassion for readers knowing what is to come, this is your second chance to sit down. The tribunal itself will not be elected by voters but appointed at the whim of the mayor except for the stipulation that one member will always come from the protected status group. Without any specialized training or education, this tribunal will have the power to collect evidence, call witnesses and levy fines up to $50,000 on violators. Sound like America? You're probably sitting down now and that is good because it gets a whole lot worse. If one finds themselves in front of this tribunal, not only will one third of the judges be biased against the accused but the entire system is set up counter to the American justice system. Yes, instead of a presumption of innocence for the accused, like witch hunts of old, the accused have a presumption of guilt and must prove they are innocent. A question screams to be answered, "What is happening in Manhattan, Kansas?"

A pastoral letter of rejection to the ordinance change was signed by over 25 Kansas preachers and pastors and was read in a local Manhattan city meeting. On December 1, 2010 several hundred Kansas citizens came together at Kansas State University for a "Faith, Family, and Freedom Rally" to fellowship with one another and pray that city officials will take a different path, and set a better precedent for other towns and states that deal with this issue. The proposed ordinance is a bad law on every level from the spiritual to city economics. If a father sees a man follow his daughter into a public bathroom and objects, he may have to pay a fine. If a business decides to deny hiring, or giving services to anyone within this protected class, they may be fined out of business. In reality, the law will be used to punish traditional Christian values whenever they come into conflict with the gay agenda. When it comes to knowing when one might be seen as committing discrimination against someone with gender identity issues, your guess is as good as mine. There are currently no criteria set up to define when a violation has occurred.

If you are simply shaking your head and giving thanks this debacle is not taking place in your town, be ready for a scary surprise in your morning paper. In April of 2010 Manhattan, Kansas, deep within the Bible Belt of the heartland, had its first gay pride parade. Then, by political fiat, the month of June was name by the Manhattan mayor pro tem as Lesbian, Gay, Bisexual and Transgender Pride Month. Now in December, three out of five liberal politicians, on behalf of a minority group with a political agenda, are about to create a liberal city ordinance more extreme than anything seen in San Francisco. This new ordinance will be used as a civil hammer to beat traditional values into submission, and the shock waves will be felt around the country. Toto, we are in a big fix, because Kansas is about to be no longer in Kansas anymore.

People in Manhattan Kansas, like people in other cities and states in this country, could now see that the homosexual agenda had hit home. Like the necessity of a strong conservative movement, the process for combating this form of liberalism began with a few citizens in Manhattan, Kansas and grew. Regular God-fearing citizens got educated, became motivated, left their comfort zones, and took a stand. In this case, it was the religious groups in the Northeast Kansas area. On December 1, 2010, hundreds of Kansans attended the "Faith, Family, and Freedom" rally hosted by the organization Awaken Manhattan on the campus of Kansas State University. I attended the rally and was amazed at the loving spirit and unity found in so many people of differing faiths who came together to ask God to help their city and its leaders make a good decision regarding a proposed city ordinance alteration. The proposed ordinance change would make gays, lesbians, and transgender people a protected class. The LGBT activists quickly organized a counter rally, and when they had shouted themselves out in a different section of the student union, predictably, they marched into the "Faith, Family, and Freedom" rally to disrupt the event in full-on Saul Alinsky style. I remembered being humbled, and certainly caught off guard, at how the gay activists who came to crash the "Christian party" were received. When I saw the activists of LGBT marching into the Christian rally and encircling the crowd, strategically placing their rainbow-painted protest signs in front of the television cameras, it made me upset. My thoughts were, "why do they have to try to disrupt a peaceful gathering?" However, the presenters of the rally welcomed the gay activists with open arms and witnessed to them about the love of God. Their disruptive intentions were diminished within the loving spirit

111

of the people in attendance. I was blessed to have the opportunity to have fellowship with so many God-fearing, kind, and considerate people at this event. I also had the opportunity to visit with former City of Manhattan government officials. These people knew me from my radio program "Conscience of Kansas," and they spoke about the years of political pressure LGBT and other liberal organizations had placed on the city to gay-ify Manhattan, Kansas. While these citizens had stood strong and denied the encroachments on traditional values, now, years later, through voter apathy, a liberal majority had made its way into power. For Kansans, specifically the people of Riley County and the city of Manhattan, a conservative movement would not come to fruition in time to block one of the most liberal ordinance changes in the country, and certainly in the state of Kansas. Some people felt that even though there was a liberal voting majority within the city government, that when faced with such opposition from the community, city officials would abandon the plan of making homosexuals a protected class. People hoped that officials would abandon the new bill, especially after it was made known that citizens could be fined up to $50,000 if convicted of a charge of discrimination against this new protected class. The ordinance allowed charges to be filed against citizens who had NOT yet committed any violations. Yes, the ordinance was that crazy and more. For those who now understand how liberals work, it was the perfect situation. Three liberal politicians in city government, working on behalf of a homosexual lobby that represented somewhere around two to five percent of Manhattan, Kansas, could now force 50,000 people to endorse the gay lifestyle without it ever making its way to the American people for a vote. That's a perfect day for many liberals, and the progressive Manhattan City Commission would not pass up this chance. In early February of 2011, the ordinance alteration was passed, and I wrote about it in newspapers and online publications across the nation.

LGBT and Rainbow Justice

As of February 8, 2011, Manhattan, Kansas has created a new mentality for the state. The message is clear: "Christians, beware." There is a new sheriff in town that goes by the name of LGBT. The acronym "LGBT" stands for Lesbian, Gay, Bisexual and Transgender and this organization and those that follow under its rainbow banners now wield the power to start a legalized process that could very well shut down local businesses in the city of Manhattan. This new ordinance alteration sends a clear message that the state itself is in an uncertain state of moral decline.

For the gay activist group LGBT, the process for passing a law counter to historical Judeo-Christian values found in the Bible Belt was simple. They just had to keep lobbying and placing pressure on city officials until a liberal voting power block was present that would subvert the majority's will for the political initiatives of a special interest group. Make no doubt about it, what LGBT and its cohorts are offering Manhattan will be painful and potentially longstanding. The consistently anti-Christian American Civil Liberties Union hosts a page for LGBT and they describe the organization as follows: "The LGBT Project fights discrimination and moves public opinion through the courts, legislatures and public education across five issue areas: Relationships, Youth & Schools, Parenting, Gender Identity and Expression and Discrimination in Employment, Housing and other areas."

So how will this discrimination ordinance alteration affect the city itself? In many ways the ordinance is still bizarrely ambiguous. It was passed before the wording was finalized. Yes, the city government went beyond the Nancy Pelosi-esque wording of "we need to pass Obamacare so you can see what's in the bill," to saying in effect, "We will pass the ordinance and tell you what the fine print reads later." If you ever wanted to see an example of an out-of-control government, there it is. What we do know is that homosexuals, amongst others, will be able to forward allegations of discrimination against business owners and landlords that may force private Kansas citizens to be brought before a non-elected human rights panel that the city mayor will appoint. The panel, which by its rules will always have an activist member appointed, will have the authority to call witnesses, collect evidence and levy heavy fines. This is a Pandora's Box and I believe its creators have no true idea of how much it will be used and misused if it is not repealed.

The ordinance allows gays to bring preemptive violation charges against citizens they believe may discriminate against them in the future. Unless science can rapidly catch up with the modern liberal version of equality, Manhattan, Kansas has created a city ordinance reminiscent to Tom Cruise's performance in the science fiction movie "Minority Report." That should be a clincher to call this ordinance insane and unenforceable, but there is more. The ordinance has a sloppy and completely incomprehensible definition of gender identity of which one of the byproducts is the need for employers to create gender-identity-acceptable bathrooms and other facilities. What will be the identifiers to designate these facilities? When a town gets to this level of absurdity, who knows, maybe a "?" placard will suffice.

I have never been more ashamed to be a Kansan or a citizen of Manhattan than I was when I saw the Christian value of morality and American citizens' freedom being trampled upon by this radical ordinance alteration. However, the anger I and others feel toward this legislation should be qualified to avoid misconception on such a sensitive subject. Most likely everyone knows a person described within the acronym LGBT. They are true members of our communities, known to us as acquaintances, friends and family. There is no doubt that Christians can, and should continue a respectful dialogue with those whose life choices violate God's laws. What cannot happen in showing respect to those we disagree with is selling out our biblical values.

It is also important to understand where this ordinance alteration stands within our community, state and nation. The LGBT-driven ordinance in Manhattan supersedes individual conversations and exchanges of ideas of morality. The legislation takes the issue of morality into the public square and the heart of our society. In this arena, the nation will be pulled toward the values we accept collectively. Here there is no room for tolerance when it comes to our core Judeo-Christian values and the tone the community sets for the future. If we are honest with ourselves, the dilemma of the ordinance alteration in Manhattan, Kansas, is not a product of a sweeping tide of homosexual support, it is an inevitable outcome when the majority of citizens become lukewarm to the necessity of placing moral conservatives into public office. While we care for those with the deviant lifestyle of homosexuality, they do not share our value system, nor can we acquiesce to their societal demands without facing the ultimate damnation of such a decision. In the end, the repeal of such an affront to Christian values as seen in this recent ordinance alteration by the City of Manhattan is not just something we should consider, it is our responsibility.

Liberals never stop, never give up. That's how they had managed to take a conservative town in the Bible belt of Kansas and make it a little sliver of San Francisco. Liberals did this, and we should not be shocked that this was their plan. However, conservatives allowed it to happen, and the people of Manhattan were having to come to grips with this harsh reality. The situation in Manhattan, Kansas, is simply proof of a larger situation that is happening in all the states of the country. The answer to the problem in Kansas is applicable to the whole nation. The people have to look to God for guidance, and take action with a determined spirit. When I say a determined spirit, I mean that people have to be willing to ask God for strength and allow him to bless them with a "spine of steel." Liberals will politically fight to the death to push their initiatives. Once they have locked them into place, such as what had transpired in Manhattan, Kansas, reversing anti-Christian laws will be hard to do. A conservative movement must be composed of people who understand the extreme opposition they will face and be ready to face it with the shield of faith. Without it, you're a political casualty on the cultural battlefield.

After the city of Manhattan's anti-discrimination ordinance had been transformed into a homosexual bill, I worked tirelessly to let people know what was happening in the state of Kansas. I did this by way of radio and my newspaper column. I repeatedly offered the liberal politicians of the city government an opportunity to debate me on the issue. My radio show broadcasts were even sent to the e-mail accounts of city officials, but we heard nothing back. I offered to debate the LGBT faction that was now ensconced within Kansas State University and I received no responses. I wanted to face these liberals and beat them on the battlefield of ideas, but without any takers, a focus was placed on a petition that was being forwarded by Christians in the community. They were hoping to repeal the ordinance. On March 4, 2001, I wrote about this bold step to push back against the homosexual tide that was taking over this Kansas community, and to document for conservatives around the country, the timeline of how quickly a town had been transformed into a homosexual Mecca.

Christians Push Back Against Gay Agenda in Kansas

Recently there has been a push by liberals to advance the homosexual agenda into pivotal areas of American life. Barack Obama's abolition of "don't ask don't tell" in the military has replaced silent service for gays with the requirement that the heterosexual majority of our fighting forces now accommodate a new, aggressive homosexual agenda if they wish to continue to defend the country. The foundation of traditional marriage in American culture is also under full assault. In another stunning attempt to force the homosexual agenda on the American people, Fox News reports that Barack Obama has ordered Attorney General Eric Holder to no longer defend the Defense of Marriage Act, the law of the land that states marriage as between a man and a woman, as constitutional. Thus we see the lengths liberals will go to achieve their goals, to fundamentally change society. What many might not be aware of is just how many parts of daily lives are being challenged by the gay agenda and the modus operandi of those involved.

If one looks closely, a repetitious pattern of presentation and action is observable from the liberal left. To start with, some radical change in traditional culture for the greater good is always forwarded, while at the same time the public at large is denied an opportunity to exercise their voices through a vote on the issue. When a people's vote does slip by the liberal machine, it is later circumvented by a governmental fiat. To liberals, the best societal decisions are best made without society. The issue of how we recognize traditional marriage, the law that Barack Obama is now declaring void without the authority of the courts, as a tyrannical third-world dictator might do, is an issue that has already been decided by the voters. The overwhelming majority of Americans have already voted for traditional marriage as being between a man and a woman. Once again, it would take a complete subversion of the voting majority to attack this Judeo-Christian pillar of American society. Unfortunately, this is not just a Barack Obama problem. The actions of this President are simply a byproduct of a growing problem that has been taking place for some time in this country. In reality,

115

Barack Obama is nothing more than the predictable fruit of the loins of modern-day liberalism, and that fruity fruit has been very fruitful.

As moral depravity is being pushed on America's defensive forces and the foundation of America in traditional marriage, liberals have been working to destroy Christian values in day-to-day business interactions. While an infiltration of homosexual ideology may have been brewing as far back as 2005, the actual blitzkrieg that struck Manhattan, Kansas, and turned the traditional town into the most liberal in the state happened within 11 short months. Within those months, the gay activist group LGBT became ensconced within Kansas State University, a month was designated by political decree for Lesbian, Gay, Bisexual and Transgender awareness complete with its own gay pride parade, and the passage of the most liberal anti-Christian discrimination law the state of Kansas has ever seen was passed by a 3-2 vote. In keeping with the liberal standard operating procedures of today, the voters of Kansas were bypassed to advance a political agenda that was, and continues to be, counter to the majority's will. Beware of anyone or any group that tells of the great things they will do that you will eventually enjoy, and then works with all their ingenuity to make sure you are excluded from the decision making process.

While the nation needs to push back the societal suicide being demanded by Barack Obama and liberal surrogates, the people of Manhattan, Kansas, are taking it upon themselves to stand up for their town's traditional values. They are doing this through a repeal petition on the anti-discrimination ordinance alteration that made lesbian, gay, bisexual and transgender people a protected class with the ability to bring preemptive charges against citizens of Kansas, thus beginning a process of mayor-appointed kangaroo courts with non-elected judges and business crushing fines. The same bill gives no protection to Christians outside their congregational buildings as "Main Street" is being transformed into "Gay Street" and all those who find themselves in violations will be severely punished. The citizens of Manhattan, Kansas, are pushing back against the gay agenda with the radical notion that they, of all things, should be able to vote on the laws that will affect their daily lives. Local Kansas pastors and other Christian leaders are currently gathering petition carriers and making their case for the ordinance repeal through the community website Awakenmanhattan.com.

As the nation decides whether or not to push back against the liberal gay agenda being forced upon the majority of America, they would do well to watch the battle that is brewing in Manhattan, Kansas. For this city in the heartland of America, the majority of citizens are going to take a stand and attempt to reverse a portion of the invasive gay agenda that is attacking not only our state, but the country. The battle that will be fought and the ending outcome may very well reflect the nation's will to hold fast to the biblical and constitutional values that have made this country great.

By the time this last article was being prepared for publication, I was contacted by Josh McGinn, the publicity face of the gay activist organization, "Flint Hills Human Rights Project." This organization had also been a part of the lobby to push Manhattan city officials to gay-ify the city. McGinn was angry about my second article, "LGBT and Rainbow Justice," which he had read on the popular Canadian conservative website "Canada Free Press." McGinn demanded a spot on my radio show to debate me on the issue. I was only too happy to oblige him. In Appendix A, I have included a complete transcription of the interview. I believe that it is the fullest discussion on the Manhattan discrimination ordinance that readers will find.

I am always polite with the people I debate on the radio. My purpose when I debate is always clear: I want to make a case for conservative values, and I want people to hear liberals tell them who they are and what they stand for. That is the harder part, as liberals know that what they believe cannot be said straight out or the great unwashed--the gun toters and Bible clingers-- will oppose them, and they will lose on their issues. Why will they lose? They will lose because the dirty gun-toting Bible clingers outnumber them. This is where I excel when it comes to radio. I create a non-hostile environment where liberals end up telling people the truth--not the liberal script, but the truth. It's a one-time shot for me because liberals seldom come back after being exposed. This happened with the Communist Jodie Evans of Code Pink when she came on my show and justified Osama bin Laden's attack on America on 9/11. The truth was shown plainly in my interview with Shirley Phelps Roper, but I can't take too much credit there, as she was almost too willing to make my points for me. All were liberals though--yes, even the cultists at Westboro Baptist Church were voting liberal Democrat before they decided everyone but them were going to hell. Create an environment where liberals will say who they are and where the American people actually fit into their agenda--that is my goal. Josh McGinn of the Flint Hills Human Rights Project not only acted in a manner consistent with how I have defined liberals within this book, but also was adamant about doing what all liberals strive to do--make sure that "We the People" are nowhere near decision making concerning major, life-altering laws and initiatives. I invite people to read the interview in Appendix A in detail and send their comments to ibbetsonusa.com. In Appendix B, I have included all the full-length versions of the Bible verses that I have referenced and often paraphrase in the articles within this book. I have used the New International Version translation, but it is only one option of many out there. I do think it is important for readers to see how liberals think and act in opposition to scripture. Giving the full scriptures found in the arguments I make for opposing liberal ideology and the call for a conservative movement keeps me and what I say under your critical eye. Ronald Reagan had it right when he said, "Trust But Verify." I am an advocate of that philosophy.

This chapter has, among other things, highlighted a direct challenge liberals have made to traditional values here in my home state of Kansas. As much as I love my state, and as active as I am in the local fight to champion conservative values, this fight is nationwide. The challenges that I present here are taking place in all communities in the country. Doubt me? Google the issues presented in this book and include your state, county, or city. Your eyes will get wide, your heartbeat will quicken, and you will get that sinking feeling in the pit of your stomach. Many of you reading this book have already come to terms with the reality that this nation is in a big mess, and you're interested in listening to someone who advocates standing up and fighting back. Good! You're needed, along with your wife, husband, sister, brother, children, neighbors—I think you get the picture. What is also needed is the mentality for victory. I have already given a usable definition of liberals, and it will serve you well. As we walk through these chapters, I will offer examples of some of the cultural issues at stake, and as importantly, I will point out the tactics used by liberals to win their arguments and to force the majority to bow down to things conservatives know are wrong. Here is one of those golden moments, and it probably wouldn't hurt to take a few notes. The standard tactic of liberals is to maximize a negative perception of their opposition. I previously mentioned the augmentation of terms like "homophobe" and how today it's not enough for liberals to frame those who want to debate the morality of homosexuality as being fearful of gays. Even though fear of homosexuals is something I have seldom seen in the Christian community, when it comes to augmenting definitions of words like "homophobe," the misuse of the words fear, hatred and violence are introduced and pushed with the term. Additionally, liberals hijack legitimate cultural movements and incorporate them into gay movements. One specific example is seen in the gay community's actions to co-opt the civil rights movement as its own. At the 22nd Annual Gay and Lesbian Alliance Against Defamation media awards, Russell Simmons of the hip-hop industry said, "You can't fight for freedom without fighting for freedom for everyone." (Mitchell, 2011). Stuck to his side like they were velcroed together was the Rev. Al Sharpton, who immediately started quoting Martin Luther

King. Sharpton quoted Dr. King by saying, "You judge a man not by where he stands in the times of convenience but where he stands in the times of controversy" (Mitchell, 2011). This is a common occurrence in the homosexual agenda: the attempt to frame civil rights and the desire to gay-ify America as the same thing. If we get down to the truth, the strategy is pretty simple. In the modern world, people know and have accepted that racism is wrong. The Ku Klux Klan in today's world no longer dominates culture. In our country today, these kinds of intolerant people are but a few beer-bellied hicks with more teeth than I.Q. points. If gay activist organizations can get mainstream America to believe being a gay person today is the same as being a black man or woman in the 1960s, they know that will be a powerful emotional hammer to culturally beat Christians into submission. The problem with that comparative argument is that it is completely absurd. Anti-discrimination laws were based on the concept that black Americans and other minority races had no choice concerning which skin color they were born with. Skin color is designated as an "immutable" quality. On the other hand, homosexuality has never been proven by science and has certainly not been validated by the Bible as an immutable quality. Quite to the contrary, homosexuality is a personal lifestyle, a life choice made by the individual. Personally, if I were a black person in this country, I would be offended by the narrative spun by the gay community that alludes to the idea that blacks and homosexuals are the same. As a white man, as an American, I am offended when charlatans such as the Rev. Al Sharpton attempt to take the words of Dr. King and make them fit into a gay advocacy sales pitch. Dr. King faced real racism, attacks on people based on immutable qualities, not life choices that run in direct opposition to the Bible. Dr. King was a Christian: he had faith in God and he believed in the Bible. I tell you with complete certainty that King would have shown the same love and compassion to the gay community that were shown on December 1, 2010 at Kansas State University at the Faith, Family and Freedom Rally. He would have witnessed to the gays, homosexuals, bi-sexuals, and transgendered people who attended the event but would have also rejected their deviant lifestyle based on Biblical values. In other words, Dr. Martin Luther King, if alive today, would be one of the leaders of the conservative movement.

If you take the conservative position in public on this issue, you will be air-bombed by the activist spin doctors. Their mode of operation will first be to minimize the Bible and its clear teachings on the subject. This will be followed by the usual psycho-babble I have termed the "inclination soup argument." This comes in various forms, but generally, it is the argument that everyone has these natural "inclinations," some heterosexual and some homosexual. They are like the letters in a bowl of alphabet soup. Life is nothing more than a quick stir of the bowl, with the possibilities infinite and beyond human control. Whatever letters come to the top first, that's your personal makeup. For example, if it's S&M well, you're a sado-masochist; if it's G.A.Y., then sorry, but you have no choice but to be a homosexual; and so on. You have no power over, or responsibility for your inclinations than that. The goal of the "inclination soup" argument by the spin doctors is to force their opposition to analyze every feeling and emotion in the entire cosmos, especially every inclination they have ever had until they can no longer tell which side is up. A seed of doubt is all these spin doctors are looking for. The inclination soup argument is a liberal construction. The answer to the inclination soup argument, no matter how it is presented, is simple. Here it is. First, there is a living God; deal with it. The Bible tells us that we are made unique and that we have within us a human nature that has a tendency toward evil. Inclinations within humanity are many and diverse, some being good and some being bad. We know this to be true. Some people have urges to be unfaithful in marriage, some adults have sexual urges toward children, some have an urge to force themselves sexually upon others. People have urges in the form of fetishes that range from what society would consider mundane to the mind boggling. The argument has been made by some medical professionals that many of these negative urges or inclinations are developmental and found in the nuturing process. I believe that homosexuality is in that group, with many others. However, even if you do not agree, even if you feel that homosexuality is a hard-wired inclination, the Bible answers this question definitively. There is no urge or inclination, good or bad, within men and women that is beyond what God has given his creation the power to have victory over. So—it doesn't matter if you are a nature or nurture advocate—God gives you the power to overcome and the ability to follow his commands. The idea that we are randomly given inclinations that are beyond our control to address is a rejection of the power of God to work through us.

Here is the last golden nugget of truth on the issue of the homosexual agenda, and it's another sensitive point because we have to focus on the choir, that is, other conservatives. Back in August of 2010, a firestorm erupted between columnist and book writer Ann Coulter and Joseph Farah, editor and chief executive officer of World Net Daily, one of the largest conservative political sites on the web. Doug Mataconis (2010) reported for *Outside the Beltway*, on the conservative infighting. The battle came after Coulter was dropped as a speaker for the "Taking America Back National Conference" hosted by World Net Daily. Coulter was dropped from the conference because she had accepted an invitation by GOProud, a homosexual Republican organization, to speak at its event entitled, "HOMOCON." Joseph Farah said about the incident, "Ultimately, as a matter of principle, it would not make sense for us to have Ann speak to a conference about 'taking America back' when she clearly does not recognize that the ideas to be espoused there simply do not include the radical and very unconservative agenda represented by GOProud" (Mataconis, 2010). Ann Coulter responded by saying, "That's silly, I speak to a lot of groups and do not endorse them. I speak at Harvard and I certainly don't endorse their views. I've spoken to Democratic groups and liberal Republicans groups that loooove abortion. The main thing I do is speak on college campuses, which is about the equivalent of speaking at an al-Qaida conference. I'm sure I agree with GOProud more than I do with at least half of my college audiances. But in any event, giving a speech is not an endorsement of every position held by the people I'm speaking to..." (Mataconis, 2010).

First, let me say that I respect Ann Coulter. We post her column linked back to her website at our master website of conservative values at www.ibbetsonusa.com, and that is not going to change anytime soon. Coulter is usually right on the issues, and I love her flair in taking on liberals. With all that said, and with great respect, I think she is wrong on this issue. Sure, she has the right to speak anywhere she wants, and it should not be presumed that she endorses the views of everyone in a crowd she may address. However, Ann Coulter is a major conservative figure, and with that position comes great responsibility. I believe that Coulter has the responsibility not to allow her star power to be coopted to promote the homosexual agenda. It's the same reason I would not allow myself to be booked to speak at a pedophile convention, even if I were there to talk about conservative values. It's the wrong image and the wrong message to send.

The homosexual organization GOProud would also infest the Conservative Political Action Conference (CPAC) by becoming one of its co-sponsors. This is clearly an action to infuse a liberal ideology into the Republican Party. This comes at a time when the GOP desperately needs to cleanse itself and get back to core conservative values. Conservative writer and lecturer Star Parker shares my opinon on this issue. In fact, she refused to attend CPAC due to GOProud's inclusion in the event. In her article in the Washington Examiner entitled, "*Gay Conservative Is an Oxymoron*," she said, "Gay is everything that 'conservative' is not. The foundation of the worldview that so-called "gay conservatives" embrace has far more in common with liberalism than with conservatism" (Parker, 2011). She went on to say, "It's a worldview that is man-centered rather than God-centered. It is a worldview that rejects eternal truths passed on from the beginning of time. Although the worldview that "gay conservatives" choose to invent may diverge with liberals, their common ground is that they make it all up. And it is here where "gay conservatives" and "liberals" fundamentally depart from conservatives" (Parker, 2011). When we look at the conservative movement that has been building for years, and has been gaining momentum through organizations from the 9-12 project to the Tea Parties and beyond, we must also acknowledge the liberal agents who are acting from within the Republican tent. These people have to go. Can homosexuals be useful to the conservative movement by voting for conservatives on Election Day? The answer is yes. Homosexuals, like other liberals who normally vote Democrat, have the freedom to vote for whomever they want. If they are drawn to vote for conservatives because a totality of their concerns are being addressed by that candidate, their votes are certainly welcome. However, as with libertarians, a conservative movement must glean votes on its own terms. Core conservative values should always stay intact. If that means losing non-conservative voters, so be it. It is a much smaller price to pay than for the party to lose its soul.

Chapter 6

Terrorism

If there is one facet of domestic and international policy that the U.S. government should apply a constant, no-nonsense vigilance to, it is the war on terror. Unfortunately, the Obama administration is worse than "out to lunch" on this issue. At least when you are "out to lunch" there is the outside hope that you will one day come back. Barack Obama and his radical support base look at America as worse than the terrorists. This is the truth, and the proof behind that statement is not only in the never-ending assembly line of initiatives that are guaranteed to fail, but also in the anti-America mentality these liberals bring to the fight against the jihadists of the world. Let's start with the administration's unwillingness to accept the fact that we have an enemy out there that wants to kill us. These spineless liberals can't even use the "words" necessary to describe the enemy. In her first testimony before Congress, Homeland Security Secretary Janet Napolitano refused to say the word "terrorism" and instead used the vague non-descript term "man-caused" disasters (Bair, 2009). When asked about why she used this bizarre wording, for what most Americans clearly see as the fight we have with terrorists, Napolitano told the German news site Spiegel Online, "I referred to man-caused disasters. That is perhaps only a nuance, but it demonstrates that we want to move away from the politics of fear toward a policy of being prepared for all risks that can occur" (Bair, 2009). In other words, to the Obama administration, the word terrorism had become a dirty word characterized by Napolitano as part of the politics of fear (Bair, 2009). Obama's administration wanted more "soft terminology" in regards to the "T-word." *The Guardian* reported in March of 2009 that the White House had e-mailed Pentagon staff that the terms "Long War on Terror," or "Global War on Terror," would be replaced with the term "Overseas Contingency Operations" (Burkeman, 2009). These word changes, and the push to simply avoid thinking with a war mentality, makes America less safe. If you think that this was just a bit of isolated word confusion for the new president, think again. In 2011, after serving almost a full term, when faced with the terrorist dictator Muammar Gaddafi and a civil war in Libya, Obama ordered air strikes in the country but again went back to non-war-like terminology saying America was involved in "Kinetic Military Action" (Allen, 2011).

124

What is wrong with these people? The answer is that they are liberals and in being so, they are weak when it comes to facing the war on terror and our enemies.

Unclear Strategy in Libya Presents Dangers to U.S.

The Barack Obama administration has remained motionless while the people of Libya have struggled and even died to replace Col. Muammar al-Gaddafi. Gaddafi, who came to power in 1969, has been a sponsor of terrorism around the world and a ruthless dictator to his people for over 40 years. Ronald Reagan called Gaddafi the "mad dog of the Middle East." His removal from power, if done in the right way, could have been a positive situation for both the people of Libya and the U.S. Unfortunately, that window of opportunity has passed and now the Obama administration, after allowing hostilities to escalate, will attempt more passive U.N. strategies to quell this radical Islamic dictator. This strategy by the White House will inevitably fail in helping freedom seekers in Libya and it will also cause complications for America down the road.

The White House has already set a precedent for inaction in this region, and the sudden change we see coming from the Obama administration gives the appearance to the world that the President is being motivated to action by other forces. To radicals such as Gaddafi and his allies this is a sign of weakness. Barack Obama has done nothing but reinforce the point that the United States will take the backseat in reducing violence among the Libyan people. In fact, the president has gone to considerable efforts to make sure that friends and foes alike in the world understand just how many military options the U.S. won't use to deal with Muammar al-Gaddafi.

Settling back into America's more familiar emasculated role within the United Nations, the United States will be limited predominantly to air strikes in Libya. Now Americans can settle in and watch the UN Security Council perform its primary function, creating resolutions that we must follow but that the radicals disregard when it is in their best interest. A little certainty of the old George Bush "shock and awe" would have rectified this situation rapidly, but alas, Gaddafi, as opposed to Saddam Hussein, has made a better dice roll when it comes to picking U.S. administrations to provoke. In fact, just what is the objective with the U.S. becoming involved in a Libyan civil war?

The White House states that the U.S. will work to safeguard the people of Libya. Are we to consider this vague mission statement a plan for regime change, nation building, or something as simple as a minor public show of assistance? Detractors of the president say that situations such as the handling of the Libyan dictator show another example of the Obama's inexperience and inability to clearly step forward as Commander in Chief of America. To others, the president's actions when it comes to Islamic nations reflect the strange bond that the president has with Muslim countries of the world. Even now, with America's new ambiguous stance against violence in Libya, the president appears to be more concerned about assuaging concerns in the Muslim world than protecting American interests and the ideals that America is known to stand for. Obama's half motions and half-hearted policy stances are painful to watch and also come with a price. Obama will fail to find the allies in the Muslim world that he is so adamantly seeking. In fact, Muammar al-Gaddafi, and especially future dictators like these that we will face, will most likely have more success than Obama in garnering support from Muslim organizations such as the Arab league. The problem with the president's failure to lead is not centered on Libya; it is a much bigger and farther-reaching problem. Within the Middle East, countries that debate aggression against America must see that our nation's leadership is clear and concise about what actions we will take to secure our own interests. That includes America's belief in the value of freedom around the world and what we will do to support those that seek liberty against tyranny. If we are weak as a nation on our core values, we invite aggressors to attempt to force their values and their control over us. This is not acceptable to the long-term security of a free nation and the people of this country should not accept the precarious position in the world that the Barack Obama administration currently places us.

When we talk about risk to the American people, an observance must be made of Obama's primary campaign pledge to shut down Guantanamo Bay, the maximum security center controlled by the United States on the island of Cuba. Obama failed to meet his promise to have the facility shut down in one year, but readers need to know more than simply that Obama is failing to come through on some of his campaign promises. Obama has failed to shut down Guantanamo Bay, but that is not for lack of trying. The main obstacle that Obama has faced in keeping his 2008 presidential primary promise on this issue is that it was a bad idea of epic proportions to start with. The Guantanamo closing was another idea launched from a liberal brain because it worked on paper as a hypothetical concept and then failed miserably when applied in the real world. In reality, the idea of shutting the facility down came from the notion that the terrorists held at Guantanamo Bay might be bad, but America--that's code for 50% George W. Bush and 50% everybody who agreed with Bush, was definitely worse for not giving these terrorists public trials. There is truly an identifiable disdain for America within this thinking. It is the rejection of the same values conservatives hold dear: 1.God, 2. Family, 3. Country. When we see how liberals operate in the war on terror, it is all too obvious that they feel an affinity with the terrorists and hostility toward this country. On January 7, 2010, I warned the nation of the dangers of following the current administration's game plan in the war on terror.

Presentation vs. Taste: Why Barack Obama is Cooking Up Disaster in the War on Terror

> There is little doubt that my pallet is not as refined as my liberal friends' and I have always found it hard to watch the gourmet shows where hours are spent meticulously preparing complex dishes that then cover about three inches of the plate. I guess you can say that while the crème de la crème is still waiting for their single mouthful of Lobster and Prawn Mornay, I will be finishing the last bites of a full plate of steak and potatoes. However, there is one very practical thing that can be learned from the fancy dishes tossed about from those exotic chefs of iron and that is the value of presentation. It is undoubtedly true that we eat first with our eyes. It is this use of presentation to the American people, our enemies, and our allies in the war on terror by the Barack Obama administration that I wish to discuss now.

> Barack Obama, since becoming president, has gone on a quest to improve what he states is a negative world image of America. To do this he has ordered the closing of Guantanamo Bay despite not having a plan for where to relocate the prisoners of that facility. The President has also, without qualification, pronounced this country a land of torturers with its use of advanced interrogation techniques and now the administration poises itself to make 9-11 mastermind Khalid Sheikh

Mohammed the most well-known terrorist recruiter in the world by way of a lengthy public show trial.

While all this is taking place, the Obama administration solidifies a transition back to the pre-9/11 reactive criminal justice style of opposition to terrorism. If we put the actions of Barack Obama in the war on terror on the plate of reality, how is he presenting America to those that want to kill us? Is there any doubt left in this great nation that Obama is inviting terrorists to our doorstep through these actions?

While American soldiers continue to fight abroad, Obama's months of indecision to send the requested troops to Afghanistan in combination with a public troop withdrawal date sends a clear message that this administration is not in the fight. The Homeland Secretary's attempt to change the word "terrorism" into "man-caused disasters" shows our enemies that we have less of a desire to get away from promoting the *politics of fear* to the world, and more that this administration operates within the *politics of the frightened* when it comes to facing radical Islamic terrorism. When U.S. Army Major Nidal Malik Hasan, you know, the guy whose business cards read "soldier of Allah," killed American soldiers on American soil, Barack Obama's first words were that we should not be quick to come to judgment. When Umar Farouk Abdulmutallab, the terrorist who attempted to blow up Northwest Flight 253 is caught, instead of screaming the war cry that Americans won't stand for this, the news is prosaic with statements that the unfortunate happening was an isolated incident in combination with Homeland Security Secretary Napolitano's mild concern over the event and praise for post-event procedures.

The bottom line is that presentation matters, and Barack Obama would do well to embrace the Reagan philosophy of "Peace through Strength" before it is too late. To those who are put out over the idea of having to hold their bowels one hour before airport landings or being made to parade in front of full-body scanners, projecting their little naked selves at the airport, all I can say is this, "you ain't seen nothing yet." As the Obama administration continues to present America as a country unable to hear, speak, or think about bringing the fight to the terrorists, frequent flyers should prepare themselves for future cavity searches with their names on them and much, much more.

The answer is as obvious as a poorly cooked Lobster and Prawn Mornay, well, more like a poorly cooked T-bone; this administration cannot handle the heat of the kitchen when it comes to fighting radical Islamic terrorists and those that aid them. While Obama twiddles and vacillates on the issue of fighting and destroying an enemy that is not going to stop, we, the American people, will be forced to eat every un-tasty dish in the form of suffering the consequences of presenting a weak front in the war on terror.

What was Obama thinking when he was gathering Code Pink bundled cash and promising to close the maximum-security facility on the island of Cuba during the 2008 presidential primary? Certainly he must not have realized that the detainees left at Guantanamo Bay, were the worst of the worst. Some of these detainees would never have cases fit for criminal court procedures. This is not a sign that they were unjustly detained. It means they were taken into custody as enemy combatants in a war zone with a different detention standard than criminals arrested in the United States. Some of these individuals cannot be released to their birth countries because those countries will not accept them. The bottom line is that some of these terrorists who were caught on the battle field trying to kill American soldiers will have to stay in a cell until they die of old age or are so old they have no desire for the martyrs' 72 virgins. After making promises to his supporters, Obama was met with a harsh reality—he would need to keep the detainees in a safe and secure facility away from the public eye, like, I don't know, Guantanamo Bay, or convince the American people it was a good idea to house these terrorists in their backyards. Needless to say, Guantanamo Bay is still open for business.

The Guantanamo Bay dilemma did not stop the Obama administration from attempting to go forward with terrorist trials taking place in the public criminal courts. The goal of the Obama administration was to have a great show trial staring Khalid Sheikh Mohammed, one of the alleged masterminds of 9/11. It was going to be an example to the world of just how kind and fair liberals could be to terrorist detainees following the evil Bush years. The problem was the same issue faced by the administration in attempting to shut down the facility in Cuba; it was a bad idea of epic proportions. On March 11, 2010, I wrote about the potential Khalid Sheikh Mohammed court trial as plans were falling apart in New York and more and more, Americans were coming to grips with the truth that Barack Obama, Eric Holder, and his congressional clown car full of liberals had no idea how to prosecute the war on terror.

Khalid Sheikh Mohammed: Terrorist Trial Space For Rent?

The future of the public trial of suspected 9/11 mastermind Khalid Sheikh Mohammed is now in question. It could be said that the Obama administration's "It's on, it's off, maybe, I don't know?" stance on the war on terror has now created yet another mini-drama. If this president did not have to be commander-in-chief, an ample portion of Obama's and the nation's woes might very well be mitigated.

Right out of the 2008 election gate, Barack Obama has been working to accomplish the impossible task of maintaining public support while being an anti-war president in a time of war, or more aptly a liberal appeaser sent to defend this country against radical jihadists. This matchup was never going to be pretty, but it has turned out to be bizarre in an almost theater-like fashion.

One after another, Barack Obama and his supporting cast have presented to the American people a series of horrifying slapstick missteps in the war on terror. Early on, the president tells the world in a series of apology tours that our advanced interrogation techniques were "torture" and begs forgiveness for America's defense of itself. Next, he sets a closing date for our most secure terrorist detention center in Guantanamo Bay with no plan for housing the terrorists currently within its walls. Just to make that bad decision a little worse, I discovered through conversations with Kansas Congressman Todd Tiahrt on my radio program the Conscience of Kansas that as many as thirty of the terrorists from Guantanamo Bay being brought to the U.S. will likely be released within the U.S. populace. This is stomach-turning information to say the least; but even worse, these released terrorist detainees would be eligible for government aid such as welfare. My conversation with Tiahrt about his work on the No Welfare for Terrorists Act dating back to May 2009 simply highlights one of many painfully bad decisions of this administration. Unfortunately for the American people, having to pay the bill for terrorist detainees to get on their feet in their own neighborhoods is not the finale of Obama's sad drama.

Trumping the administration's ill-thought dress rehearsals of softening words pertaining to terrorism and their grandiose mental confusion on when the system "worked fine" versus when the system "worked terribly," as seen last Christmas, we have the issue of Khalid Sheikh Mohammed. In November 2009 Obama's Attorney General Eric Holder announced that the alleged mastermind of 9/11 and other conspirators would be brought back to the scene of the crime for the "trial of the century." The idea of giving terrorists of the magnitude of KSM the world's microphone to recruit new followers to Islamic Jihad through a long protracted public trial has never set well with the public. Jane Mayer of the New Yorker documented a gathering of several hundred in New York in December 2009 in which protestors to the terrorist trials, some family members of 9/11 victims, viewed Holder's KSM trial announcement. Adding insult to injury, by January

2010, the New York Times was reporting that the cost of the KSM trials would exceed more than 200 million dollars a year.

Whether or not it is a product of a lack of political support, growing negative public sentiment, or the huge financial burden, the Obama administration appears to be considering throwing the public KSM trial in the trashcan. What does this potential change in the administration's plans tell us? The answer is that we are more likely looking at the will of the American people than the thoughtful deliberations of this administration. If this is the case, this potential change would seem most positive and even worthy of celebration that the will of the people can still overrule poor decision making from Washington, right? Even my own personal yardstick for gauging when good things are happening in this country, when the ACLU is screaming of injustice, further begs the need for celebration, but despite this evidence I would urge pre-festival restraint.

Two reasons support holding off breaking out the cake and party hats. The first is that the KSM trials may still go forward if public sentiment decreases or if the administration decides they have passed the fool's point of no return on this national security blunder. The second reason with the furthest-reaching implication is that despite the final decision on the issue of the KSM trials, the world, and most notably our enemies can see very easily that this administration is more than weak; they are completely lost when it comes to fighting the war on terror. The coupling of liberal ideology with poor planning on major strategic decisions in this fight may very well spell a tragic end to The Barack Obama Show well before the curtain closes on his term as president. In the end, we should be happy if the future public trial spots for KSM remain vacant and are replaced with a military tribunal; however, it is far from an overall victory, as the same mentality that created these sad follies remains.

America has been at war with radical Islam for decades. Most Americans did not come to the reality of this war until September 11, 2001. In my 2007 book *Living Under The Patriot Act: Educating A Society*, I document a decade of Islamic attacks on the United States and its interests prior to 9/11. Our failures as a nation to defend our people properly led to the thousands of American dead on 9/11. This is another in a series of painful truths. Since September 11, 2001, Americans have started to educate themselves on Islam and for many, myself included, this religion raises difficult questions for a country that welcomes everyone from around the world with open arms. I have studied the Koran and as importantly, I have brought specialists in the field of Islam from around the world on my radio show to discuss this religion. I have come to the conclusion that Islam at its core is not a religion of peace. This religion is fundamentally at odds with western culture. Islam brings with it a call to action that when followed equates in almost all instances to violence against westerners. This is not saying that all Muslims are terrorists. I have lived with Muslims. I sat for hours with Muslims who cheered at the TV screens for American troops as they defeated the forces of Saddam Hussein. Muslims cannot all be bad or all hate America and I stand by that. What I do say is that there is an element of violence that is validated through the usage of the Koran. In March 2009, Khalid Sheik Mohammed and his co-conspirators accused of the attacks of 9/11 submitted what has been called the "Islamic Response to the Government's Nine Accusations" (Spencer 2009). Within this document they used the Koran to justify the terrorist attack on America (Spencer 2009). Robert Spencer, who documented the Islamic response in his 2009 article in *Human Events* entitled, "*Latest Jihad Plot Shows Need to Know Koran,*" illustrates the connection between the teachings in the Koran and Islamic terrorism tied to 9/11, "In God's book (the Koran)," asserts, "he ordered us to fight you everywhere we find you, even if you were inside the holiest of all holy cities, The Mosque in Mecca, and the holy city of Mecca, and even during sacred months. In God's book (the Koran), verse 9 [actually verse 5], Al-Tawbah [the Koran's 9th chapter]: Then fight and slay the pagans wherever you find them, and seize them, and besiege them and lie in wait for them in each and every ambush." Osama bin Laden's communiqués also quote the Koran copiously. In his "Declaration of War against the Americans Occupying the Land of the Two Holy Places," he quotes seven Koran verses: 3:145; 47:4-6; 2:154; 9:14; 47:19; 8:72; and the notorious "Verse of the Sword," 9:5. In a sermon broadcast in 2003, bin Laden rejoiced in a Koranic exhortation to violence as being a means to establish the truth: "Praise be to Allah who revealed the verse of the Sword to his servant and messenger [the Islamic Prophet Muhammad], in order to establish truth and abolish falsehood." The "Verse of the Sword" is Koran 9:5, the passage quoted above about slaying the pagans. For additional information on this subject I would recommend "The Complete Infidel's Guide to the Koran" by Robert Spencer as well as his book, *The Politically Incorrect Guide to Islam.* I have had Robert Spencer on my radio program, and he is a vast well of knowledge on the subject. As importantly, he has the backbone to talk to the American people honestly on the issue. We have to come to terms with the radical Islamic war currently taking place on America.

The area around New York where the twin towers originally stood, where new structures will someday stand again, is holy ground. For some time before major construction at ground zero took place, there was a considerable amount of dubious monkey business involving the

Cordoba Initiative. Yes, you remember it probably as the issue of the Mega Mosque. This was the workings of the dark side of Islam if there ever was such a thing. Under this plan headed by Imam Feisal Abdul Rauf, a guy who looked like he should have been a personal aide to Darth Vader, post-9/11 Americans were pushed to the limits of their tolerance concerning the encroachment of Islam on American "Holy Ground." In a completely foreseeable move, conservatives fought to keep the mosque from being built in this area. Also completely foreseeable was that liberals sided with Rauf and company. I believe that the radical imam wished to make a symbolic statement of the triumph of Islam over the west with the mega mosque strategically placed at Ground Zero, and I laid out this charge in my July 30, 2010 article, "Mega Mosques and the Territorial Mark."

Mega Mosques and the Territorial Mark

Right now at ground zero in New York a battle over the construction of buildings following 9/11 is raging. It is hard to believe that almost nine years following the Islamic attacks that took thousands of American lives, post-9/11 construction has moved at the speed of a dying snail. Even more perplexing than the failure of New York officials to take on aggressive construction projects to breathe life back into areas destroyed by 9/11 is the proposed mega mosque building project only blocks away from ground zero.

It's times like these that a person has to shake his head and wonder, "Are you just trying to provoke me?" From Voice of America News, Carolyn Weaver reports on the plans of Imam Feisal Abdul Rauf, president of what has been called the Cordoba Initiative to create a mega mosque and community center near ground zero. In Weaver's report, Imam Feisal Abdul Rauf attempts to frame the mega mosque as though it will be a cultural meeting point for as many non-Muslims as followers of Islam. With the long history of Islamic intolerance of what they consider non-believers, Rauf's sales pitch demands a high level of scrutiny. To get further compliance, Rauf claims that those who oppose a mega mosque being built on the ashes of 9/11 are Islamophobes. This is an insult to America's dead and deserves a healthy rebuke, which I am ready to give.

Without question Imam Rauf is attempting to crack the political correctness whip on the backs of Americans in the hopes that fear of the bigot brand will allow Islamic expansion into what Pamela Geller of Atlas Shrugs has properly termed a "war memorial." The idea forwarded by proponents that unity and tolerance can be achieved by building a mega mosque where Americans were butchered by Islamic radicals has the same tasteful appeal as building a Nazi gift shop at Auschwitz. So why create a religious supercenter in the most inflammatory place it could be built in America?

The answer is to make a religious statement of supremacy by expanding mosque construction in areas of cultural and historical significance. This is not just an issue within the United States. James Delingpole of Human Events talks at length about the Islamic push for mega mosque construction near the site of the 2012 Olympics in England. On Pajamas Media Television in an interview with Baroness Caroline Cox, councilor Alan Craig, who spearheaded the opposition to the London super mosque project, aptly alluded to the fact that the mega mosques go far beyond benign meeting places of worship to what can be interpreted as overt symbols of Islamic expansion.

Once again showing her moxie in the face of the politically correct whips, Sarah Palin called for New Yorkers to oppose the mega mosque at ground zero. After Sarah Palin, GOP gubernatorial candidate Rick Lazio stepped up in opposition to the mosque and called for Attorney General Andrew Cuomo to investigate Imam Feisal Abdul Rauf. If preliminary research on Rauf is any indication, the attorney general would be wise to take a long, hard look at the Imam who is rolling out the construction plans for the super mosque in New York.

As Aaron Klein of WorldNetDaily reports, Imam Feisal Abdul Rauf appears to be nothing short of a proselytizing Islamic radical. According to Klein, Rauf has publicly blamed America for 9/11, refused to recognize Hamas as a terrorist group and even was quoted as refusing to admit that Muslims carried out the terrorist attacks of 9/11. Even Rauf's 2004 book titled "What's Right with Islam is What's Right with America" had a radically dark Arabic title when published overseas, "The Call From the WTC Rubble: Islamic Da'wah From The Heart of America Post-9/11."Imam Feisel Abdul Rauf's books, in combination with the super mosque project, congeal into nothing short of a two-headed snake that will strike all in its domain or a rabid dog raising its haunch to mark new territory.

Either way it's dangerous, deadly business that carries the unique, foul odor of anti-Americanism. The American people have no inclination, requirement or duty to be tolerant of such an aggressive affront to the dignity of our dead by those who would perpetuate the same mentality that has brought such pain to our people. The territorial mark of a mega mosque at ground zero in New York should be met with complete and utter rejection.

While I am restrained when it comes to laying a blanket label of bad intentions on all Muslims, I am not so restrained when it comes to judgments of Sharia law in the United States. Sharia law is incompatible with American law and should never be allowed to hold sway in any U.S. court, period. I find the idea that any group or individual would have the audacity to push Sharia law onto American culture so offensive that when I think about it, I immediately need Tylenol. Unfortunately, this is a common trick the Left uses to win major issues without even having to fight. How is it done? Do something so outrageous, the average person wouldn't even believe it possible, let alone fight it. Barack Obama has made a presidential career doing this, and on the issue of pushing Sharia law in America, anti-American groups such as the Council on Foreign Relations (CAIR) and the American Civil Liberties Union (ACLU) are working diligently with other liberals to bring down America through a transformation of our court system. Like a broken record, when the chips are down, these liberals once again take the American people's right to speak through the ballot box and place it in the hands of an activist liberal cabal. On November 13, 2010, I wrote about Oklahoma's fight to keep Sharia law out of their court system.

Oklahoma: When Sharia Comes Sweeping Down the Plains

During the recent mid-term election, voters across the country voiced their will on more than just which politicians or political party they wanted to see in power for the next term. Voters in Oklahoma voted on whether or not Sharia, Islamic law, should or should not be used or considered within the state's court system. Seventy percent — that's right, seven out of ten Oklahoma voters — said no to Sharia and international law, and within days Oklahoma's chapter of CAIR, the Council on American-Islamic Relations, filed a lawsuit against the Oklahoma State Election Board. As reported by Rachel Slajda of TPM Muckracker, Muneer Awad, director of the Oklahoma branch of CAIR who filed the suit, says that the new Oklahoma law violates his First Amendment rights, including his personal desires for actions to be taken after his death.

Two questions should be forwarded to Muneer Awad, American Muslims and visitors who feel that a rejection of Sharia law within the American court system is worthy of court litigation. The first question is, what are the true motivations for the opposition of the American justice system applying its own laws within a sovereign nation? The second question is, just what country do you think you are living in? Omar Sacirbey from the Religion News Service reports a conversation with Sarah Albahadily, a 27-year-old American-born Muslim woman, who said after Oklahomans voted on State Question 755, barring Sharia law from American courts, that she felt less at home in the state. Specifically, she said, "It's disheartening, even though it was expected, you still feel the blow." Statements like these leave me in a state of bewilderment. How can the enforcement of American law within America be felt as an emotional blow? What would be the end result of subverting American law with a Middle Eastern form of law such as Sharia?

In a summary supplied by the Council on Foreign Relations, Islamic Law in Sharia, known as "the path" in Arabic, is described as a guide for all aspects of a Muslim's daily life. The conflicts coming from having Sharia in American law

135

would be immediate. There is little doubt that to place a foreign legal system that dictates all matters of familial, financial, religious and criminal matters will bring drastic, detrimental conflict to the American legal justice system. From the background supplied by the CFR, we only have to look to what punishments are called for under "hadd" crimes as prescribed by Sharia law to bring the point home.

Five different crimes fall under the "hadd" category: unlawful sexual intercourse, false accusation of unlawful sexual intercourse, the consumption of alcohol, theft and highway robbery. Punishments for such offenses under Sharia may include flogging, stoning, amputation, exile or execution. Sound like the American way? Sounds more like a trip back in the Dark Ages. Sharia also embodies the well-documented honor killings for daughters and wives who were deemed to have brought shame to the family, not to mention genital mutilation, adolescent marriages, polygamy and gender-biased inheritance rules. Do people like Muneer Awad feel that these aspects of Sharia are necessary for First Amendment rights in America's Constitution to be valid? Would subverting American law for individuals who commit honor killings or genital mutilations add to the "homey" aspects of the Sooner state? While the dangerous trend these days is to attack the exercising of state rights, Oklahoma voters deserve answers to questions such as these before their voices, and their state, are blacklisted alongside others such as Arizona.

Some that may wish to push the Sharia agenda at worst, or to be apathetic to its dangers at best, say that Oklahoma's lawmakers and voters are premature to address this issue as it has not yet been a factor in Oklahoma courts. Really, this question is of little importance when compared to Oklahoma's right to deal as a sovereign state with the issues it finds important. If we were to poll the estimated 30,000 Oklahoma Muslims along with Oklahoma's total population of 3.5 million citizens, I believe that Sharia law would be strongly rejected by a majority of all Oklahoma residents. But even so, groups like CAIR and their lackeys in the American Civil Liberties Union are framing the issue of the affirmation of the American court system as unconstitutional and the safeguarding of all American people as an exercise in Islamophobia. It appears that something dark and sinister may be afoot within the upcoming Oklahoma Sharia litigation, and Americans should be privy to the truth. Groups like CAIR and the ACLU should be made to more fully explain their motivations for opposing state's right in Oklahoma and its people's desire to uphold American law.

We got him! Osama bin Laden has been killed by American forces in Pakistan! On Sunday, May 1, 2011, the news outlets began to tell bits of the story about how intelligence gathering had led to a special U.S. military operation in Pakistan that ended in the death of Osama bin Laden. The facts of the U.S. military mission were sketchy—in fact they still are today--but Americans were told that the number one most wanted terrorist in the world had been brought to justice. That alone was reason to celebrate, or was it? Immediately following the initial reports of bin Laden's death were warnings that Americans should be careful not to celebrate this monumental American victory. Political correctness was in overdrive, and while the reasons for avoiding celebration had no substance, certainly many arguments were forwarded. I wrote what I thought was a well-crafted, articulate argument about why decent, reasonable, and humane Americans should be happy that the country was safer with Osama sleeping with the fishes instead of creating threat videos. I took some heat from the usual liberals and also more than a few of the politically correct RINO Republicans. If I had it to do all over again, I would not change a thing.

Osama bin Laden Killed by U.S. Forces, America Should Celebrate

The inevitable has taken place. Osama bin Laden has been killed by American forces. The details are still limited but as reported by FOX News, bin Laden was killed in a firefight on the ground in Pakistan. It is reported that no Americans were injured during the firefight that took bin Laden's life. As I type this column I can hear the celebrations outside my window here in the heartland of Kansas. Celebrating the death of bin Laden calls for a short discussion on how Americans should act in the aftermath of the U.S. military operation in which a human life was taken. When it comes to the death of the nation's number one terrorist, Americans should celebrate, should be happy. Allow me to expand on this line of thinking.

There are no illusions that the death of bin Laden will end attempts by terrorists to attack America. For some time terrorists have been trying, and at times succeeding, in acts of terrorism around the world. Many of these acts have been conducted without any input by bin Laden. The death of bin Laden will not end terrorism. With that said, the symbolic nature of bin Laden to terrorists has been twofold. The first being the successful attack on America he orchestrated on September 11, 2001, and the second being this terrorist's ability to evade American forces. Bin Laden's evasion from justice has had consequences on America and other countries as he continued to release periodical threat messages that received world coverage. The message to terrorists today with bin Laden's death is that when you mess with America, it's just a matter of time before you will be brought to justice. This is a powerful piece of symbolism in America's favor that will inevitably outweigh attempts to frame bin Laden as a martyr. Now back to celebrating.

There will be some that will forward the idea that we should be restrained in our joy over the demise of a death dealer like bin Laden. Some will say that America's celebration over a dead terrorist will provoke a higher response by al-Qaeda. Americans should brace themselves for the possibility that terrorists will attempt a response to the death of their symbolic leader. However, America's avoidance of celebrating bin Laden's death would not decrease radical Islamic terrorists from wanting to kill us. These radicals always want to kill everyone who does not think exactly like them. To the radical Islamic terrorist, a breathing American is a killable offense.

Next, some people may wish to diminish celebrations because Osama bin Laden was dispatched during the presidency of Barack Obama instead of George W. Bush. I would recommend against this for two reasons. First is the notion that withholding celebration when it is warranted somehow politically hurts a president with whom many do not agree. This is a false assumption that leads to poor actions. We can see this from history when liberals turned their backs on celebrating Americans when Saddam Hussein was ripped from his rat hole and brought to justice by U.S. military forces. Liberals withheld their joy during the capture of the Iraqi dictator simply out of spite against George W. Bush. These shallow political acts should not be repeated at this historical moment.

Lastly, celebrating the death of bin Laden is a hallowed bonding processes by which Americans continue to remember the war on terror that was brought to our shores and the innocent lives that were brutally taken on 9/11. It is a time for us to give thanks to our military and for the country to come together to celebrate a long-awaited moment of justice. Osama bin Laden is dead; let the celebrations begin.

There are many issues surrounding Osama bin Laden's death that are still unknown to the public. Some information that is important to ongoing terrorist investigations will, and should, remain secret. I hope we will kill or capture additional terrorists using information from papers and documents found at bin Laden's residence in Pakistan. Documenting a full history of this portion of Osama bin Laden's reign as the leader of al-Qaeda has tremendous importance to future generations that will study the war on terror. With that said, Barack Obama's decision to quickly bury bin Laden's body at sea in combination with withholding the death photo of the terrorist is extremely odd when placed in the context of history. The administration stated that the sea burial of bin Laden was done in accordance with Islamic law. Many Americans would have wished to have had a visual verification of Osama's death as was given to the Iraqi people when Uday and Qusay Hussein were killed by American forces. Others find it strange that the Obama administration would give full Islamic traditional burial rights to a radical who is not supposed to represent the "religion of peace." On May 10, 2011, I wrote about Barack Obama's break with history in not allowing the death photo of Osama bin Laden to be chronicled in the public record. I also talked about the politically correct merchants who would have Americans all but erase this portion of the history of the war on terror for the silly notion that terrorist will love us if we bow to their intolerance.

Bin Laden Death Photo: Obama Breaks from History, America Losing Spine

It is said that a picture says a thousand words. When it comes to today's politically correct world, presenting some pictures may say even more. President Barack Obama's refusal to submit the death photo of the number one terrorist behind 9/11, Osama bin Laden, is a fundamentally flawed decision full of negative consequences. The President's decision appears to be based on a concern that terrorists around the world will be inflamed to a higher level if bin Laden's death becomes public through pictures. This argument is weak and without supporting evidence. Certainly the idea of withholding potentially inflammatory photos for fear of angering terrorists around the world went out the door years ago with the overwhelming photo coverage of human rights violations at Abu Ghraib. If documenting this portion of American history through photos was deemed reasonable, how can withholding Osama bin Laden's death photo from the American people and history be justified?

The President also seems to believe that releasing bin Laden's death photo is in itself an act of selfish aggression beneath the dignity of the American people, which he has termed "spiking the ball." Someone should walk the president through American history, which is in complete opposition to this line of thinking. Historically, America has consistently used photos to chronicle the history of the deaths of those that have brought terror to this country. This has been a fundamental byproduct of our free speech that is recognized through our Constitution. This freedom to document history through published photos may not be pretty, but it was never feared nor denied to the American people.

In 1892, the infamous outlaws of the Dalton Gang were shot dead by local citizens in Coffeyville, Kansas. The death photos of these outlaws brought to justice were circulated through print worldwide. Documenting the deaths of bandits such as these through published images and photos was commonplace. Almost four decades later Americans would see death photos of gangsters such as John Dillinger to the St. Valentine's Day Massacre in newspapers across the country. Americans recorded the photos of the deaths of fascists like Benito Mussolini during World War II, and decades later monsters like Che Guevara were placed into historical context through the same means.

The idea that a handful of government officials would withhold visual verification of the death of the biggest villain of modern times is only surpassed in outrageousness by the possibility that Americans will stand for it. The Obama administration's purposeful denial of visual verification of this terrorist's dead body needlessly sows the seeds for myth, folklore and conspiracy theories. Does this make America safer? Of course not. This bungling administration is confused about the proper priorities within the war on terror.

Our country's history has not always been beautifully photogenic, but it's been our history and many have given the ultimate sacrifice to safeguard the freedom we have to keep it accurate and truthful. When citizens see pictures of African Americans being hung from ropes along roadsides during the terror of the Ku Klux Klan, it is unsettling to view, but also a true part of our history. Should we remove these photos from public consumption because somewhere someone will be offended? Only cowards and fools would endorse such actions.

President Barack Obama should do the right thing and release the death photo of Osama bin Laden. It is an action rightly done, not for the purpose of blood lust or to celebrate death for death's sake, but to place this part of America's history into an accurate context. Americans can handle the photo as they have been seeing the end results of what happens to those that terrorize Americans since the days of the Daltons. Those that view our publications from around the world can take from it the valuable lesson that America is the land of the free, and free people need not be denied reality for fear of being politically incorrect. The issue of the Osama bin Laden death photo release is now less of an observance of America's stomach or heart, but of the country's spine.

There has always been a special relationship between the citizen and the soldier in America. With the exception of Vietnam, where parts of the nation temporarily lost itself in a youth movement of anti-Americanism, and the treasonous actions against the military by Democrats during the George W. Bush presidency, the citizens of America love and embrace our fighting forces and try to do right by them. On the issue of doing what is right by the military, I want to devote a few words to 1st Lieutenant Michael Behenna. His story offers an example of a low point in American spirit that must be corrected with a strong conservative movement. Behenna is confined in a military prison in Leavenworth, Kansas, with a 25-year sentence for killing a terrorist in Iraq. I invite people to visit defendmichael.com for more information on his case. Having gone over all the public records and spoken to his family both on the phone and in radio interviews, I maintain that Behenna's incarceration defies logic. I believe it is a case not of incarceration due to facts, but of incarceration due to political correctness on the battlefield. In the following article, I make my case for Behenna and for the personal responsibility I believe Americans have to the men and women of the armed forces.

Protection and Reward: The Case of 1st Lieutenant Michael Behenna

America is truly a blessed land. This is not a secret, as people from all parts of the world try everything from walking the deserts without water to paddling in trashcans through the ocean to reach the place where the "American dream" happens. While there are many factors that bring about America's continued prosperity such as the free market, our capitalist system, our constitution with its valuable principles, and the tolerance found within the Christian foundations of this nation, these things have flourished only because America has remained free.

Even in the nation today where we face the ongoing struggle to maintain the components of America's success, we must never forget the cost in American blood and sacrifice that has afforded this country the stability to develop and establish what is truly the envy of the planet. What are the responsibilities-and dare I say the duties-of the U.S. citizenry to those who guard the outposts of this country's defensive lines, those who walk the patrols in foreign lands where our enemies lurk while we the American people go about our little errands of life?

The case of 1st Lieutenant Michael Behenna, a soldier convicted and sentenced to twenty-five years in prison for the alleged murder of suspected Al Qaeda operative Ali Mansur in Iraq is a disturbing story on several levels. The story itself is painful to me as a Kansan since I learned that Behenna has been in military prison in Fort Leavenworth (yes the same facility in which Barack Obama wanted to house terrorist detainees from Guantanamo Bay) for almost a year and I knew nothing about Behenna or his case. The minimal news coverage about his story is unsettling.

I learned that Michael Behenna came from a stable family with a mother who is a U.S. Attorney and a father who is a retired Oklahoma Bureau of Investigations agent. Behenna excelled in the military, and while in Iraq served as a platoon commander. His most recent officer evaluation before the Ali Mansur shooting incident was stellar. In fact, the comments for his potential for promotion made it abundantly clear that Behenna was a soldier on the fast track upward. Now barring parole, Behenna, who was twenty-five years old at the time of his sentence, will be forty years old by the time of his release. The question that screams out in this case is, "how did this happen?"

What is known is that Behenna's platoon was plagued with the threat of roadside bombs and insurgent attacks and on April 21, 2008, his platoon was ambushed and two of his soldiers were killed. Ali Mansur was believed to be responsible for the attack and was later detained and questioned by Army Intelligence. In a strange set of events, Ali Mansur was released by Army Intelligence and Behenna was ordered to transport the suspected Al Qaeda member back to his home. Instead of taking Ali Mansur home, Behenna attempted an interrogation for additional information from the suspected Al Qaeda member and during this interrogation Ali Mansur was shot and killed.

In hopes of shining more light on the case, I was given the opportunity to talk about the incident with Michael Behenna's mother Vicki on my radio program "Conscience of Kansas." Vicki Behenna, an articulate woman, stated that her son pleaded self-defense in the case saying that Ali Mansur had attempted to take his weapon during the interrogation. She further said that the prosecution's expert during the trial, a Dr. Herbert MacDonnell who was not called to testify in the case, corroborated Behenna's trial testimony that Ali Mansur was in a standing position when shot versus the prosecution's assertion that he was in a seated position. This crucial witness was not made available to the defense during the trial. Behenna's case is on appeal.

Since the sentencing of Michael Behenna, a clemency letter has been sent to Fort Leavenworth, Kansas, by politicians James Inhofe, Frank Lucas, Tom Coburn, John Sullivan, Tom Cole, and Dan Boren. For myself the case of 1st Lieutenant Michael Behenna seems painfully similar in many ways to the stories of Ramos and Compean, the soldier-related Haditha shootings, and Navy Seals in the Ahmed Hashim Abed incident, among many others. In many of these cases those who are charged with America's security were placed in almost untenable situations in which mistakes and errors could easily come to fruition while mercy and justice lagged painfully far behind.

The question that stands before Americans today is what is owed to those that protect our lives and freedoms? Is proper media coverage a mandatory precursor to justice in cases like Behenna's? Should the public demand the freedom of soldiers accused, if not convicted in defense-related cases in the war zone? Should the American people demand that those who defend our lives be given at least the benefit of the doubt? For those who put everything on the line, should protection come with reward? The answers to these questions must be based on the value we place on the protectors of our liberty. If we hold them dear to our hearts, if we find merit in the toils of their labor, then we must face the debt that we owe to them; we must take up the mantle of responsibility to insure that their sacrifices for us are not in vain.

I had the opportunity to interview Allen West in August of 2010. One of the wonderful perks of being a radio host is that you get to meet patriots. In my opinion, Allen West is the definition of what the conservative movement needs. West is an articulate man with courage, honor and commitment. I believe he knows that we are in a battle for the future of the country and he sees that Americans need to step up and be accountable. I am naturally drawn to conservatives with backbone and I was happy to hear that West was going to Leavenworth, Kansas, to speak on behalf of Behenna and nine other American soldiers being held on similar charges. On March 2, 2010, I wrote about Allen West and the Leavenworth 10.

Lt. Col. Allen West: A Voice for the Leavenworth 10

Is somebody watching over you today? Is there someone somewhere that is willing to put your well-being ahead of theirs? Those are powerful questions that we seldom ponder here in America. Why? The answer is that safety, security and most importantly freedom, the delicacies sought in so many places in the world, are things we in America nonchalantly pile upon our plates daily like hungry diners at an all-you-can-eat smorgasbord. Say what you will, but the reality is that even in the worst of times we really have it good. However, America, the magnet for so many people of the world, has been maintained and has flourished by the blood of the American soldier. The soldier's willingness to fight and if need be, die on foreign soils against vicious enemies for the nation's survival is often underestimated.

The war on terror brought a realization to most Americans through the terrorist attacks of September 11, 2001, that we had to take a stand against radical Islamic extremism. In one of President George W. Bush's best moments as the leader of the free world, Americans took an overdue offensive stance against terrorism. American fighting forces, along with others across the world, have been fighting a brave battle against the scourge of Islamic terrorism. Unfortunately, the battle to defeat terrorism has been as much a battle within as on the outside. In a political environment not seen since Vietnam, the American soldier has been placed in the very untenable situation of being charged with finding victory in the battle zone, without being able to incorporate the normal tools by which victory is attained. Political correctness on the battlefield handed down by those in government without the belly for war or simply American victory, has threatened the lives of American soldiers in more ways than one.

About a year ago I learned about 1st Lt. Michael Behenna, a sterling military officer that is now in the military prison at Fort Leavenworth, Kansas, for killing a known terrorist in self-defense in the war zone of Iraq. The injustice that took place in the Behenna case was so counter to logic, let alone fairness, that it calls into question the whole military justice system. I soon found out that nine other soldiers find themselves imprisoned in Leavenworth for similar situations. In a surreal move to appease the desires of political correctness, a mindset that is awash with liberal guilt and anti-Americanism, our soldiers are now given prison sentences instead of their deserved medals of honor. The shame of these actions will come back to haunt this nation for decades.

One of the pressing fears of those that wish to find recourse to free these imprisoned soldiers is that public attention may become focused elsewhere with the upcoming downturn in military forces in Iraq. In a move to increase public attention to the plight of what has been coined the "Leavenworth 10," a freedom ride has been schedule in Fort Leavenworth, Kansas, for September 4, 2010. Among those that will speak at the event is Lt. Col. Allen West.

I spoke with West on my radio program Conscience of Kansas and was impressed with his commitment to these soldiers despite being involved in a busy political season. In 2003, West was serving in Iraq and during an interview with a suspected Iraqi terrorist, the battalion commander fired his weapon near the individual that was refusing to give up critical information. These actions lead to an accumulation of intelligence being collected which no doubt saved lives from West's battalion. The actions of West were aggressive and for the liberal weak-kneed of the world, not politically correct, but they were effective and American soldiers were saved at the cost of scaring a terrorist. Many would say, myself included, a more-than-fair trade. Lt. Col. Allen West was relieved of command and had to struggle to avoid being sent to prison himself. Again, reward was replaced with punishment for American soldiers that are looking out for you and me. It was easy for me to find common ground with Michael Behenna and Allen West, as their heartland ties and love of country shine through immediately in their words, actions and the ways in which they have fought to do right for those they have sworn to protect.

Americans would serve themselves and this country well to meet the soldiers that make up the Leavenworth 10 at L10freedomride.com. In doing so I believe you will find a reflection of the American spirit that we must support and defend until these soldiers are freed in these backward days of political correctness

Chapter 7
Women and the Conservative Movement

A strong conservative movement in this country-- a movement that will have the staying power to last for years and allow people with values like those of the Founding Fathers to find their way into all levels of society—is what this book is about. This kind of movement involves the entire family unit. I'm talking the entire family tree, the entire city block. I think we should attempt to get the entire city to buy into the values of responsibility, work, prosperity, limited government, and unlimited human innovation, as well as the belief in the value of God and the love of country. To make this happen, we must have not only the involvement of women, but also their leadership and inspiration. I learned some very valuable lessons about what women could do when I was a Kansas police chief. In many ways, women have had to struggle to get their para-military style black boots in the door of law enforcement. As in many jobs previously denied to women, female police officers show their worth every day. While a law enforcement officer, I had the opportunity to see female officers confidently work their way through high-risk situations that would have been impossible for many males. I saw female officers overcome the feelings of uncertainty brought forth by male partners and even departments that were struggling to accept them. When I left law enforcement in 2002 to return to academia, I had no idea that in 2010, I would be touring the state of Kansas interviewing Kansas police chiefs for my doctoral dissertation. It was a rewarding research project for me in many ways, one of which was the opportunity to sit down with female police chiefs commanding huge budgets and large numbers of officers, as well as chiefs who ran small agencies. I was as impressed, and educated almost a decade later to talk to female police chiefs in 2010 as I had been talking to female road cops back in 1995.

There are smart, strong, tough, moral women in this country waiting to lead Americans to a better place, and we need to find them and lift them up with our support. We have some very dynamic female politicians fighting the good fight right now. I am going to talk about some of these female cultural trail blazers, as I am very proud of them. I am also going to be painfully truthful and not shy away from a little discussion of the "political birds and bees." It's something that needs to be done, and if you have made it this far in the book, don't stop now.

The country yearns for conservative values to be restored to their original dominance. People can feel it in the air—an expectation that something good is about to happen, and that it must happen now. With that said, the conservative ideals of the individual supersede issues of sex, beauty, flair, and other outward characteristics. Great leaders are first observed because we recognize that their hearts are true. They are in it to win it and they truly believe in the causes they advocate for. Those who model and can articulate genuine conservative beliefs, be they male or female, will draw support from the public. Now to something you've heard before, but something that cannot be stated enough. Victory in the culture war is a numbers game. We have to have more than them. Some still ask the question, "Is this culture war really an us versus them kind of thing?" The answer is this: you had better believe it is. It is a numbers game at the ballot box, it's a numbers game with your purchasing dollar, it's a numbers game at your local PTA meetings, a numbers game in all important facets of life. A conservative movement is not about eking by with a reasonable amount of victories on most of the issues we care about. It is about absolute, overwhelming victory. It's about winning through total domination. Liberals cannot be allowed any backroom options, any strong arm tactics, any weasily weasel room to do anything but shake hands and go home to their candle lit Marxian shrines in teary-eyed defeat. We have to be aggressive, we have to man-up and to do that, we need women.

In strategic terms, there are three valuable resources women bring to the table for a conservative political movement. The first is the practical element of additional numbers at the ballot box. The second is that women are as tough as nails; more on that to come. Third, strong conservative women are absolutely inspirational. Some would say, well, Paul, you mean women can bring other women into the political fold, right? Yes, that is true, but strong conservative women who stand on their values, inspire men as strongly as women. The values always lead the way, but there is a unique magnetism that surrounds the female patriot. Let's show a few examples.

Sarah Palin, former governor of Alaska and Vice Presidential candidate in 2008. When you mention her name, people spring into one of two camps. There's the Sarah-Palin-oh-I-love-her-so-much-I-hope-she-runs-for-president-in-2012 camp, and there's the Sarah-Palin-oh-I-hate-her-so-much-I would-eat-glass-before-I-would-vote-for-her camp. I bet even liberals would say I am accurate with these two assessments. Ever wonder why Sarah Palin elicits such strong emotions in the poltical arena? I can tell you why, and it is one reason that if she ran for president, I would vote for her. Sarah Palin has a clear platform. She advocates small government, the free market, and the Constitution. She is not afraid to drill a bunch of American oil for Americans. She is a pro-lifer with a life story to back up her advocacy of that position. Palin is the kind of lady who would shoot a wolf and not suffer a month's depression. Because liberals reject the principles of the Founding Fathers, to be a conservative makes them angry, and to be consistently conservative brings them to a crazy-eyed rabid froth. Liberals hate Palin because she is consistent, not a liberal ally every other day like John McCain. While we are touching on the subject of moral weakness, let's spend a moment of reflection on the election of 2008.

There has never been a vice presidential candidate who has been attacked as viciously, or as personally as Sarah Palin was in the 2008 campaign. Many of the attacks thrown at Palin by Democratic operatives were personal in nature. It was like liberals were willing to take the advances women had made in politics over the last 50 years and drag it all back into the dark ages. From the liberal smears that Sarah Palin's child Trig was not her own, to the "Nuclear Missile Launch" sized reports about the costs of her wardrobe while running as VP, to Obama's low-brow statements about putting "lipstick on a pig," Palin took personal attacks that would have broken many men. She not only took the attacks, but also maintained a positive message about this country and what we could achieve through conservative values. With all that said, the Governor of Alaska had one insurmountable problem in the 2008 campaign. She had a chain hooked to her ankle that was connected to an aged RINO in John McCain. This was a political death sentence. Had Palin been the presidential candidate, I truly think the election would have come down to the wire. In 2008, liberals hated Palin because they could see she was politically dangerous to their agenda. After the election, liberals hated Palin because Americans wanted to buy her books in unprecedented numbers. Next, liberals hated Palin because she had a successful reality show, but the biggest hate of all resides in the liberals' fear that Palin will end up someday on a political ticket and derail the modern liberal agenda. On February 18, 2010, I wrote a piece in an ongoing set of articles on "Palin hate." This article was written during the buildup to the midterm election of 2010. In this article, I was addressing an atrocious hit piece by one of the *New York Times* lipstick-less swine, Frank Rich.

Palms, Knuckles, and Fingertips: A Rich Assessment of Palin Hate

Oh, it is indeed a hard time to be a liberal. The storm clouds of destiny are so close one can feel the humidity of the humiliation that is about to rain down on the liberal left. The thunder, of course, is the American people who have had enough of uncontrolled spending and the quickstep to socialistic left with which Barack Obama and his political supporting cast has taken this country with an arrogant indifference to opposition by the American people. So, as is the case in a free country, our system will be used to wash away these destructive forces and the nation will begin to heal itself and hopefully, be wiser for the experience.

I have written about Palin Hate many times and have been observing its evolution as liberals attempt to come to terms with their upcoming ideological defeats in 2010 and 2012. This documentation has been a dirty business with many twists and turns and as always, with each writing, a little more is learned about both Palin and her attackers. The latest attack comes from liberal New York Times columnist Frank Rich. For the most part Rich blindly stabs his trident at Palin like most of the frothing left that knows they hate the former governor of Alaska for some reason or another but fail to make a coherent argument. To continue a documentation of the evolution of Palin Hate, I will give you an assessment of Rich's most overt thrusts at the Palin camp.

First, Rich does what all liberals do when they see red. He does what liberals accuse conservatives of doing; he bashes women. Out of the gate and in defiance of every feminist who ever voted democrat, Rich frames Palin as the evil, maniacal plotting female. In fact, when talking about Sarah Palin and the incident in which she wrote crib notes on her hand for a speech and was later made fun of by White House court jester Robert Gibbs, Rich takes pity on giggling Gibbs who he sees as a helpless pawn in Palin's elaborate plan to gain backlash support from the American people. In fact, Rich eludes that Palin's only quality of note may be her plotting nature when he says, "you had to wonder if Palin, who is nothing if not cunning, had sprung a trap." All I can say to Frank Rich on that component of his Palin attack is that he pushed the point home very aggressively, "women, you just can't trust them," I'm sure the feminists would all be proud.

At this point, Rich's attack echoes the usual subliminal and overt liberal talking points of the left which include intolerance for financial success, anti-capitalistic spew, guilt by association, bathroom yardstick talk of who has the longest "conservatism," perpetuating the one-dimensional view of the Tea Party movement, Americans being brainless cattle, and finally the always popular liberal slap at Christianity.

149

The attacks by Frank Rich on Sarah Palin anger a majority in this nation. He probably does more to promote Palin to the public stage than his cohort, the press secretary, in that he shines even more light on the desperation of the modern liberal today with his multiple-layered attacks. It is important to remember that Frank Rich is playing the best cards that he has against Sarah Palin which when placed on the table appear to depict that Palin is a tricky financially successful woman who believes in God and has hordes of Tea Party followers. This is the best that a New York Times columnist can do after examining everything from the palms, knuckles, and fingertips of the Palin crib note incident.

In the end it is hard not to take at least some pity on Rich who is reflecting not the death of real journalism but the death throes of a liberal ideology that has been exposed and is being rejected by the American people. Palin, as well, should not be elevated to some position of the divine but simply as a person who has a message that rings true with the majority of the nation, a majority which is now about to bring a long-needed cleansing rain to this country.

Some liberals have told me, Paul you just like Sarah Palin because she's hot! Ironically, usually in their next breath they say that Palin is also stupid. You know, all body and no brains—that line. I will be completely honest: I think Sarah Palin is a very beautiful person. I think Michele Bachmann is beautiful. I would rather look at them all day for free than to be paid to make my eyes focus on Nancy Pelosi or Barbara Boxer for an hour. I find patriots like Palin and Bachmann appealing to watch and listen to because they love this country. I love to watch Governor Jan Brewer in Arizona stand up to Barack Obama for failing to secure the border; what a woman! I learned in high school that a girl who smiles is much more appealing than a girl who frowns. It is not raunchy or distasteful to say that women who stand up tall for America are simply more appealing—dare I say, sexier—than those that want to destroy it. Truth be told, the women patriots of today also lead with an almost indescribable mixture of elegance and determination. What America-loving person wouldn't want to watch this in action? As the midterm election was almost upon the country, I wrote an article supporting several strong conservative women. The article was entitled: "Let's Hear It for the Girls! Women and the Conservative Movement." The title of the article was inspired by Deniece Williams' song "Let's Hear It for the Boys" from the soundtrack of the hit movie *Footloose*. I thought it was a clever title for an article that was paying homage to female Republicans going to battle it out in the 2010 midterm. As it turns out, the feminists were greatly offended by the title, and they flooded my e-mail box for several days after its publication. Following the example of Sarah Palin, I sucked it up, kept smiling, and continued on.

Let's Hear It for the Girls! Women and the Conservative Movement

We are currently watching the beginning of an American return to conservative values. What is unique about this return is that it is being led by an increasing number of politically savvy women. Political positions in almost all local, state, and national levels of government have been occupied by women for many years but the overwhelming majority have been filled by liberal Democrats. This is about to change.

Sparked by conservative women like Michele Bachmann, the first woman to be elected to the U.S. House of Representatives from the state of Minnesota, the challenge for women of breaking the "glass ceiling" has been replaced with the reality of breaking the liberal female glass ceiling. Currently Republican Governor Jan Brewer of Arizona is locked in a stare down with President Barack Obama over SB 1070, which deals with illegal immigrants. It's no longer a question of separating the men from the boys, but more aptly the conservatives from the liberals, the strong from the weak. Jan Brewer is currently winning her stare down with the president, and Arizona's SB 1070 may in fact be a fundamental catalyst for securing the border in America's future.

Much praise must be given to Sarah Palin, who invigorated the nation with her conservative values and positive, enthusiastic vision for the country. The Palin phenomenon is still infectious today. What she also did by stepping onto the national stage was educate the nation about a woman's ability to govern and fight for core beliefs, and to do so without losing her humanity.

So what will this year's conservative women bring to the table for the primary races in 2010? Many of the Republican women who are poised to unseat longtime Democrats are tremendously successful business leaders from the private sector. Republican Carly Fiorina running for the Senate seat in California against Barbara Boxer is a former Chairman and CEO of Hewlett-Packard Co. (HP). California Republican Meg Whitman won her gubernatorial primary and is the former CEO of eBay Inc. Economically bankrupt California now has the opportunity to elect into high levels of political leadership two dynamic women who have been successful in business and know how to make a profit. Can I hear an "Amen!"

The conservative women of this year's midterm election will be propelled by the Tea Party movement. You know, that movement that Nancy Pelosi said doesn't really exist? The Vegas odds are that Senate Majority Leader Harry Reid will roll "snake eyes" in his attempt at re-election against Republican candidate Sharron Angle. Though we will never know for sure, the GOP's candidate in the primary race, Sue Lowden, would have most likely sent Reid home a loser, yes, another conservative, yes, another woman.

Additional Republicans challenging influential Senate seats include Jane Norton in Colorado, Linda McMahon in Connecticut and Kelly Ayotte in New Hampshire. When we look at these ladies of liberty, these women of worth, we see that their primary victories have been hinged upon their abilities to articulate the conservative message: limited government, controlled spending, adherence to the Constitution and traditional American values. What you do not hear from these conservatives is that they are victims of everything, or that they deserve the American people's votes because of who they are. Instead, they are taking the conservative route in their platforms, staying issue-driven and appealing to the American people with what they have already accomplished and how it will apply in their future service. As the country moves back to conservative values to survive as a nation, let us not forget that many of our champions will be wearing skirts. Let's hear it for the girls!

I decided to include my article about the Values Voter Summit in this section of the book. The Values Voter Summit is really nothing more than a conservative get-together with the intention of kicking the tires on a few potential presidential candidates. I talk in this article, published on September 24, 2010, about why presidential candidates never announce their candidacy half as fast as we would wish them to. The fact is, once candidates announce that they are running for president, they start aging in dog years. The attacks are immediate. For example, look at the voracious liberal campaign attacks that were unleashed on Delaware Senatorial candidate Christine O'Donnell. O'Donnell made some campaign mistakes and missteps, but the onslaught she had to withstand was disproportional to her campaign errors. In short, she was treated in an overly harsh manner for being a conservative in a blue state.

Values Voter Summit: Why Winning is Not Enough

The recent Values Voter Summit in Washington gave people a chance to hear from some of the potential Republican presidential candidates for 2012. Indiana Congressman Mike Pence, the lesser known of the political lineup that spoke at the event, took first place with 24 percent, narrowly beating former Arkansas Governor Mike Huckabee who received 22 percent of the votes from the 700 plus attendees of the event.

While straw polls have no real validity as a gauge of the future political waters, they do show us that the Republican Party has begun to think about the future. It is now that the GOP and the American people must do some careful thinking. As much as we all would love to know the primary candidates now, strategic reasoning places most of those declarations further down the road. The most important reason for this is that when politicians announce their candidacy, they are immediately placed under attack, often attacks frivolous in nature, and must expend valuable time and resources defending their names. Strategically, this is a fight best scheduled for months before an election, not years. While this kind of baseless mud throwing demeans the process, it has unfortunately become so common that we are shocked when politicians at any level of government simply square off on their platform issues. At my last count, Delaware senatorial candidate Christine O'Donnell, who just won her primary, is currently accused of being a mentally unstable, litigious, satanic witch who improperly uses campaign funds to gain the allegiance of a radical right-wing Tea Party movement. Did I miss anything? A stroke of the keys on your computer in a week will probably bring forth accusations that make these look tame, and a presidential candidate will have it much worse.

As much as I feel for whomever will take on that monumental task of being the Republican presidential candidate for the primaries and later, the winner in the general election, I am much more concerned about losing the country. In the bigger picture, that is the challenge at hand. Here are some fundamental truths along the pathway to the 2012 presidential election: Barack Obama will be extremely hard to beat in 2012. Any mentality to the contrary is almost as detrimental to the GOP as being part of an ACORN voter registration drive. On my radio program *Conscience of Kansas* I spoke with Lt. Col. Robert "Buzz" Patterson, author of the book "Conduct Unbecoming." Patterson said of Obama that "he is the most anti-American, most radical president we have ever elected by far." Now remember, Patterson worked directly with former president Bill Clinton. Despite the painful accuracy of Patterson's assessment and the growing discontent found in Astroturf-free groups like the Tea Party, Obama and the Democrats have several ways to achieve victory in 2012. Republicans have only one.

Here are some more 2012 election truths: Barack Obama is nothing if not a superb campaigner. Let not the lackadaisical John McCain presidential campaign diminish the real effectiveness of Obama's campaign machine when put into action. We would also be wise to understand that power achieved is never easily relinquished. If the Republican Party fails to place truly conservative candidates in the primary, Obama will win. If the American people allow third-string democrats in the form of RINOs in the Republican Party to surpass true conservatives in the primary, Obama wins. If the American people vote a strong conservative through the primary and the party fails to adequately disseminate those values and how they address the issues of the day, Obama wins. Lastly, and possibly the most overlooked potential for defeat during the course of this upcoming 2012 general election battle, even if Republicans defeat Obama in the general election, if our party's candidate does not have true conservative values, we lose, we lose, we lose.

It might sound that pessimism is the word of the day, but that is not so. Barack Obama is indeed beatable, and he deserves to be placed in the annals of history with democrat failures such as Jimmy Carter. Like many unhappy Americans today, I look forward to voting in the 2012 election. Heck, I want to video tape my trip to the polls and put it on YouTube, just to be able to relive the moment and to anger liberals till the end of time. However, the Republican Party must have a true conservative candidate to show voters the clear delineation between their values and the socialistic values of Barack Obama.

The Values Voter Summit is but one of many chances for politicians in the Republican Party to prepare themselves for the scrutiny of the American people on both the right and the left. If Mike Pence and others can truly model the congressman's own words at the Voter Summit that priorities are to be a Christian, conservative and a Republican, they will find the support of the Tea Party, they will be equipped to address the economic concerns of this nation.

They will also have the strength from faith necessary to handle the liberal onslaught and defeat the Obama political machine. This is the Republican Party's only true option to victory in 2012.

I have talked about women who are currently standing up for conservative values and will be the future of the conservative movement. While I am excited to see their achievements, it is very important to never forget the couragous conservative women throughout history who forged a way for our modern-day lady patriots. On January 14, 2010, I wrote about England's Former Prime Minister Margaret Thatcher. It is not often that I look to other countries for inspiration. I usually find more than I need right here in America. However, Margaret Thatcher, often called the "Iron Lady," is nothing short of exceptional. Like Winston Churchill, she has grit. If you wanted to see a woman champion the free market and literally eviscerate liberal arguments with style, Margaret Thatcher never disappointed. If you are able to find any of Margaret Thatcher's interviews and debates, you should watch them and learn. Her optimism about the free market and what it could accomplish in England is timeless. Her ability to call socialists "socialists" to their faces is priceless. As Prime Minister Tony Blair was a steadfast ally and friend to George W. Bush through the storms following 9/11, Margaret Thatcher was the perfect ideological ally for Ronald Reagan during the tumultuous years of the Soviet Union. On January 14, 2010, I was highlighting the conservative female stalwarts of both politics and punditry and I laid the groundwork with a historical observance of the "Iron Lady." Enjoy.

A Thankful Observance of the "Iron Lady"

Today, when we watch the courageous actions of women who stand for conservative values in this country, we often bring up names like Sarah Palin, Ann Coulter, and Michelle Malkin. These women often gallantly rebuke the feminist fallacies and liberal lies of today in ways that make people proud not just to be men or women, but proud to be Americans.

It is not just their smiles, their wit, their skirts, or their grit that make these women ladies of interest, but the culmination of these tantalizing factors with the all-important center-piece of conservative values that make their thoughts, struggles, and victories interesting to the world and of value to public discourse.

As is the case with men, the women of today who champion conservative values owe a great deal to the stalwarts that precede them. Those that have not only battled the socialistic minions of their times, but have also forged a historic path that leads to defeating enemies of freedom with superior values. Despite my ever-eager desire to highlight Americans in these positions of distinction, when it comes to a contemporary display of leadership through conservative values, much can be gained by remembering the work of England's Prime Minister Margaret Thatcher.

Thatcher became the prime minister in the 1980's during an economic slump and period of national malaise. Her party name, "The Conservative Party," was a reflection of her values, and she spent her time fighting the trade unions and championing her beliefs in the free market. If you take a stroll among the video archives of the many interviews Thatcher took part in with the liberal mouth pieces of the 1980's, you see the same classic confrontations as today: apathy vs. innovation, victimization vs. accountability, and pessimism vs. optimism.

Despite being the first female prime minister in the country's history, there was never a concern of whether or not she could carry the mantle of power in England, and her strong verbal debates during the rambunctious procedures within the House of Commons contributed to her nickname "Iron Lady." While some in England floundered on the issue of fighting communism, Margaret Thatcher acted with bold clarity on her belief in the dangers of the Red Menace and stood against the Soviet Union for the betterment of her country. Unlike the flaccid nature found within the U.S. administration today, Thatcher refused to embolden the terrorists of her time by showing fear and apathy. Even after narrowly escaping an assassination attempt by IRA terrorist bombers on October 12, 1984, at the Grand Hotel in Brighton, England, Thatcher never flinched in her stance on strong national security.

There is little wonder that a leader of such quality would find an ally such as Ronald Reagan. Reagan, who was also rejuvenating a nation suffering from recession and liberal dysfunction, together with Thatcher, did more than perpetuate a continual relationship between countries that have shared so much history together; they showed the world the economic and social rewards of flowing conservative values.

Thatcher spoke at length about the values of personal responsibility and standing up for what you believe in, and she embodied her beliefs for her terms as prime minister of England. It could be argued that beyond the grit of Winston Churchill, the Union Jack has never flown with such bold grace in modern times as it did under the guidance of Prime Minister Margaret Thatcher, a truly remarkable women.

Chapter 8

Abortion

It's just a choice, the right of a woman to control her body. Abortion is framed as an expansion of the civil rights movement and women's suffrage and all other things consequence- free, bright and wonderful. Why do liberals support abortion while conservatives oppose it? It goes back to the fundamental principles of conservatism: 1. God, 2, Family, 3. Country. Without God, the lowest order of human activity can and will be legitimized. The Prophet Jeremiah was told by God the value of the individual before birth, and the personal relationship that the Creator has with his creation through every stage of life. Specifically, the Bible says, "Now the word of the Lord came to me saying, before I formed you in the womb I knew you, and before you were born I consecrated you; I have appointed you a prophet to the nations." (Jeremiah 1:5). If God considers each unborn child unique and important to him, should we not be a people who do the same? Let me get a bit more specific; if we wish for God to bless this nation, should we as a people not show respect to the children that the Lord God Almighty forms individually in the womb?

All life is precious, and as we get older, we understand more and more the fragile nature of our own existence. There are many places within and outside this country where Americans are at risk of losing the precious gift of life. Right now, we have men and women serving in the military who are in the combat zone defending this nation. Many of our soldiers are in places where life is considered cheap, and we mourn as a country the dead who are brought back home having given the ultimate sacrifice. Today, children and teenagers join gangs in the inner city of the United States where they are placed at tremendous risk of being killed. An almost endless list could be constructed of the number of situations that heighten the chances of losing one's life. With that said, there is one place where the chance of dying is so great that it dwarfs every other situation we could ever think of. The place where Americans are at the highest risk of dying, by far, is in the womb. These victims cannot increase their chances of survival by complying with information found in any manual or survival guide. They have no weapons to fight back against their aggressors. These victims are absolutely innocent; after all, they are babies.

As a nation we have allowed liberals to turn American culture from its Judeo-Christian beginnings, where abortion was treated as God views it—as a mortal sin, into a culture where the killing of babies is thought of with no more care than tossing out the garbage. We can only speculate concerning the number of talented individuals with special gifts to give to the world—people who could have been a Thomas Edison, Jonas Salk, George Washington Carver, or Shirley Temple Black—who have simply been tossed into the trash. A conservative movement brought to its full potential would have the numbers and power to stop abortion in America. I believe this. If I had the choice of victory in only one of the many challenges that face the country, it would be here. On February 11, 2011, I wrote an article entitled, "Abortion in 2011: From Tax Breaks to Heartache." This article shines light on just how far the nation has fallen from grace on the issue of abortion.

Abortion in 2011: From Tax Breaks to Heartache

Since the United States legalized abortion in 1973 in Roe v. Wade, approximately 40 million abortions have been conducted in this country. These death toll numbers, which continue to mount, dwarf the statistics of Americans killed in war, crime, accidental death from handguns, you name it. As we enter the year 2011, legalized abortion in America is by far the leader in institutionalized death. Prior to 1973 abortion was more than simply illegal, it was a socially shunned activity for both the pregnant mother and the covert abortionist. Today not only have the tables turned on the legality of taking the life of a baby in the womb, but the decades that have passed since Roe v. Wade have seen a continual desensitizing of Americans to the ramifications of abortion.

Since the recent mid-term election the Republican-controlled House has been working to pass the No Taxpayer Funding for Abortion Act. Among other things, the bill would stop internal revenue credits for expenses paid for medical care of the taxpayer or the taxpayer's spouse or dependents for abortion. Furthermore, this bill would stop tax deductions through health benefit plans that include coverage of abortion. The bill is considered only a symbolic action for Republicans in the House of Representatives, since the Democrats will most certainly vote down any similar action in the Senate. It is a little bit too easy to simply look at the political maneuverings here and forget the actual tragedy that has become America.

We as a country are debating whether or not there should be tax break eligibility for taking a human life. In a country founded upon Christian values, we are calmly discussing, and for the opposition of abortion, losing the debate on society's right to force all citizens of this country to fund the death of generations of children. This desensitization of the American conscience is inevitable as abortion continues in America and the effects accumulate.

To bring this point home, we simply have to observe how mildly the people of this country respond to the killing mills of abortion practitioners when things goes awry in our post-Roe v. Wade world. In the recent Pennsylvania case of the abortion clinic ran by Dr. Kermit Gosnell, the abortion doctor who is alleged to have killed seven babies by inducing birth and then cutting the babies' spinal cords with a pair of scissors, the public's outrage is more technicality based than an affront to national moral values. Had it not been for a separate federal drug investigation on unlawful pain medicine distribution, the clinic would most likely still be in operation. Even the most egregious of operating abortion clinics fail to stir concern or curiosity from regulating entities. Gosnell, who was allegedly responsible for the death of an adult, Karnamaya Mongar, was shocked when he found himself on trial for eight counts of murder as this whole strange case unfurled.

Gosnell reportedly told a judge at a recent arraignment, "I understand the one count, because a patient died, but I didn't understand the seven counts." In this case, despite the abortionist's heinous actions within his clinic, Gosnell appears to feel he is simply guilty of deviating from standard operating procedures. In reality, those seven babies brought to his facility were slated to die when their mothers entered the abortion clinic. Gosnell simply failed to follow the institutionally accepted killing rituals. It's that simple, and that terrible. Even one of America's most notorious late-term abortionists, George Tiller, was openly embraced by a mainstream church in Kansas at the heart of the Bible Belt.

The undeniable truth is that abortion exists in opposition to everything America stands for, from the Bill of Rights to the Christian foundations of this country. Unfortunately, in failing to recognize the loss of moral values that have allowed abortion to be legalized in the United States, we are doomed to watching the country spiral further toward the devaluing of human life, creating future heartache. What is necessary for America to awaken to the desperate need to repeal abortion? Will it take having killed more babies than the living population of the country before the people's conscience is stirred into action? As incredible as that seems, that bloody number will most certainly be reached in time.

The truth is that in time those that oppose abortion in America will no longer be losing the debate on this issue because the debate will be over. The opportunity to change the tide will be lost either through additional legislation or irreversible national malaise. Re-establishing America to greatness in 2011 will not be accomplished through stabilizing markets or lowering unemployment rates. Yes, America's economy is struggling but the souls of its people are in much worse shape. The reemergence of America can only be accomplished through aligning the country's belief system with that of the Creator that has made America a blessed land.

While legalized abortion on demand is a relatively new thing here in the United States, enough time has passed that many people do not understand the incremental steps taken by liberals to completely reverse America's law. It did not happen all at once. Readers will remember at the beginning of this book two important points that were made about how liberals operate. The first was how liberals minimize their activities to avoid facing opposition from this country's moral majority. Second, was the fundamental truth that liberals will never give up trying to achieve their goals. If they are not politically beaten and consistently held at bay, they will advance their agenda, even if in small steps, to an ultimate victory. Here is how liberals made abortion legal. According the National Right to Life organization, in 1959, The American Law Institute (ALI) presented a proposal for a model code for state abortion laws. The new code proposal asked only to legalize abortion for the mental or physical health of the mother, or pregnancy due to rape and incest, and fetal abnormalities. In 1967, Colorado Governor John A. Love pushed through an abortion law in the United States that permitted abortion in cases of permanent mental or physical disability of either the child or mother or in cases of rape or incest (NRLC, 2011). In 1970, New York Governor Nelson Rockefeller reversed the state law that had been in existence since 1830, which had prohibited abortion except to save a woman's life, and replaced it with abortion on demand for up to the 24th week of pregnancy. In 1973, the Supreme Court issued its ruling in *Roe v. Wade* finding that a "right of privacy" was "broad enough to encompass" a right to abortion (NRLC, 2011). On the same day in the case *Doe v. Bolton* the term "health" was defined to mean "all factors" that affect a woman, including emotional factors, psychological factors, familial factors, and the woman's age (NRLC, 2011). From this point on abortion on demand was mainstreamed into American culture.

If we advance to the current day, we see that liberals are attempting to continue the industry of death through embryonic stem cell research. In this case, it is through removing cells that could be used to create life, as has been done with the Snow Flake Babies (Cosgrove-Mather, 2005). In an article written on September 20, 2010, I chronicled the abortion industry's continued push to desensitize the country on issues surrounding life and its blood trail of progress.

Embryonic Stem Cell Research: The Blood Trail of Progress

With a recent federal appeals court decision temporarily lifting the ban on embryonic stem cell research, the question of destroying a life to save a life is again thrust back into the realm of public debate. As reported by medical AP writer Lauran Neergaard, the National Institutes of Health will rapidly resume embryonic stem cell research as well as remove holds on grants and contracts allowing the use of embryonic stem cells.

The stance from the White House on this debate has been predictable. Former President George W. Bush's position against federal funding for embryonic stem cell research was a part of his pro-life stance and heavily based on his religious belief in the sanctity of life. Barack Obama, the president who said in 2008 at a rally in Pennsylvania that if his daughters ever made the mistake of getting pregnant he would not want them "punished with a baby," has predictably taken the modern liberal stance on this issue in support of federal funding for embryonic stem cell research.

Those that advocate the federal funding of embryonic stem cell research attempt to wrap their argument within the notion of helping society. Who doesn't want to do that? In fact, if we believe the rhetoric from our recent past, like the bold words of John Edwards, who alluded to the fact that if embryonic stem cells could not make us supermen, they could at least make "Superman" actor Christopher Reeve rise up and walk after being paralyzed, it would almost be cruel to refuse such miracles so close at hand. Of course, if embryonic stem cell cures did not happen, it would not be because the science was not there, or would never be there, but because narrow-minded individuals like George W. Bush lacked the understanding to allow the careful and restrained usage of stem cells in limited situations like embryos discarded by patients of in vitro fertilization clinics. So much was to be gained if we had the will to bring this brave new world to fruition.

Of course those that accept this premise have not only bought into the John Edwards lies of instant embryonic cell miracles but also the much darker lie that comes from prioritizing one life over another. To get a sobering look at the deadly progression that comes from degrading life for societal improvement, two names come to the forefront in modern times: Margaret Sanger and Adolf Hitler. Margaret Sanger wrote the book "The Pivot of Civilization," which is so full of eugenic madness that even the organization she founded, Planned Parenthood, has to distance itself from its very pages. It is a frightening book to say the least. Sanger wished for society to be free of the feebleminded and their tendencies toward poor economic status and societal violation. Her answer: society would never suffer from the ills of the mentally defective if those individuals never existed. Instead of embryonic stem cell miracles, selective breeding would bring about societal improvement if we were enlightened enough to grasp it. What was the natural progression of these eugenic beliefs? Not just Planned Parenthood, an organization that specializes in death, but a government that forces its citizens to pay for its operation.

Margaret Sanger's book preceded Adolf Hitler's racial eugenics piece in "Mein Kampf," but they are solidly compatible with their focus on eradicating what they believed were out-of-control, undesirable elements in society. We all know from history that the progression of purifying Germany came in the form of the "Final Solution," which just happens to be not too far from the mentality of Sanger's modern day Planned Parenthood which teaches, "eradicate what is not desired."

Sanger and Hitler were truly sister and brother to a common set of eugenic values. Both treated those they designated as defective as less than human, inconsequential and tainted. One focused on intelligence and the other on race, but when it came to the cold calculations, from Sanger's desire for quarantines and forced sterilizations to Hitler's usage of intern camps, both embraced their blood trail of progress. This eugenics mentality lives and its natural progression is seen today in the modern abortionists who help female teens fit better into their prom dresses or avoid missing spring break. It is seen in the zero-growth environmentalists who calculate the value of babies as having no more worth than any other natural resource. It is a deadly progression of cruelty in which the most brutal actions are depicted as societal improvements. Sanger's morons beget Hitler's troublesome Jews which beget Obama's idea of punishment, which ultimately beget the embryonic stem cell industry waiting to go full bore.

What common factor has been missing throughout this entire observation? What critical void exists in this debate that allows those that advocate degrees of value for human existence to entertain credibility? The missing piece, the all-important component that has allowed, and continues to allow, such abominations that encapsulate the embryonic stem cell debate is the self-imposed absence of God. When God becomes part of the debate, life becomes sacred and murder becomes sin, not a matter of choice or the restructuring of society. If the current debate on embryonic stem cell usage remains an issue dictated by science alone, its progression may find an ending point worse than past atrocities.

Chapter 9
Political Correctness

How do I make you shut up? That is what liberals contemplate when conservatives get so fed up that they start to stand up for themselves and for their country. What is a minority with an ideological view so twistedly un-American that it will lose in any fair political fight to do to control the political agenda in this country? Liberals have been quite crafty and effective in finding the answer to this question. First, they never push any agenda at face value-- yep, that's a loser. Next, they craft a platform that uses patriotic or ambiguous wording to avoid being sniffed out immediately as America haters. People will reject liberals if they are straight with them, so, to beat the people, liberals trick them, and here are a few of the tricks in their playbook. If liberals can't shut conservatives up directly, they manipulate them so that they will silence themselves. How? One of the useful tools liberals have unleashed on this country is the implementation of political correctness. I have called it the "mental neutering" of the nation, and here is how it works. People in America start out their lives with what I would call common sense knowledge of what is right and wrong, as well as the belief that they should stand up for their values when they are threatened. However, through political correctness those who challenge the liberal minority on any topic are denigrated, demonized, and treated as outcasts. In the short term, people may see wrongs in the world, but they start to withdraw from speaking freely and challenging liberal ideas as they don't want to be judged as being "out of line." To avoid having harsh criticisms leveled against them for speaking their minds, conservatives teach themselves to hold their tongues when they really know better. This self-imposed silence allows liberals to win battle after battle simply by default. Liberals spin falsehoods and shape the culture in ways they want and conservatives sit there in silence, hoping to be deemed reasonable. This is insane! It gets worse over time as liberals continue to frame the world as they wish it would be. After enough time, some conservatives fall prey to believing that the liberal view of the world is in fact reality. Interestingly enough, political correctness is a one-way street. It always works to the benefit of liberals at the cost of conservative values.

Naturally, the rule of thumb for a conservative movement is to always avoid being politically correct, but let's make sure we know what that means. Being politically incorrect does not mean being angry or divisive. Political incorrectness doesn't involve shouting or breaking the family dishes. It simply means telling the truth, conveying truthful information through intelligent, honest dialogue, and challenging the unreasonable with logical arguments. Being politically incorrect does not mean that compromises can't be attained; it just means that the road to compromise will be traveled honestly. Honesty is the key here and it is what liberals fear. On November 23, 2010, I wrote about how political correctness is hurting the nation when it comes to security at the airports and the privacy we should have with our own bodies.

Political Correctness and Your Body: Why TSA Security Measures Won't Fly

This just in: TSA airport security personnel have now reaffirmed, after thousands of overtly aggressive body pat-downs, that elderly grandmothers and little children are still not attempting to commit terrorist attacks by carrying explosives onto planes. The growing discontent at the government's new intrusive security measures are now being seen throughout the country. The reasons people don't like it can be broken down into three areas of discussion: efficiency, invasiveness, and the strategic end results.

No one likes to be held up at the airport; however, most flyers are willing to accept delays that can be logically explained. For example, if the landing gear is about to fall off the plane, people have no qualms and show no resistance in patiently waiting while the issue is resolved. That is, people want to be safe while flying and will readily accept being inconvenienced if a reasonable case can be made for the situation. The problem comes when there cannot be a reasonable articulation made between extreme flyer inconvenience and passenger safety. Imagine if a plane with landing gear problems required all passengers to have a forced colonoscopy. The differential between the observed airline safety issue and the requirements placed on passengers would be so great that most flyers would refuse to comply. Welcome to the modern world of TSA security measures and what have become the unfriendly skies.

Prospective passengers in many airports are now being faced with having to go through full-body scanners that render the flyer practically naked to be photographed and observed by strangers. The long-term physical effects of radiation exposure from these scanners are unknown, along with their usefulness in detecting plastics and other materials terrorists use. As of now, full-body scanners do not make a case for security that equals or surpasses their offensive nature. Without more evidence of their practicality, TSA might as well request naked photographs of all passengers at the gate and save them the time of passing through the costly and time-consuming machines. However, the full-body scanners are quickly falling behind in public distaste to the full body pat down.

By now most Americans who have not experienced their own horror story at the airport have heard the tales of those who have been poked, prodded, and even fondled while trying to get on a flight. Stories of the handicapped being forced to stand on defective limbs while security personnel inspect their leg braces or the cancer survivor made to remove her prosthetic breast for inspection brings home the egregious nature of the new protocols. With the current system that is now being put into place, TSA cannot expect future increases in efficiency to mitigate the invasive nature of the experience to any noticeable degree.

It is in the strategic nature of the enhanced security protocol at the airports, and the argument made to passengers for their compliance that TSA utterly fails to make their case. They fail not just in the possession of full-body scanners or the implementation of enhanced pat-downs, TSA fails because blanket implementation of these protocols does not give airline passengers a degree of safety equal to or surpassing the violation of human dignity that they entail. Individuals seeking alternatives, such as Republican Representative John Mica of Florida, say the answer can be found in replacing TSA agents with private security guards. Mica's reasoning for such changes is based on the idea that private industry through competition would increase quality and efficiency.

This is possible, but only if several fundamental strategies are put into place. More diligent inspection of passports and pre-travel documents along with observations of passenger activities and actions at the airport will go far toward true airline security. This goes hand in hand with observing sets of characteristics that identify what has been congruent with modern-day terrorists. At this point in time, this means placing higher scrutiny on Muslim males that are traveling from known terrorist locations over elderly American grandmothers in walkers flying to see their grandchildren for the holidays. To call this racist is to be misguided. To deplete critical security resources to invasively search people who do not fit any criteria of a terrorist simply to be politically correct is more than wasteful, it is reckless. It is reckless because it places all passengers at higher risk as security personnel decrease their attentiveness while searching individuals who are obvious non-threats.

Those that would place all airline travelers in front of the full-body scanners and rubber gloves of TSA personnel cite the case that if the current profile of the modern terrorist is actually observed instead of denied through blanket security procedures that those that wish to do Americans harm will simply use different actors to conduct terrorist activities. The current evidence does not support this line of thinking for terroristic airline incidents. If this does change and grandmothers, Girl Scouts, American vets, and even farm boys from Kansas like myself fall under the profile of terrorists who blow up planes, then adaptations can be made, and protocols altered. The new protocols would come with, most importantly, a logical argument to be made for the reasonable balance of security measures and airline safety. Right now, we are all getting the equivalent of the unwarranted colonoscopy.

The Rigoberto Ruelas suicide in California was an incident that I felt required a discussion about not only personal responsibility, but also how political correctness is used as a tool to punish the innocent. I received a lot of reader mail from people who had family and friends who had committed suicide. I feel for their pain; however, if we cannot speak truthfully about who is responsible—and yes, to blame—for suicide, we shut the door to speaking the truth on many important issues. This kind of political correctness must be overcome; it must be defeated.

Death before Truth: Political Correctness in America

If you want to see the pervasive nature of political correctness in America today, the national public outcry following the Rigoberto Ruelas suicide in California is a salient example. Ruelas, a fifth grade teacher at Miramonte Elementary School in south Los Angeles, is believed to have committed suicide after receiving poor ratings in a teacher-rating database that was posted in the Los Angeles Times. Specifically, Christina Hoag of the Associated Press reports that Rigoberto Ruelas was described by friends as being distraught over scoring "average" in his teaching effectiveness in English and scoring as "less effective" in the area of math. Ruelas had an overall score of "less effective." As Ruelas' body was found in the Big Tujunga Canyon area in the Angeles National Forest by law enforcement officials, the question, "who is to blame?" cascades across the nation.

The apparent suicide of Rigoberto Ruelas brings about the usual pain and anguish of such events. Having worked numerous suicide investigations as a criminal investigator, I understand there are many common elements that family and friends suffer through when individuals choose to take their own lives. One of the common themes is an attempt to rationally explain how such a tragedy could take place. With the attempt to find explanations for such traumatic events comes the common quest to assign blame. This is when the politically correct operatives step out of the woodwork to point the public toward those they wish to be held accountable.

I feel true sadness and sympathy for the family, friends and students who grieve Ruelas' death. However, the attacks on the L.A. Times for reporting Ruelas' sub-par teacher ratings are not deserved justice, rather the implementation of political correctness. Within political correctness, value judgments of almost any kind become taboo, especially those that account for personal conduct. Ironically, it is politically incorrect to even talk about political correctness.

The Ruelas case brings the point home. Who is to blame for the death of Rigoberto Ruelas? If we take the example being modeled by the teachers union, it is not only the unfairness of the evaluation system that found Ruelas lacking as a teacher, but more so the audacity of the L.A. Times for reporting his deficiencies. Nowhere in the teachers union's politically correct assessment of this incident do we hear them talk about holding teachers accountable for their own actions. As is the case with political correctness, those who publicize a value judgment are treated as the offenders while the problem itself is allowed to grow and build. Following political correctness, no problem is too big to ignore. The Ruelas case reflects this. As reported in the Associated Press, it was not just Ruelas who had teaching issues at Miramonte that the L.A. Times made public. The Miramonte Elementary School itself ranked as "least effective" in raising test scores, and only five out of 35 third to fifth grade teachers at the school were ranked as high as "average." The problem was widespread but would have remained hidden from the view of parents and the public without publication. So, is the L.A. Times the culprit in this story, or is it some really bad teaching? You won't hear any apologies from the teachers union United Teachers Los Angeles for Miramonte's poor teacher performance. Instead, they are demanding that the L.A. Times stop posting teacher evaluations. Without the now-controversial publication, educators such as Ruelas would still have been evaluated on the criteria of respect and likeability. Is this the yardstick of evaluation that is in the best interest of the students of Miramonte? It certainly would have been more politically correct.

Taking political correctness to the next level, the teachers union has called for a boycott of the L.A. Times. The idea that teachers should have their own report cards and accountability made public will now be put to the test. The unfortunate reality in this case is that the students of this school have lost a teacher, and their pain is justified. Family and friends are without someone they care about and their mourning is difficult to bear witness to. However, in the case of suicide, the responsibility falls with the individual, as this is a personal act, and a very selfish one at that.

If this teacher truly killed himself in reaction to a poor teacher evaluation made public, a politically incorrect truth needs to be accepted. It was not a poor evaluation or the L.A. Times' decision to publish it along with other educators' results that ended the teacher's life. It was Ruelas' personal decision to leave this world instead of addressing it that is causing the pain felt by family and friends today. It was his decision to run from a poor performance evaluation instead of improving himself or challenging the criteria by which he was evaluated. In the end, it was a very selfish decision of this teacher to abandon those that held him in such high regard for the false belief in escape. This is an important lesson that the teachers union could be addressing, instead they are obscuring true issues of accountability by evoking political correctness.

He may rape girls in nightclub bathrooms, but hey, he's a great quarterback! He was only killing dogs, and now you want to take him off the field? They (athletes) all take drugs, what's the problem? We hear this tripe every time a major sports figure is found in some cocaine-filled hotel room full of fifteen year-old hookers. It's truly an entitlement belief system that some people are believed to be above the law, but it is also a political correctness issue. Using words such as I have at the beginning of this paragraph will enrage certain people more than the atrocities committed by some of the athletes people tend to hold in such high esteem. On February 11, 2010, I addressed this important issue while talking about the world of politics. This is easy to do because politics is truly a contact sport, and Americans must always keep their eyes on the ball (the truth), no matter where the contest is being played.

Give Me the Ball! Entitlement in the Political Field

Hardly a day goes by that we do not hear about a famous sports player breaking societal rules for his or her own personal deviant desires. Whether it is marital infidelity, unscrupulous financial dealings, or just the case of the sensationalized beloved being jerks to their followers, there is an undeniable trend that some believe that all is owed to them no questions asked.

Of course this is not just a phenomenon predominant in the sports industry. It is a mental state of mind that brings about the arrogant belief of entitlement, the idea that a person deserves everything at once just for being who they are despite their personal actions. Cases of entitlement gone bad at times catch the public's attention with out-of-control sports figures, those who fail to conform to team rules and create general chaos on and off the field, and then complain that they were not given their fair share of time to play, bonus dollars to perform, or face time in front of the camera.

The transition from sports to politics is made easily by listening to the actual architect of the entitlement philosophy (the modern day liberal). Even today, the microphones are still warm from the liberal breath of former Bill Clinton political mouthpiece James Carville and his statements that allude to entitlement. Carville said about this year's Super Bowl that other than people living in Indianapolis, anyone who did not root for the New Orleans Saints was less of a human being. With his snappy Cajun style of banter, Carville fused the New Orleans Saints football team with years of economic and racial inequality to frame a football team that Americans should not just support because of love of team, but because they deserve to win because they are who they are, entitled.

This same bold challenge to defy the entitled at the ballot box was recently thrust at Scott Brown in his historic upset win in Massachusetts. Liberals found it distasteful that a Republican would have the audacity to even run in an election on a ballot that once held the name of Ted Kennedy. We see the same entitlement mentality on the defiant lips of people like Bertha Lewis from the infamous brothel-builders at ACORN. The idea that their organization should be punished with investigative probes or withdrawn governmental funding is a foreign concept that has no potential to become a reality, because in the minds of the entitled, they are deserving of the rewards they receive simply by their state of existence.

Whether it is the million-dollar crybabies that derail great sports teams, or the loudmouth politicians that throw away party voting majorities, or anywhere it is found in society, the entitlement mentality will continue to be a destructive force. While the "entitled" of the world are doomed to their own self-designed demise, their effect can be minimized if we educate the next generation to reject this flawed, destructive mindset. For the future of our youth, we must reject the notion to allow entitlement to continue despite the volume with which we are instructed otherwise. We must take the time to show our children why liberalism itself creates such negative by-products as entitlement, and highlight the ever-present examples of individuals who go down in flames clutching blindly to entitlement as though it will save them. Despite the pervasive nature of entitlement within the culture today, it is not unachievable to create a future where success and all the adulations that come with it are based on what one does by his or her own hand, and not through the blind fallacies of entitlement.

Chapter 10

A Moment for the Pharisees

The Westboro Baptist Church--I hate these people. The damage this little cult of misfits does to the country is hard to count, and the world would be a better place without them. WBC hurts the conservative movement because opportunist liberals often seize the chance to place this organization in with mainstream Christians. You've heard the talking points by liberals that Christians are mean and intolerant. It is not surprising that in substantive debates on religious issues, WBC will often get thrown into the discussion by the Left to supposedly prove the nasty nature of Christians. This is simply a tactic to minimize Christians; it's like calling conservatives "Nazis." Once it's thrown out there, the idea is that people don't have to listen to the side with the wild label wrapped around its neck. The truth is that no mainstream Christian organization identifies or has any affiliation with WBC. Not any branch of the Baptists or any other Christian denomination or non-denominational church will touch these folks. The members of WBC are truly lepers to the Christian world. WBC hurts the conservative movement because liberals often place these nuts as part of the political Right. The term "right wing" or "radical right wing" is a common descriptor use to psychologically place the "Fred Heads" of WBC a little closer to the Republican Party and any other conservatives. The truth is that until Fred Phelps and WBC turned into complete nut bars, they were liberals. Should I repeat that? Did I miss your good ear? Fred Phelps and clan were die-hard Democrats. Let's savor that for a moment. Fred Phelps ran in 1990, 1994, and 1998 for Kansas Governor on the Democrat ticket. Fred Phelps also ran for U.S. Senate from Kansas as a Democrat in 1992. Wait, there is more. Guess who the Phelps' crew campaigned for in 1988? It was none other than Democrat Al Gore. At Hillbuzz.com, readers can look at pictures of Al Gore, Fred Phelps, and company working the Democrat campaign trail. Politically, WBC is a liberal organization. Religiously, its members act like the Pharisees and the Sadducees. The Bible is valuable as a survival manual for life and exposes the self-serving ways of this group. I invite you to read my April 15, 2010, article entitled, "The Westboro Baptist Church: In the Footsteps of the Pharisees and Sadducees" and tell me if my assessment of this group is correct.

The Westboro Baptist Church: In the Footsteps of the Pharisees and Sadducees

In the aftermath of the court's reversal of a multi-million dollar judgment against the Westboro Baptist Church for picketing a soldier's funeral, we in America are left with many questions about where justice can be found. Despite many within the country that believe that the cult from Topeka, Kansas, should not be allowed to heckle and damn our nation's military dead at their funerals, for now, the courts have decided that these protests are protected under the constitution. Equally painful to so many, myself included, is the court's decision to force the Al Snyder family, the family that brought the private lawsuit against Westboro, to pay over $16,000 of the Phelps family's court costs. It would seem that the courts have said to grieving military families across the nation that attempting to stop the Westboro Baptist Church from joyously telling them that their loved ones are in hell will be a costly endeavor on all fronts.

Does this recent court ruling in some way justify the work of Westboro? Has God reached down to shelter his faithful flock with their colorful signs and punish the wickedness of the world as is so often indicated from the members of this group from Kansas? The answer to this question is found in the same document they use to damn all of humanity: the Bible. When we find ourselves at a loss to fathom groups like Westboro, it is the wisdom and modern applicability found within the Bible that exposes them and shows their true place in the world. It is amongst the holy hypocrisy of the Pharisees and the Sadducees of the Bible we find Westboro's equivalent.

The Pharisees and Sadducees were the religious experts of their time, and like Westboro and their colorful signs, these religion enforcers wore special colorful robes to be easily identified among the masses. You might say the colorful robes were their trademark. The Pharisees and Sadducees took great effort to garner attention for themselves in public spectacles on street corners that were meant to show their righteousness, and more importantly, the disparity between them and the masses of the spiritually lost. Are you seeing the similarities yet? Jesus admonished the Pharisees and Sadducees for their lack of compassion, and in their intolerance, for turning people away from God. The Lord could see that these public super holy rollers acted for their own glory and not his. Jesus as well understood them, and admonished them for what they really were, a "brood of vipers."

I remember interviewing Shirley Phelps Roper in 2008 on my radio program *Conscience of Kansas*. The cult lives only 40 miles from me here in Kansas and despite many friends who feared for my physical and financial safety against these well-known litigious fanatics, I invited their congregational spokesperson to the program and debated the issues as best as can be done with members of this group. In fact, if I have any YouTube fame at all, it is as the radio host that turned Shirley Phelps Roper's microphone off a record number of times. During my interview with her, among the many judgments she laid upon me, I remember her saying that I would have been one of the people cheering the crucifixion of Christ. If the truth be told, it was in fact the self-absorbed Westborian-like Pharisees that saw Jesus as a threat to their power base and worked so hard to destroy the son of God. If the sacrificial lamb were to return today, he would have Westboro at his doorstep with the signs of the Sadducees saying "God Hates Jesus."

I don't know if this biblical perspective gives any consolation to the Snyder family or those who will suffer at future military funerals at the hands of a bunch of Kansas Pharisees and Sadducees. What I hope is that while the high court's struggle with where free speech begins and ends, we take to heart what eluded the Pharisees, Sadducees, and their modern equivalents. That is, while sin, judgment, and damnation are biblical realities, so are love, mercy, compassion, and the opportunity for God's grace. Both exist and are relevant to humanity, and to imply otherwise is to be worse than a fool; it is to be a hypocrite. It is to be a Pharisee or a Sadducee.

When WBC was fined millions of dollars for damages in protesting a fallen soldier's funeral, I cheered along with the nation. Finally, these terrible people were going to get theirs. When they won their appeal and the father of the fallen soldier who originally brought the lawsuit was told by an appeals judge that he would have to pay the Phelps' legal costs equaling thousands of dollars, my heart sunk. It seemed that there was just no fairness in the world. On October 16, 2010, I published an article that was a reply to *Detroit Free Press* columnist Mitch Albom. Albom, like me, felt that something had to be done about these twisted people from Topeka, Kansas. What we had were different ideas on how to handle them. Albom wanted to back these protestors up ten miles from each funeral, while I wanted to throw them in prison. This is not a new proposition for me, as I have made my case before for giving the Phelps' crew extended "alone time" via the penal system. However, in this article I forwarded my proposition for incarceration against what most often is the way people try to deal with WBC, which is to try to force them through law to back up and back off our soldiers who have made the ultimate sacrifice.

Westboro Baptist Church and the Ten-Mile Proposition

The Westboro Baptist Church... need I say more? The nation watches as the Supreme Court deliberates on the limits of free speech in America involving the right of families to bury the dead in peace versus the need of the little Kansas cult to disrupt military funerals and tell grieving families that their dearly departed are going to hell. Going to hell, mind you, because somewhere in the world, a homosexual exists.

The rhyme or reason behind the actions of the Westboro sign-wavers is so contradictory to the Bible and to logic itself that their actions may never be brought to a reasonable understanding. The big head shaker when it comes to this group of peculiar proselytes is Westboro's overwhelming indifference to actually bringing any converts into their fold. This group shows up at a location and tells people the equivalency of, "God hates you, you're going to hell and we're not; have a nice day." This appears to be the Westboro mission statement. I know; I live only 40 miles from these dirty damnation designators and their central compound in Topeka, Kansas. I have had them shake their signs at me in Wichita, Kansas, while attempting to go to church, and I have been in spitting distance of them at Kansas State University. I interviewed Shirley Phelps-Roper on my radio program *Conscience of Kansas* in 2008 and I still receive positive feedback from YouTube viewers who enjoy the moments when I turn Phelps-Roper's microphone off to break up her rants and filibustering.

The point here is not to rehash a debate about the deviant inner workings of the Westboro Baptist Church; I would not drag readers into that gutter. The point is also not to have a high noon theologian-style standoff with WBC on who will get their comeuppance come judgment day. What is of importance here is whether this country should allow WBC to continue to harangue military families and call it free speech. Do we undermine the Constitution and what the First Amendment stands for if we say that unpopular speech, even the near-fighting words of WBC, can be squelched? Westboro, as the Saul Alinksy tacticians that they are, now bank on our Constitution to save them in their hour of need. Should they be silenced at the risk of silencing legitimate voices down the road in places like the Internet, Tea Party gatherings, and conservative talk radio?

Detroit Free Press columnist Mitch Albom laments about the Westboro issue and comes to a couple of interesting conclusions with which I partially agree. First, Albom concludes that the Supreme Court will most likely rule on the side of the Westboro Baptist Church. I agree that this will happen. Based on this conclusion, Albom forwards the idea that the current state laws pushing protestors to distances of 500 feet or more should be changed for groups like Westboro to 10 miles. Albom's idea is that at that distance, Westboro would be made ineffective and they would give up their activities due to a lack of attention.

At first thought this might seem like the way to go, and my knee-jerk reaction, like Albom's, is to make "distance" the defense for military families from Westboro's brand of hateful speech. But alas, after further thought I believe that this would not bring about the desired effect and might possibly have a myriad of unintended negative consequences. We have to recognize that Westboro members, like a nest of vipers, are extremely crafty. They know the law and they use it to their advantage very effectively. If they were physically banned for 10 miles they would most likely affix jumbotrons to public walkways where they could flash their signs and scream insults at the dead via satellite. The point is that they would not give in, they would not give up; they would adapt to the letter of the law to continue their protests. Worse yet, the slippery slope issue is again brought forth. These are the points where Albom's strategy fails to hit the mark.

Despite my disagreement with the current option, I do not come to the table without any solutions to the Westboro question. Westboro should be shut down, but not on the issue of free speech. They should be shut down because their protests are in fact an act of treason. Westboro's military protests are open acts of treachery and clearly a breach of allegiance to the nation. Westboro, through their psychological warfare against the military, show a clear pattern of undermining the war effort and thus aid and comfort the enemy. Akin to passing out pamphlets at military recruiting stations to join al-Qaeda, Westboro passes out the threat to

American families that if their children serve and die for this country, their cult may be attending the funeral. WBC protests disrupt communities, turn the local populace against the police who must protect the protestors from annihilation, and bring never-ending pain and anguish to grieving families of fallen soldiers. Arguably worse, Westboro's funeral protests plant the seeds of fear into America's bravest families who can only wonder if their fallen loved one will be the next on the Westboro Baptist Church hit list.

In the end, we can and should leave the Constitution uncut and uncompromised on this heated issue. I guess you could say that when it comes to the Westboro Baptist Church, the answer is already on the books, and jail will bring far more justice than the 10-mile proposition.

Chapter 11

Border Security and Immigration

If a person wants to see a salient example of liberals being able to perpetuate a political victory over time, it is visible in the open U.S. southern border. Despite several pushes by the American people since September 11, 2001, the southern border remains porous. This is an issue that screams to be resolved by a strong conservative movement. Ironically, compared with the massive construction projects that have been accomplished throughout history in this country, double fencing and a strong military presence at the border would be a cake-walk. The open border is a failure of both Republicans and Democrats and it is a prime example of why some Republicans need to be put out to pasture and why all Democrats must be dominated. End result--a secured border. A word for conservatives debating the issue with liberals who say open borders are an issue of compassion: the continuance of illegal immigration has nothing to do with compassion; in fact, it is an act of cruelty. In my May 7, 2010, article the issue of kindness and cruelty at the border is brought before the American people.

Illegal Immigration: Is it Kind to be Cruel?

What the media coins the "tough" new Arizona immigration law, SB1070, forwarded by Governor Jan Brewer, has once again pushed to the forefront the argument of, "just what is the proper course of action when dealing with illegal immigration?" The American Civil Liberties Union (ACLU) says the new law is unconstitutional. Ultra-liberal Mayor Gavin Newsom of the sanctuary city San Francisco is working to boycott Arizona in an effort to force the state to scrap the new law. In what has to be seen as a bizarre political move, Arizona Democrat Congressman Raul Grijalva has decided to boycott his own state.

Whether it is the ACLU, liberal mayors in San Francisco, or an Arizona Congressmen who wishes to make his next political race very interesting, the overarching theme is that it is cruel to enforce immigration law and kind for the borders to remain open. To believe this, does one has to redefine those terms? You decide.

In the back pages of the New York Times, law professor Kris Kobach, who helped draft the new Arizona law, dispels the case for harassment in the state's requirement of immigrants to show proper documents. Remember, this is not groundbreaking as it has been federal law since 1940 that aliens carry registration documents. Kobach outlines the state's restraint on police authority in requesting such documents. It must be during proper investigations after a totality of circumstances leads an officer to a reasonable suspicion to make these requests. Every day U.S. citizens are asked for identification documents during police investigations. Ever been pulled over for speeding? Filed a police report on any event? Americans are neither shocked nor do they find it cruel when asked by the police for identification or other documents. Because Arizona requires one to be a legal resident to get a driver's license, in any situation that involves a question of immigration, police must presume that a person with a valid Arizona driver's license has legal status. How very kind of Arizona to do that.

While the legal opposition to Arizona's new law is an empty argument, the basis for it — the question of kindness versus cruelty — still remains. Is it cruel or kind to deny states the right to enforce their own laws? It would seem that those that promote illegal immigration in the U.S. have decided that citizens of Arizona are acceptable casualties to drug dealers, human traffickers, gang activity, and the list goes on. Phoenix, Arizona: Hostage Capital of the U.S. is another title of distinction that can be directly tied to illegal immigration. Is it cruel to say that Arizona's fate is Arizona's business, or is it kind for a mayor in San Francisco to attempt to dictate the state's laws through strong-arm tactics?

Lastly, is it kind or cruel to perpetuate the shadow class of illegal immigrants, a group whose lack of standard legal identification and lawful entry places them as potential criminals and terrorists at worst, and as an unwarranted drain to the economy at best?

As it stands today, it appears to me that it is through a series of cruelties that both the U.S. citizen and the illegal immigrant attempt to find and hold on to the bounties of the American dream. Both sides suffer through a system that promotes illegality, victimization, and distrust. So, the question remains, is it kind to be cruel?

There is weak, and then there is really weak when it comes to securing the southern border. Barack Obama makes both groups look strong. When I wrote my July 9, 2010, article on border security, the country had already been watching the battle taking place at the Arizona border for some time. Arizona Governor Jan Brewer had overseen the crafting of S.B. 1070, a law that among other things, would allow law enforcement officers during the course of a lawful investigation to ask people for identification papers, including those that would pertain to citizenship status. Arizona, a state that has been literally overrun by illegals from the southern border was simply attempting to enforce immigration and criminal law that the Federal Government had refused to take its responsibility to enforce. Predictably, the Barack Obama administration fought Arizona's attempt to secure its border. Then, to make matters worse, during the battle over S.B. 1070, the Obama administration had signs placed 80 miles from the U.S.-Mexico border and about 30 miles from the Arizona state capital that read, "Smuggling and illegal immigration may be encountered in this area." You can't make this stuff up!

Barack Obama: Securing the Border, One Sign at a Time

No one likes to be opposed. As people, we pick a side of an argument we believe in and try our hardest to win. That's life, but there are differing ways in which we oppose one another and some are much more inflammatory than others. See if you agree. Is it not more frustrating, more infuriating when someone attempts to trick you to win an argument? Is there not more respect given to those who say, "You're wrong, I'm right, and I will prove it!" versus someone who attempts trickery and poorly devised schemes to win an argument while congratulating you on your hard-fought victory?

I say it is better to be defeated than to be duped and defeated. When it comes to the issue of border security Barack Obama is attempting poorly crafted chicanery on the citizens of this country. Obama is not the first to fail the American people on this issue, but he is the first to fail them in such an insulting manner. Before we shine the light of accountability on Obama's bamboozling bag of border tricks, we should look at the failures to secure the border that preceded his presidency.

Through the time and effort of average Americans in the Minuteman Project the nation received video footage of the undeniably massive influx of illegal aliens crossing the border. If ever it was in question, the will of the American people to be safe and secure in their own nation has now been made clear. The U.S. border must be secured.

On Oct. 26, 2006, the Secure Fence Act was passed. It stated that within 18 months the government was to have secured the border through the use of physical barriers, border patrol agents, unmanned aerial vehicles, ground-based sensors, satellites, radar coverage, cameras and additional checkpoints. Just to make sure there was no question about the end goal, the term "operational control," which is referenced throughout the law, was defined as "the prevention of all unlawful U.S. entries, including entries by terrorists, other unlawful aliens, instruments of terrorism, narcotics and other contraband." So why is the border still wide open? Here is where the trickery starts. Instead of going full bore to complete the project, funding became a political wedge issue as double fencing became single fencing, and by the time the Obama administration was faced with the border security issue, fencing at all was seen as impractical. As reported by the Associated Press back in 2005, then-Arizona Governor Janet Napolitano was already undermining the fence option with statements such as, "You show me a 50-foot wall and I'll show you a 51-foot ladder at the border. That's the way the border works."

In a very foreseeable progression in the government's failure to secure the border, Arizona passes SB1070 to protect its state from an onslaught of illegal immigration. The current Arizona Governor Jan Brewer, once again with a majority of American support, forces the government's hand to take action. Even with the self-proclaimed transparent Obama administration at the helm, like painful déjà vu, government trickery again replaced government action. In response to Brewer's meeting with Barack Obama and the promise of government aid to secure the Arizona border, the president's response was to post warning signs in the desert, 80 miles from the U.S.-Mexico border and about 30 miles from the state capital. The signs read, "Smuggling and illegal immigration may be encountered in this area." No kidding, Sherlock! As reported by CBS news, Governor Brewer now stars in a new video showing the warning signs at her state's border as she gives the president both barrels for his lackadaisical response to this growing threat.

I can identify with her anger because it is not just opposition to securing the border that Obama is showing, it is opposition presented through an intelligence-insulting ruse. The Obama-border-sign fiasco is the biggest slap in the face to America on this issue so far and it will not be forgotten quickly. The economic and physical security of Americans is not a joke to be placed on signs at the nation's edge. After what has been years of failed policy on border security, Barack Obama is redefining the concept of "adding insult to injury." You can put that on a sign

Has it always been this way? Has the American government always refused to require immigrants to enter the United States legally? Is it historically common place for immigrants who enter the United States to come with an entitlement mentality that this country owes them a better life? The answer is no. America's history on this issue shows a country that used to know its own worth and treated entrance into the United States as a privilege and not a right. Furthermore, past immigrants coming to the United States treated this country much more respectfully than today, obeying immigration laws and entering without an entitlement mentality. These immigrants of the past are the backbone of the country today.

Analyzing the Open-Border Mentality

How special is America? Is it truly a unique place where people can find opportunities for a better life that surpass those of other countries? Many think this to be true and the country has had a long history of being a welcoming place for people from all across the world. From 1892 to 1924 the port of New York at Ellis Island processed over 20 million foreign immigrants to legally enter the country. According to the National Park Service's Ellis Island site, as many as 11,747 immigrants legally entered America in a single day in 1907. It is estimated that as many 100 million Americans are descendants of the process of legal immigration that took place at locations such as Ellis Island.

Unfortunately, the mentality that gave America such a large infusion of hopeful and hardworking immigrants to this country has vanished and has been replaced with something much different. For one, immigrants entering America through Ellis Island came in with no preconceived beliefs that the United States owed them anything. Instead, immigrants entered the country with gracious humility to seek out the "American Dream."
Traditional immigration encompassed a mutually respectful exchange between country and immigrant for the right of admittance. Foreigners had to show that

they had a trade or other ability that would be useful to the country in order to be allowed in. Also, immigrants had to show that they were not carrying harmful communicable diseases that would be a detriment to the American people. Some immigrants were held for observation due to fear of disease and about two percent of those seeking to enter the country were turned away. America's policy at that time was most certainly pro-immigration but it also encompassed a secure border element that is sorely lacking today. The next time you're faced with an argument for open borders by someone who declares we are all descendants of immigrants, remember that a majority of this country's classical immigration was conducted legally.

Today's open-border mentality has been steadily moving toward an entitlement belief system that combines the thinking that America, for some inexplicable reason, owes everybody everything and that the country's financial pockets are bottomless. This open-border entitlement mentality has not only enveloped immigrants that enter America through our southern border, it is also a heavily entrenched mentality for many within the U.S. government. The idea that America needs illegal immigrants to do America's work is still touted despite the crushing unemployment rates of the last two years. The open-border mentality has been tested by time and continues to exist. No matter whether a Republican or Democrat is running the country, the border remains unsecured and the American people continue to pay from their own pockets, suffer from a lack of security and be forced to endure the open-border propaganda machine.

Recently Americans were shown a presentation meant to highlight the futility of the fence at the Mexican border. Fox News aired footage of two women scaling a four-million-dollar-a-mile security fence in eighteen seconds at the southern border. The message being sent is that attempts to secure the border are futile. What is less evident in this visual of the fast-moving climbers circumventing the border fence is the missing concertina wire at the fence's apex let alone the lack of funding for double fencing that has fallen to the wayside since 2006. If one can break away from the open-border mentality, what is actually shown in such depictions is that the American government is extremely successful at failing when they really try.

To maintain the current open-border mentality that secure borders are akin to hatred of immigrants, an idea that would have been rejected by the immigrants processed at Ellis Island, it has become acceptable for government officials to spend their times downplaying incidents such as the daily gun battles that occur in places like Laredo, Texas, by the Mexican drug runners. The open-border mentality requires a person to accept as economically reasonable the $1.6 billion being spent for welfare, public safety and healthcare for illegal aliens in Los Angeles County alone. Sadly, U.S. citizens are more likely to receive a bundle of airmail(ed) marijuana via catapult than a secure border.

America has never had an inability to secure the border. If the government desired, we have the means to create a southern border that would allow only recognized and processed immigrants into the country as we did at Ellis Island. What we have is a mentality problem that starts with how some perceive the worth of America and its relationship with those that wish to visit or become part of this wonderful country. The immigrants that came to Ellis Island came with respect for America. Respect of country leads to a respect of a country's law and its people. The idea of illegal immigrants covertly entering America to give birth to children that will eventually receive citizenship and social benefits that must be paid for by the descendants of Ellis Island's legal immigrants is more than a painful irony. In the end it shows us the dark side of the current open-border mentality, a mentality that perceives the value of America as less than what has been traditionally held by the immigrants that have made this country so great. We will all pay if we allow this mentality to dominate our actions as a nation on the issue of border security.

It's time to grow up! As adults we can no longer live in the fantasy world our children play in. We do not have that luxury. That is in part why liberals can't be placed in charge of the reins of power within this country without adverse effects. This book has laid out the ideological conflicts between liberals and conservatives based on the principles of conservatism: 1. God, 2. Family, 3. Country. The articles within this book have brought a plethora of examples of the issues at stake and the battles being fought for the future of the nation. We know that there are many more issues of importance and in the future we will see new things that we must address. Either a conservative or a liberal ideology will be used to address all these issues. Conservatives have the statistical majority, and we can decide that our values will be utilized when a major decision must be addressed. While liberals are free to create theoretical utopias where unions don't exploit their workers and dictators don't behead the intelligentsia, the first time there is a point of contention, conservatives have to live in the real world, and we must be accountable as adults. Our ideological makeup forces us toward accountability and a quantifiable bottom line. Here I come with the responsibility pitch once again. If we fail, we can't blame it on society, or the "Man," or even the Bossa Nova. It's all on us. The upside is that the rewards will be real and earned by our own hard work and not off the backs of others. It's time for a conservative movement to take over this country and put the children to bed.

When I Was A Child, I thought like the Obama Administration

Remember when you were in grade school, or dare I say high school, and you found yourself in a humiliating situation after having failed to read the day's assignment and being called to expound upon your of knowledge in front of the class? If this happened to you then you don't need me to frame how things transpired, since for most, this was a situation of distress, confusion, sadness, and shame. The memory of facing the class and trying to repel each of the teacher's questions like incoming missiles can create a sheen of perspiration on the brow even today.

Some people find they relive these situations in their dreams from time to time when the sandman decides to deal them a dirty hand at bedtime. For most, the saving grace that allows us to break free from such situations is that we grew up and took on the responsibility to prepare for the tasks that we face today. This truth is eloquently stated in the Bible in Corinthians, "When I was a child, I talked like a child, I thought like a child, I reasoned like a child. When I became a man, I put childish ways behind me." How the Obama administration could gain from following these wise words!

Arizona's new immigration law SB 1070 is being attacked by liberals around the globe as racist, overreaching, barbaric, draconian, and the list of descriptors is almost limitless. From the White House, President Obama called the law "misguided" and now jumps back and forth on the issue of whether or not Arizona's law promotes racial profiling. Attorney General Eric Holder and Homeland Security Secretary Janet Napolitano, both highly critical of Arizona's law, recently admitted in public forums before television cameras that they had not even read the 10-page bill they had been condemning. I wonder if they felt silly, like children who had failed to do their homework and were then called to

186

the front of the class to give their report. To many it appeared so, but to me they were more frightening than anything. Should the American people require that they stay after class, or even be held back? Way back? When I saw how little the facts really mattered to these government officials when it came to how they dealt with Arizona and the America people, I began to see the childlike mentality that dictatorships often encompass.

This is a scary place where deliberation and decision making is devoid of fact and reason and based merely on party line politics and the whims of the White House. The words in Corinthians come back to me with modern-day applicability: "When I was a child, I talked like a child, I thought like a child, I reasoned like *the Obama administration*. It's a painfully accurate fit.

I would say that reading the laws would bolster the credibility of the White House's opposition to laws, with which they disagree, but the problem here is much deeper than understanding that "reading is fundamental;" you also have to care about the people and respect the rule of law. As Fox News reports, John Morton, assistant secretary of homeland security for U.S. Immigration and Customs Enforcement, stated that illegal aliens from Arizona may be rejected for processing based on his view, which subsequently falls in line with the White House's stance that Arizona's law is not the solution to the illegal immigration problem. Has John Morton read the law he now rejects? Well, he certainly has not been briefed on the specifics of Arizona's SB 1070 by Obama administration officials such as Eric Holder and Janet Napolitano. It is apparent that right now America has an administration quick to turn in their verdicts and slow to do their homework.

Chapter 12

A Conservative Movement: Goals, Rules, and Guidelines

Traditional Americans are in a war of ideologies with liberals for the soul of the country. Our future and the future of our children, and their children will be decided by the actions we take today. This war will be hard fought by both sides, there will be ideological casualties and conservatives will lose friends and certain opportunities that are held in liberal control along the way. Nothing of importance is accomplished easily, this is a fight. With that said, conservative Americans should take heart that they are on the right of side of history and that their mission is naturally more likely to succeed than that of their left leaning opposition. Yes, liberals have damaged the country, but let's take a moment to put that into perspective. In reality, the Left has only chipped its way into select niches of society--places like newspapers, television, universities, the courts and other pivotal locations. From these positions, those on the Left work tirelessly to expand the liberal agenda. These are important parts of society that the Left dominates; but even with these pivotal positions to espouse Marxian big government ideology, liberals fail to bring a message that resonates with a majority of Americans. Why is this so? Remember that it is the liberal, not the conservative who is attempting to change the natural order of America, to turn the country on its head. Leftists wish to reinvent this country. It is the modern liberal's intent to psychologically attach the totalitarian hammer and sickle to the stars and stripes of the American flag. It is the extreme nature of the changes that the liberals wish to make in America that will be their undoing. Conservatives simply want to restore the country to its original glory. Our job is much easier because the country naturally yearns to be brought back to God, to be blessed by His love and protection. Our intentions with a conservative movement are validated by history and inspired by the Divine. Liberals have the challenge of forcing a foreign Marxian philosophy onto a land naturally inclined to oppose it. Within the natural state of America, liberals are swimming against the current while conservatives swim with it. So be determined, but also bring a spirit of joy as we go to battle against this foe, because we are going to win. Now let's look at specific strategy.

Political and Spiritual Goals

The conservative movement has already been building. Our job is to swell the ranks and stay focused on the final objectives. The end goal, politically, is to have overwhelming numbers at the polls. A growing conservative movement keeps focused locally, and then looks to state and national growth. The first goal is to win local elections. Why local elections first? Local elections ranging from school board to city mayor affect people's lives as private citizens quickly and more directly. Here is an example; Barack Obama passes Obamacare and it is years before it goes into effect. Your city council in your town passes a hike on trash fees, and you may see a bigger bill the next month. I gave the example of the homosexual agenda as it was being forwarded in my town in Kansas. You have probably seen these types of liberal proposals in your town. If not, you will. The culture at large is affected from the ground up. Our towns, counties, and states, while often treated as inconsequential are like the roots of a tree. They affect everything from the trunk, to the limbs, to the leaves. If the roots fail to receive life-giving water, the tree withers. If the roots become poisoned, the tree dies. When towns and counties refuse to allow liberals to encroach on conservative core values, it is a powerful message. Victory spreads like life-giving water from the roots throughout the entire tree. The tree becomes stronger until it can handle any storm, any ill wind.

Spiritually, the goal of the conservative movement is to bring the nation back to God, to create a country that is not looking for ways to minimize the creator and His creation. God exists in government, business, the private sphere and the public square. To deny the American people this divine relationship between God and his people will not stand. America must continue to be a nation of tolerance of all religions, but to the world, the United States must be clearly known by deed and by action as a Christian nation. Again this is a battle first fought and won locally. Christian households make for Christian communities, which then can demand that God remain at the state and national levels of government.

Growing Our Numbers

The Tea Party and 9-12 organizations have been successful because they mirror in many ways church groups. That is, they are small and localized within individual towns or grouped by counties. I recommend that groups stay relatively non-bureaucratic. If your Tea Party group becomes so bureaucratic that you're paying dues or other fees to belong, you're not in a conservative organization; you're in a union. There are several valid reasons for keeping groups small. First, groups needs to have longevity; if you have to travel 80 miles to some gathering spot, the costs and time involved will limit your participation. A simple-to-reach centralized residence or social gathering spot makes regular meetings easy. Second, small group meetings allow for fuller communications and less infighting. Third, leadership positions become less political because small groups are more like families. Small groups can still be highly organized and have their own group and individual e-mail lists, treasurers, and highly effective goals and strategies. Small groups can still assist and inspire other groups in the area. When it is strategically effective to do so, small groups can coordinate around the country for massive rallies.

Finding the People

For the purpose of growing numbers, small groups have an advantage over mega-organizations in that they are invested in their communities. They know the people they live with and who in their communities should be approached to join the good fight. Conversely, people in the community who see local conservative events are less hesitant to approach local community members to ask questions, and potentially put their money and time into a cause. Small towns are full of places with people waiting to join the conservative movement. Start with the churches. All church attending members of the core conservative group should solicit their church to participate if they feel the calling. The articulation of the conservative principles of: 1. God, 2. Family, 3. Country, will open the door to physical and financial support. You will find that church members will not be ignorant of the political and the cultural landscape of the country. Support will flow when inquiries are made. The next locations in both small communities and large cities are social organizations such as the VFW, Lions, Rotary, and other social clubs. It is best if core members of the local conservative movement who are members of these social organizations speak privately with a few perspective members at a time. This is a non-aggressive way to ask for help. Never rule out the elderly for assistance with the conservative movement. In fact, seek them out. Senior citizens often have time to spend working on projects. Many have their own assets that will assist the movement which they will share willingly if asked. Most importantly, the seniors of this country know America from periods of time when it was a better place. They understand the need for a restoration of conservative values, as many were raised on those values, and appreciate them.

Technology and the Conservative Movement

When we talk about using small groups to help build a massive conservative movement, it is hard to shake the idea of five, ten, fifteen, or thirty people sitting in a living room or a steak house whispering quietly to one another. Tremendous things have been accomplished by groups of this size, but small groups can greatly increase their influence with the usage of modern technology. Thankfully we live in a technological age where one person can communicate to thousands of people with a push of a single computer key. This can be done cheaply and can have massive effect. A few simple steps can immediately improve a group's chance of getting new members. Here are some ideas. Free social-networking sites such as Facebook allow activities, mission statements, contact e-mails, and many other things to be reachable on the World Wide Web in a matter of minutes. Through Facebook, a person can search out other likeminded organizations to coordinate with, or seek out relationships with people in their area. A person can create his or her own free website that can accomplish the same internet presence. An Internet presence is a must in today's world. Every conservative group should seek out and identify its best bloggers. These are people who have the computer skills to use the group's designated Facebook page or another site to write about the events or programs that their group is working on. Potential new members want to know, and need to know, what the conservatives in their area are doing. Video-tape the Tea Parties you put on in your area and put it on YouTube. This is easy and fast and people will watch your videos and want to know what your organization is doing next. YouTube videos can be embedded on other people's websites and this can create a snowball effect of viewership. Text messaging can be used to coordinate people for events. There are almost limitless ways to advertise your group and events that are taking place.

Beware of costs that may come with certain Internet, radio, and television advertising avenues. Word of mouth and local phone calling are still among my favorite techniques as well as the "ride to the event." All successful campaigns use phone calls to voters the night before the polls open and give rides to get the voters to the polls the following day. Technology is just another way to implement innovative thinking. Use it for all it's worth.

Never Lose Your Joy

Conservatives have the right to be mad; our country is being torn apart piece by piece. The God-given emotions of anger and frustration have been catalysts that have gotten many people off their tails and helping to grow a conservative movement, but that is not the whole story. The conservative movement is also powered by the love of country and respect for how the Founding Fathers set up this nation. The movement is filled with reverence to an all-powerful God that inspired men from different backgrounds to come together and create a Constitution that has held together this free and blessed nation. I have said for some time that conservatives are happier people than liberals. We don't come out of the womb with picket signs and loud speakers screaming for a Marxist regime. The goal for a successful, long-lasting conservative movement is to keep a positive attitude despite getting angry when the Left does something crazy. Conservative events must always include laughter and a certain sense of playfulness. Find a way to insert some fun into every major and minor gathering. There is always time in any battle to smile, laugh and encourage one another. Remember, in the end, we are going to win.

A Guide to Debating

Every group within the larger conservative movement will have people who do certain things better than others. Diversity is part of the beauty of creation; we are not all alike. Find your talents and use them. Some people will be natural speakers in front of their own cohorts while others have the talent for debate; both are very valuable to the movement. This section is for those who are called upon to debate the Left. There are certain strategies that will serve you well when debating liberals. First, always be prepared. If you are going to debate on a certain issue, and you know the topics in advance, practice what you will say out loud. Like giving a speech, people do better when they practice what they are going to say. In a debate, never expect your opposition to validate your position. Even though we are naturally inclined to want to nod along when people speak, make sure you don't nod at your opponent's statement unless you actually agree with what is being said. For example, do you really want to nod in agreement while the liberal across the table from you is talking about why we should have four more years of Barack Obama? People notice as much what your body indicates as what comes out of your mouth. Train both to be accurate instruments of your beliefs. Avoid yelling and talking over people; this makes for poor television and radio and demeans you as a speaker. With that said, never let a liberal filibuster, or talk during your designated time to be speaking. If this starts being a problem, politely cut in when your time to speak has arrived, or make it apparent to the debate moderator that your opponent is stealing your time. Conservatives have the moral and logical high ground on the issues of the day. Never give that high ground up in a debate. How does one lose the high ground in a debate? There are four major ways this happens:

1. The Drive-by: This is where a liberal demeans your point or position with a poorly constructed attack and then drives on to a new subject, where the majority of his or her speaking time is spent. The strategy is that you will put all your energy into debating the new point while the first issue is allowed to stand. This can be called losing by deception but in reality it is losing by default. Never let a liberal win by default. Go back to the original point, challenge it, address it, debunk it, and then move to the next issue. In Appendix A, you will see examples of **The Drive-by** tactic in my debate with Josh McGinn of the gay activist organization, Flint Hills Human Rights Project.

2. The Political Correctness Retreat: If you are honest and truthful in a debate, you will most certainly have a liberal at some point demand that you retreat for the sake of political correctness. This usually comes as you are validating a statement. Let me give you an example that is common place. A debate commentator asks you to best describe the administrational policies and practices of Barack Obama. You say that you believe that the Barack Obama administration has created more socialistic policies than free market policies. You are about to validate your assertion with examples when the liberal you are debating goes into a violent seizure full of protest yelling things like "Oh, I can't believe you would say that...!" or through wild gesticulations he or she says, "That's what they always say, it's because he's black....!" The idea with these kinds of outbursts is more than just to stop you from laying out your immediate case; liberals want you to be reluctant to continue talking on the issue later in the debate. Don't fall for it! Remember, you have the high ground; you are right. Stay on topic and logically lay out the facts. If the opposition continues to respond with outbursts, overtime he or she will be seen by the viewing public as desperate. In other words, his or her tactic will be exposed.

3. Debate Welfare: This is a common tactic liberals use in debates. Even very smart people fall into this trap so pay very close attention. Debate welfare occurs when a liberal introduces a subject of his or her choosing and frames a question around that subject in which the answer can only fit his or her ideological belief system. The liberal takes his or her created question and then demands that you give an answer. The way to beat this kind of trap is not to play the game at all. Am I saying just refuse to speak and sit there in silence? Of course not; that is losing by default which we already know is bad. Remember, conservatives have the high ground and from time to time you simply remind liberals of that fact by denying a faulty premise that is being presented to you. All the things I am talking about have happened to me in public debates on radio and television. Here is an example of debate welfare. A liberal was debating me on television, and he was getting angry; this happens a lot. Out of the blue, this individual demands that I explain how we can downsize the military to avoid a future economic crash from over-spending on defense. Think about that sentence, and remember that in the debate world, you often only have seconds to figure out what to do. Also, most people have a natural inclination in debate situations to want to rapid-fire answers back to their opponent. I fought the urge to shoot back an answer and stopped long enough to think about the question. I told him I rejected his premise of a necessity to downsize the military. I followed-up with a clear and concise explanation of the benefits of a strong military. I then closed with laying the responsibility on him to explain how weakening the military was in this country's best interest, and I demanded his answer as he had demanded mine. The individual was unable to make a case for military downsizing. I had won that point of the debate by simply not giving away the high ground I already possessed. I refused to subsidize debate welfare.

4. The Poor Man's Jedi: Have you ever seen the movie *Star Wars,* in which the veteran Jedi master Obi-Wan Kenobi is confronted by the less than intelligent storm troopers at the fictitious Mos Eisley Spaceport? If so, then this movie comparison to liberal debate trickery will make perfect sense. If not, I will do my best to explain. In this science fiction classic the wise old Jedi master uses his mental powers (the force) to make others agree with his suggestions. Waving his hand in the air the Jedi tells the storm troopers that are searching for the droids in the Jedi's traveling group that "These are not the droids you are looking for." As a result of his power (the force) the storm troopers simply repeat the Jedi's words in agreement, having been tricked into thinking the Jedi's suggestion was their own. Now, liberals are NOT Jedi and I could make the argument all day that the force is not with them. However, they often attempt to be Jedi's during debates. How do they do this? In a debate, it is common for a liberal to state what conservatives would believe if they were actually liberals. For example, a conservative might have a liberal say in a debate, "I am sure that my opponent would want to raise taxes to help the poor," or "I know my colleague would never wish to see children turn to crime when a social program could be used to save them." This is not stated as a question but as a fact. Throw a cloak over these liberals and have them wave their hand in the air and you have **The Poor Man's Jedi.** What is the desired effect? The hope is that you will either agree with the statement or stumble around long enough trying to figure out how to respond that your indecision will weaken the credibility of your answer. Don't let this happen! This is another reason to practice debating out loud and prepare for different kinds of questions. If you know your subject, you will know the answers to the important questions. Stick to them. Speaking the truth without fear of violating political correctness is your power to defeat The Poor's Man's Jedi. Tell your opposition you disagree with his or her assessment of your supposed thoughts and beliefs. Disagree with authority and give a clear explanation of why you feel differently. If the liberal feigns shock when you take a different position from what he or she described, this is just another trick and you can either brush it off as trivial or feign shock at their shock that you do not think like a liberal.

Whether debating, organizing, making phone calls, or simply being there for support, every man, woman, and child is needed if we are going to save this country. A conservative movement is ideologically led by people who are fully invested in a specific outcome. I hope that this book has been informative and educational, and I hope it has gotten you fired up. Find people in your town, church, or social organizations who believe in conservative values--the principles of 1. God, 2. Family, 3. Country--and put your time, money, and physical efforts into winning the future. Pray to God for strength to be brave as you tell the truth and make a stand. Never let a liberal take your joy. We can expand a conservative movement in this nation. The opportunity to bring superior numbers to the polls for local to national elections is completely attainable. It's been done before and if we are to save the country we love, we have to do it now. The future is ours to win or lose. We must stand up together and defend the conservative values of America. It's time to fight the good fight!

Appendix A
The Ibbetson McGinn Debate

This is the debate between Paul A. Ibbetson and Josh McGinn of the Flint Hills Human Right Project aired on March 8, 2011, on the Conscience of Kansas Radio Program KSDB Manhattan at Kansas State University. Josh McGinn is a spokesperson for the Flint Hills Human Right project. You can find their website at http://www.fhhrp.com.

Ibbetson: All right ladies and gentleman today we have a special guest in Josh McGinn. Josh McGinn is of the Flint Hills Human Rights Project. This is a gay activist organization here in the Flint Hills of Kansas and Josh we would like to welcome you here to the Conscience of Kansas radio program.

McGinn: Thank you.

Ibbetson: Well Josh, I got an e-mail from you here a while back in regards to one of my articles I wrote in the Canada Free Press. An article entitled, "LGBT and Rainbow Justice." You told me that, let's see, you said, even though you have a worldwide view that regards some people, including myself and all those young and old like me as deviant and therefore underserving of equal treatment, I would be happy to come on your show and try to dispel some of the myths and rumors that you have spread. In particular, the claim it (New Manhattan City ordinance alteration) will drive out churches and businesses given that 39% of the population of the United States grants all this to its citizens, similar protections that Manhattan has proposed. I do not know of an exodus of Christians and businesses from those areas due to non-discrimination laws. You could start by refusing to broadcast that lie to your listeners. It said here, (continuing with the e-mail) also unless you or anyone else here in the community can prove that you do not have a sexual orientation or gender identity you could stop calling the ordinance a homosexual bill.

Ibbetson continues: I think it concluded with, of course I understand how those who have not experienced true persecution due to their orientation or gender identity would assume that such persons are not real but please if you would, if you consider nothing else, please appreciate that your attitude does cause harm. I understand that you do not take anything as evidence unless it comes from the mouth of God or Bill O'Reilly. Still I felt it was my duty to witness to the hurtful consequences of your propositions regarding the LGBT people.

Ibbetson addresses McGinn: I wanted to make the opportunity to talk about that, to talk about your thoughts, to give you a forum to discuss the issue. I might start though, by actually telling you my position. Sort of witnessing to you a little bit so you know where I come from. Because when you said that I've got to listen to everything from God and Bill O'Reilly you may have been a little angry (laugh) when you said that, but you are not completely wrong though Josh. The Bill O'Reilly part, no, not so much, but I am a Christian, I believe in God, I believe in the Bible.

McGinn: Yeah.

Ibbetson: That's where I come from, so you know my spot.

McGinn: Right.

Ibbetson: It's always best to tell people where you are coming from as opposed to letting them describe where you come from because it leads to inaccuracies. I am not perfect Josh; I make mistakes, the Bible talks about Christians as being that way. But, I'm trying, I'm trying to follow my belief system and I use the Bible as my guide.

McGinn: Right.

Ibbetson: That is the guide I go by. So, that's my position. I have the feeling that if you and I were to sit down and talk about a myriad of life issues from movies to books to activities we would probably have several things in common. We would probably find many areas that we would agree on and passions in life that we would share. I, I just have no doubt about that. When we come to this issue though, this is where we have the conflict, but the conflict for me is not an individual conflict. I think it is important to get that out there because there is as much misrepresentation of Christians, certainly my positions. I get angry e-mails all the time from folks in the gay community. My opposition is with an ideology, with a belief system and what I think are the ramifications of that and definitely, what I feel is my responsibility, my individual responsibility and that is where I find opposition.

McGinn: Ok, Well, I just want to say that, of course that first e-mail, I was pretty angry. I had just listened to a long interview that you had had with Mr. Barkey on your show. And yes, I completely agree with your right and to some level your duty to have your beliefs and to hold your beliefs. So, yes I agree that on an individual level, I think you and I are both just trying to live our lives right. To come to a better understanding I hope. I do appreciate your responses and your e-mails and I got that indication from you all along. Um, after we started communicating. I guess my issue is, like in that first e-mail, at least the first part. When it comes to the ordinance, is just how it is discussed, I think skews the issue unfairly. So, like you first bring up, or from the e-mail I talk about how usually my opponents, they talk about as if it (new ordinance) were granting special rights to LGBT people and only to LGBT people and it is assumed that it is at the expense of everyone else in this community. I take a certain amount of exception to that because the ordinance specifically protects sexual orientation and gender identity, not just lesbian, gay, bi-sexual and transgender but also heterosexual people that have the normal male and female gender as well. Now, that kind of discrimination probably does not occur very much. So, it is probably difficult for us to think that that might be covered by that ordinance but it is. Also, the ordinance already protects people so they cannot be discriminated against based off of religion. So, a lot of times when this ordinance is discussed they talk about how it protects certain activities which I would say from the start is untrue, it no ways says that a business cannot still have appropriate standards of dress and of conduct on the job. So, I just want to be clear about that...

Ibbetson: Can I jump on just a point...

McGinn: Sure, sure.

Ibbetson: When you say it protects Christians, the ordinance talks about organized religion such as churches and activities within your churches being protected, but one of the big bones of contention is the issue that we know that Christians don't just stay hoarded up in their church buildings. They moved about in town, they do commerce, they do business, they live and have their lives in the community. There is nothing in this ordinance that says citizens outside of those organizations, citizens that may own a business, citizens that may be a landlord, may have a bakery, you know, people having their lives outside of the church that are Christians that have Christian beliefs, there is no, nothing in this ordinance that gives them, to me, anything but being at risk and that is one of the points that people have brought up. I mean, what if you are a business owner that happens to be a Christian that runs into a conflict, what is going to happen to you?

McGinn: Right, well I am glad that you bring that up and I am glad that you do mention that religious organizations are exempted. Actually what I was talking about, was just that part of the law that already says that you can't be discriminated against because of your religion, not that as a religion that you can discriminate. So, a little bit two slightly different things. Um, first of all as a Christian or as a Muslim or as a Jew or as an agnostic or whatever you cannot be discriminated against in work or in housing. With the exemption, yes it only covers religious organizations, but, more specifically, sexual orientation and gender identity, an additional exemption was sort of granted within those organizations, so even the positions that aren't directly related to religious purpose such as pastors but even a church secretary, churches can still discriminate in those positions as well as on the basis of sexual orientation and gender identity. When it comes to the community, you are right, that this (new ordinance) does restrict the person's ability to discriminate if they are a landlord and they don't want a homosexual or transgender person to live in their apartment building. It does restrict their right to do that. It also restricts a religious person's right, or I wouldn't consider it a right, but a privilege to discriminate in employment because of a person's sexuality or gender identity. But the problem with that criticism is just that religious people already have to tolerate people that have different beliefs and may have even different practices. Because religious people already have to tolerate people of different religions so, as offensive as it might be to tolerate a gay person working for them, a religious person already has to tolerate a pagan person working for them or an atheist working for them and I think that necessarily a pagan or an atheist does have different beliefs and identifies differently, and also has certain practices that a Christian would disagree with. But, they can't discriminate on that basis against a pagan and this would be the same thing when it comes to a person trying to hire a homosexual. But again, I just want to reiterate, because I think that this is a large source of the fear surrounding this ordinance, businesses and landlords can continue to have standards of conduct and policies, they simply have to apply them equally to all people. So, if you don't want the homosexual couple kissing in your work place, then that's fine, but you just cannot deny, you can't say, well that is ok for a heterosexual couple to do, but a homosexual couple PDA (public display of affection) is not allowed. It has to be equal across the board.

Ibbetson: Well what this ordinance allows, it is allows members, anyone in this, I say LGBT simply because they were one of the banner carriers pushing this ordinance. So was your organization (Flint Hill Human Rights Project) as well, I spoke to former members of city hall from years past and they said LGBT was the group that was actively lobbying for this ordinance alteration. I will tell you some of my immediate concerns. One, when you talk about tolerance and Christianity, I think Christians are very, very tolerant people as far as inclusion. This is my opinion, that our country was based on these Judeo-Christian values you see it in our criminal law, crimes against murder and theft and all these things. You see it within the Bible you see it within city ordinances but the Bible, from a Christian perspective is pretty clear on its position on homosexuality, and where it stands, and the charge that Christians have to obey the commandments that are therein. So, when it comes to Christianity, being tolerant of people as far as caring about people, being kind to people, being civil to people, being non-violent to people, that's all in the Bible. But the Bible does not say to be tolerant of what God says you're not supposed to do or what God calls a sin or an abomination. It's a major block (point of contention) to say well, they (Christians) have been accommodating others things so let's just put one more on the heap, because the one we are putting on the heap is pretty clear cut in the Bible. To me Josh, it's like the equivalent of telling Christians, denounce God, tear up your Bibles, burn down your churches and go walk in the gay pride parade. Now, some people would say well Paul, your just over the top, all we are wanting is a little bit of tolerance, all we are wanting is just for you to meet us half way. Just to kind of turn a blind eye to some of your Bible stuff, we don't want you to go all the way. But actually, the Bible says that's even worse, that is what the Bible calls the "Luke Warm Attitude" which God rejects worse than the hot or cold person.

McGinn: Right.

Ibbetson: So, what you are asking Christians to do is to really renounce their beliefs if they believe that homosexuality is a sin. It's not a small insignificant tiny little clerical step like where are we going to park in the parking lot or something. Christians would bend over backwards to not have a problem on something like that. This is a core belief issue.

McGinn: Right. Ok,

Ibbetson: Just so you know where I am coming from.

McGinn: Right, so I will try not to get into a biblical discussion because that could go on for centuries as it has.

Ibbetson: Ok, feel free to talk about anything you want, I brought tons of scripture. I am confident on my position on that but it's not simply that it (Manhattan ordinance alteration) goes against what you are going to find in mainstream Christianity, but it is also an issue of due process. You know when we look at this gender identity (ordinance definition) inside of this ordinance, that the citizens of Kansas are going to have to try to understand and adhere to and be financially liable potentially to, it says, (gender identity definition is read), means a person's good faith, and continuing presentation of a person's related identity, appearance, mannerisms, or other gender related characteristics, which may, or may not be consistent with a person's biological sex. I'm thinking, Josh, what the heck did that say?

McGinn: Alright.

Ibbetson: I mean, you could say that in Klingon and it would mean the same amount to me and it seems unfair to hold people. I mean we had the city council talking about states that had twenty page definitions of this trying to nail this down.

McGinn: Right.

Ibbetson: And they couldn't do it. They (city of Manhattan) tried the simple way, which was uh, three lines, three or four lines and I have no idea what they are talking about.

McGinn: Ok, well, I do think we should talk about the due process issue.

Ibbetson: Ok, sure.

McGinn: But, to try to get back to what this asks Christians to do. So, the only thing I will say about the Bible interpretation on the issue of homosexuality is that the idea, the term homosexuality which is between two consenting adults, love between two consenting adults of the same sex it did not come around until the 19th century. So a lot of the sexuality that the Bible is discussing is, the practices at the time involved adults and children and temple prostitution and also some of the verses deal, you know, talk about lust, and I would just say that I think that's the more important message to get from that issue. I think that illustrates that Christians interpret the Bible itself differently and so there is a wide range of Christians, even around this issue as to how it should be interpreted.

Ibbetson: I suppose so Josh, but with all due respect, that seems like a lot of spin to me. I'm not telling you that you need to be a Christian if you are not a Christian and I have already told you that I am not a perfect Christian, but the Bible says thou shalt not lie with a man as one lies with a female. I mean, even for a simple little country boy like me, I get the meaning of that. The Bible says, if there is a man that lies with a male as one lies with women, both have committed a detestable act.

McGinn: Right, but in that same chapter it also describes how abominable shell fish is, and how abominable it is to wear clothing with different materials and so I think we just need to look at the context in which the Bible was written and that was really focused on the law and yet there is also an entire other more radical part of the Bible that is more focused on how we are to love individuals the best.

Ibbetson: Yeah, but the thing about it is Josh is that you can say, well, parts (of the Bible) don't apply but the Bible keeps coming back to the same thing over and over, it so repetitious. In 1st Corinthians 6:9-10, it says homosexuals won't go to heaven. It says, or do you not know, the unrighteous will not inherit the kingdom of God. Those that deceive, fornicators or idolaters, homosexuals, nor drunkards, revilers, or swindlers. It says a lot of people aren't going to go to heaven for these sins and it includes homosexuality. Now, it goes on and on and on and it starts through Genesis on through the New Testament, we clearly have the designation of what traditional marriage is and why God created Adam and not another Adam. He created Eve and so forth. I don't claim to be a theologian…

McGinn: Heterosexual marriage is important because we do need procreation but I would just say whenever a Bible uses the term homosexual, I feel like the fact that that word is only 150 years old and before that there were much different ideas about sexuality and what it meant when the Bible was discussing those terms. It's been interpreted in many different ways by even going back as a far as the (organization name) and many other theologians going back a long way. I mean you have the Episcopal Church, you have the ELCA, you have many of the Presbyterians, you have the Methodists, the church of Canada, you have many churches across the spectrum of Christianity and I think this is where it gets to a question of even within Christianity there is disagreement as to how we are to treat homosexuals. What is the government's responsibility and I believe that the government's responsibility is to treat all individuals with the most respect as possible. So, that's where....

Ibbetson: Yeah, I agree with you Josh...

McGinn: What a homosexual does on their own time in their private life and I don't think this debate should get into that because it doesn't really deal with that. This only deals with what a person does in their public life and businesses can still have standards of conduct and I encourage them to do so. It gets back to my point, in all these other cities across the country 39% of the population of the United States are covered by laws that protect gender identity and sexuality and you have that in areas like Iowa, Illinois, and Colorado. Minneapolis has protected for gender identity since the 1970s and you don't see these fears becoming reality when it comes to a lot of the issues.

Ibbetson: Let's back up...

McGinn: When it comes to defining gender identity, a lot of these areas have been able to do it for years and even decades in many cases...

Ibbetson: Let me address that.

McGinn: Ok.

Ibbetson: Let me first go back to the Bible and I would say I believe that the overwhelming majority of Christian thought would fall into line with what I am saying. I'm not a theologian; I don't claim to be one. Shirley Phelps Roper asked me one time if I was one and I said no, but I do believe that God is right.

McGinn: I admire you for getting into a debate with her.

Ibbetson: Well you know Josh, it was another time that I disappointed the gay community. I went toe to toe with her because I believe she is crazy.

McGinn: Right.

Ibbetson: But, the homosexual community came out and said, are you going to be our advocate Paul? You know you really took her on (Shirley Phelps Roper) fine and I said no, I'm not, and here is the reason why. I draw my conclusions myself and I would tell you I believe the Christian community by and large, 99% believes this stance that I am telling you on Christianity (homosexuality and the Bible) and while they (organized religion) may quibble on certain areas of the Bible, I don't think you are going to find any place in the Bible where it says that God finds man sleeping with man as pleasing as opposed to an abomination or detestable which you get in the King James and the New International version. I don't think that you are going to see a place where the Bible says God created Adam and then created another Adam or that God created man for man and said that it would be well. I mean you are just not going to find that. I think you are hedging (attempting to rationalize) that when you say that there is a debate within the Christian community. But you know, even with that said Josh, what you do in the privacy of your own home I, I don't want any part of.

McGinn: I don't want you in any part of it either.

Ibbetson: So, we are in agreement. But that is not the case with this city ordinance. This city ordinance is not a privacy issue; it is a public square issue.

MsGinn: Exactly, exactly.

Ibbetson: So, that is why Christians are up in arms over this. It is something that we are going to have as far as a group societal stance and while you say, well we have had these things in these others states and other places. In Kansas we haven't. In Kansas the city attorney said on television that this is the first time Kansas has ever had an ordinance like this one. On KSN3 (television station) they had on television, the same episode that you actually spoke in, they said that this would be the farthest reaching ordinance in Kansas. So, when I tell you that I think this is going to have ramifications here in the Bible belt of Kansas, you can't say well it worked in Indiana, or it worked in California, because I'm not talking about there. I'm talking about Kansas and it is yet to be seen what it will do in Kansas.

McGinn: You're, you're right. I would just say that I just think that it is legitimate to look at previous states and how their experience has been done and how it has worked. I would just say that the language of this amendment is the same as Kansas state law except for that that deals with gender identity which we have never protected before, I agree. I think that the exemptions and protections for businesses and for religious people are pretty far reaching and do allow for a great deal of leeway in enforcing this law. And when it comes to the public versus private, just going back to that, again, that's totally what I agree with. That is where, I think when we get into these debates about what people are doing behind closed doors, I think we have lost sight of this because we are not really dealing with that. We are really dealing with what people do in businesses and what is appropriate in businesses and that doesn't change due to this amendment except for, here is what might change. A person might be able to put a picture of their true family on their desk. A person might be able to bring their partner, their true loved one, with them to a Christmas party or holiday party or whatever you want to call it. That is all that will change and that is where I feel growing up in a Christian household, and being a Christian myself that it should not be beyond, I don't see why it is beyond any Christian's ability to tolerate that. Now, I agree that when it comes to the more private issues, that is something churches and families should work out by themselves...

Ibbetson: They have been doing that for a long time. I mean look at this aggrieved person (within the ordinance). Josh, I mean, you sound like an intelligent guy and I am sure you are. This aggrieved person definition in this ordinance says, an aggrieved person is any person who claims that the person being, or has been injured by an unlawful discriminatory act or practice, or believes the person **WILL** be injured by an unlawful discriminatory act or practice that is **ABOUT** to occur. Now, how, listen, I am a former Kansas chief of police. I used to have to put cases together to send to the district attorney for prosecution. If I had ever gone and said look, we got this guy over here, got this woman over here, they haven't done anything, but I am sure they are going to do it. Let's prosecute them to the fullest extent of the law. Let's just put them into court, let's just call them into questioning. Let's just give them a summons and make them go in front of a panel. The district attorney would throw it out, would laugh me out, and I would be given a stern warning don't ever do that again. Because, in Kansas, in America, in our system for criminal punishment, you have to have substantial evidence, you can't have just hearsay. This law gives what's call preemptive charges, and it doesn't really matter whether you are brought in and the investigations that can hang over people which range from 4 months to 6 months, that they can hang over people in this ordinance. How can you justify preemptive charges being brought against people here in the state of Kansas?

McGinn: Ok, so this is good, we are getting into a due process issue. First, I just want to be clear, that this is some language taken from the Kansas Act Against Discrimination. So, this is what applies to all classes of people regardless their sexual orientation or gender identity. Now, if you have a problem with the language of the overall act against discrimination then that is kind of a separate issue and...

Ibbetson: Well, let's take that issue on, do you think that's fair, that someone from the gay community can accuse somebody from the community here in Kansas, in Manhattan preemptively and say, I think they are going to do something bad, let's drop a $50,000 fine on them.

McGinn: Ok, ok, so, see that's a bit of an exaggeration because they cannot drop a $50,000 fine.

Ibbetson: They file a complaint and they can start the gears of this process, they can do that can't they Josh?

McGinn: Exactly, they can file a complaint before discrimination occurs and that is how it was explained to me by a legal person who knows more about the law then I do but has worked in this kind of law, because this is a phrase, basically, about to occur, that is a legal phrase and is used in other laws. Basically, what it is, is, there is no way that a business that hasn't discriminated yet is going to get fined for something that hasn't happened.

Ibbetson: (laugh) Well you say that Josh, and of course we don't have this legal person here to talk to we only have you. You say this can't happen but here it is (ordinance alteration) that allows the process to take place.

McGinn: Allows the process to begin.

Ibbetson: I'm asking you as a rational sane person, is it right to be able to bring charges against someone who hasn't done anything yet? Is it right to do that? Is it fair?

McGinn: Well, I think this is what it is getting at. It's getting at, it allows a person the ability to start collecting evidence and giving that to the city before they are fired basically, probably is where it might occur. Generally this is never used, first of all...

Ibbetson: (laugh) That doesn't console me much, that doesn't console me much Josh.

McGinn: It is consistent with state wide law and basically if a person is about to get discriminated against, and they want to build a solid case because they have to still prove a case before a hearing board of their peers, other citizens, sort of like a jury.

Ibbetson: Yeah, a lot like a jury.

McGinn: Right which is right, I believe in the jury system.

Ibbetson: Yeah, but here is the problem. I do to Josh, I believe in the jury system and I believe in the court system which has a judge, which has a lawyer and a prosecutor. Both the judge, lawyer and prosecutor are all trained people, they go to law school, they get law degrees. They are trained to go through this process to make sure it's fair. Both the defense attorney and the prosecutor advocate for their side and the judge delegates that it is a fair process. That is not what is happening here. Here we have a seven person panel that is not elected by the people, is appointed at the whim of the mayor of which only three of the panel are required to sit over one of these hearings of which one must be a member of the minority group. So, if you have an issue with this ordinance, if you are like me and you look at it with a dubious eye, you see 33% potentially, of this jury could be against you. These people (panel members) have no special training, they have no certifications, and they are going to be able to do what a judge can do. Authorize warrants, authorize subpoenas, authorize people to be able to give testimony, grab evidence...

McGinn: Collect evidence...

Ibbetson: And in the end they are going to render a judgment.

McGinn: A fine, sort of like a zoning board.

Ibbetson: Oh yeah, Josh it's not a $5.00 fine, I mean let's not minimize it.

McGinn: Well zoning boards don't just do $5.00 dollar fines.

Ibbetson: These are fines from $10,000 up to $50,000.

McGinn: No, they, it can be much less than that. It goes all the way up to $50,000 but if that, if that is the amount that is awarded, it has to be proven. Like any...

Ibbetson: Well, in the law it tells you what the fines are for the different kinds and it started up on my deal with $10,000. Obviously, to me, $10,000 is a lot of money, $50,000 is a lot of money. To a business here in Manhattan, that could put you out of business. But even before that process happens, even before this quasi, I would call them kangaroo courts, because I look at them from the perspective of criminal courts and what it takes to have justice in our criminal justice system versus this. Nobody has got any say on who is in there and what their motivations are. It just seems repetitious Josh that in these situations, the people never get a say. It's a special interest group, one or two activists in government. You know this whole petition they (the Christian community) want to pass out, it's not calling for violence against the gay or homosexual community. I have not ever done that I would challenge you to ever find that I ever have, but it's asking for this wild and crazy thought of letting the people vote on the issue. What would be wrong with letting the people vote in Manhattan, Kansas, on an ordinance that is going to drastically affect their lives?

McGinn: Ok, Just to conclude on that, on that hearing board, I would like to say again, it's like any city hearing board. That the penalties do go up to $50,000 but any penalty has to be justified, otherwise it can be challenged in court. I just want to be clear about that, it doesn't have any quota system for how many people have to be on it. The language says it has to reflect the community which is basically when you choose a jury. It is supposed to reflect the community of your peers.

Ibbetson: Yeah, but Josh, Josh....

McGinn: I don't think that board is that radical...

Ibbetson: When you pick a jury in criminal court you have what is called Voir Dire, and that is where the professionals vet out people to get a jury. It's not one guy, it's not Mayor Snead, out here saying this is what I think will be representative, this would be arbitrary to our criminal justice system. Yeah, we do have panels from a lot of things in Manhattan, Kansas, whether or not to put flowers at the park, whether or not to see how wide you're going to have the swimming pool. But this is a little bit different deal. This is where you are going to mark people as gay bashers.

McGinn: Well there is no way that this board can say that someone is a gay basher, it can just say that they discriminated unlawfully against a gay person but that gay person has to completely, the burden of evidence is still on that person and I think that that is something that is really forgotten and that it is just that they make an accusation and then it can be done and then there is no justice there. But they prove that discrimination occurred, they will be advised by the city's legal advisors, they will be educated and trained when it comes to this kind of law. It will exactly resemble the statewide discrimination, anti-discrimination board when it comes to hearing these cases except for now, people, if they have a complaint, businesses as well as individuals, they won't have to go to Topeka. The process should be shortened so it will be able to be resolved more efficiently, and most of these cases are solved before they even get to the hearing stage by city staff.

Ibbetson: Josh, you're, I don't doubt that you may believe all those things, but you are giving me hypotheticals that are one, not tested in the state of Kansas so you can't prove what you are saying and two, you are giving me the very rosy, rosy scenarios.

McGinn: Most discrimination cases in Kansas are handled...

Ibbetson: let me...

McGinn: Most of them are resolved at the city level with city staff without going to a hearing board.

Ibbetson: Let me explain how it works when you get arrested and brought in for a criminal crime, allegation of rape, allegation of theft, allegation of being a drunk driver. Those things do not stay anonymous. The next day it gets out. Human nature, it gets out. When you go through any kind of trial or proceeding for a crime, you take baggage with you, even if you are acquitted, that was the guy that was in the rape case trial. That's how that works, it's not as though that people that are alleged, that go through this process, and win so to speak, are not going to be damaged people because they will always be remembered, aren't you the business that had to go through the gay discrimination thing yeah, yeah. That's what happens and you (gay special interest groups) have to take some accountability to the ramifications that will surround allegations even if you get found innocent.

McGinn: Well, that is what I think is so good about this is because those sorts of rumors already occur but now they are completely unsubstantiated because there is no way to prove whether discrimination actually occurred. This is a way for businesses to be exonerated where they can come back and say hey, I actually didn't do anything unlawful. Right now, what actually happens is businesses will discriminate and it's just a rumor. That happens already, now there will be a way, for businesses to prove that they don't discriminate and that's what I think is good about this system.

Ibbetson: Well let's talk about how discrimination and how people will not discriminate against gender identity people. When we look at gender identity and this four line, or yeah, four line definition that the city has decided to opt with, the American Psychiatric Association Diagnostic and Statistical Manual for Mental Disorders, they list gender disorder as a mental disorder, an axis 1 disorder which puts it in the same category as schizophrenia and what is it, bipolarism and they recommend therapy. But this bill (city of Manhattan ordinance) recommends that they (gender identity people) become a protected class with this preemptive strike ability. How do you justify that?

McGinn: Ok, well, I am glad that you brought that up and basically I just want to be clear about how disorders are formed and a lot of times disorders are formed because of the environment we live in and the reaction that that causes. So, that's what I just want to be clear that most people that are transgender, the medical community does not consider that they have a disorder, it is usually only when they are, during, in the transition process or, before they are in the transition process that they might go through, or they might experience a disorder. But it's not stereotypical, it doesn't occur to every transgender person it usually occurs to people who face a great deal of discrimination and rejection because they are transgender.

Ibbetson: Not in the American Psychiatric Association, not by their definition...

McGinn: It does not define every transgender as mentally ill...

Ibbetson: No, but it does not say they don't have a problem until someone discriminates against them. It talks about a long time disorder where someone thinks they are another gender.

McGinn: Right.

Ibbetson: They (American Psychiatric Association) don't recommend discrimination ordinances, they recommend therapy for this. They put it in the same category, like I said, an Axis 1 category of clinical disorders including major mental disorders and learning disorders and I ran through the list. So, what you're telling me is that you don't agree with the American Psychiatric Association's labeling and their recommendations for these folks?

McGinn: Well they're not, they're not, they don't all have a disorder. So, only some do have that disorder. Usually they do get therapy. All transgender do have to go through a great deal of therapy but most of them actually come out of that if they have to go through it in the first place. They are not mentally ill. It's just for a period of time, when they are challenging their, uh, when they start to assert their true gender identity, that can become very difficult for them and yes, all transgender people do have to go through therapy. That's something that is important like, that this ordinance doesn't just protect anyone. The group of people that this protects is very, very, small and their very identifiable.

Ibbetson: Is it fair? If you are saying that this mental disorder is a periodical period for these folks through a stage or whatever. Is it fair for citizens of Manhattan to be held financially liable for the decisions or the allegations brought by people that may be going through this period that you are talking about where therapy is warranted and used. Is it fair to ask people to decide whether or not their actions are going to be perceived (laugh) and I would just try to grapple with this uh...

McGinn: No you're doing a good job...

Ibbetson: Well it says (referring the Manhattan city ordinance), a person's good faith continuing presentation of a person's gender related identity, appearance, mannerisms, or gender related characteristics, which may, or may not, be consistent with a person's biological sex. That to me is the equivalent of the word "guess." Guess which personality Sybil **(authors note: the name *Sybil* is a 1973 reference to a book by <u>Flora Rheta Schreiber</u> about the treatment of Sybil Dorsett (a <u>pseudonym</u> for <u>Shirley Ardell Mason</u>) for <u>dissociative identity disorder</u>, then referred to as *multiple personality disorder*)**, is going to have today and if you don't, we are going to put you through this kangaroo court. I ask you, is it fair? I can't do it, as a Christian, as a heterosexual Christian, I cannot go to my city attorney and say, you know, just today I feel like somebody did me wrong, or they are going to do me wrong and start a process. I am not protected in that fashion, to be able to bring that allegation; they would laugh me out me of...

McGinn: If you were applying at a homosexually owned business, and they fired you or during your hiring process, said something disparaging, or, it's not just disparaging...

Ibbetson: Really, disparaging words?

McGinn: Or, indicated that you were going to be disqualified from that position because you were heterosexual, then yes you would be covered. Granted that situation doesn't occur often but there are cases in Manhattan that do hire mostly heterosexual people so, yes that situation is rare. In the 1960s and before it was probably rare for a white person to get discriminated against in the south.

Ibbetson: But I tell you what, that argument won't fly with me Josh. That argument won't fly with me Josh with the civil rights because I don't accept the idea that these (homosexuality, etc.) are immutable qualities. I don't accept the idea of the gay gene or that, a black man obviously has no choice of what his skin color is going to be, I see that as....

McGinn: Then getting back to what I said before about religion being protected, religion is not immutable. So, I don't agree that sexuality is not immutable.

Ibbetson: So, so...

McGinn: So this might be a personal question, but when it comes to how you were first attracted to your significant other was that something that you chose completely or was that something that, so I want people, I hope that people think about their own experience and they realize that is the same thing that happens with homosexuals. That it is really not in their control but even if it wasn't in their control, religion is in a person's control, military status is in a person's control. Family status is largely in a person's control whether they are married or single or divorce and those statuses are still protected.

Ibbetson: If you have a business, say you have a cake making business in Manhattan and a gay couple comes in and wants to have a big setup and you (a Christian business owner) say, look, I'm a Christian, I believe in God, the Bible says that this is a sin and I don't want to be an enabler or a part of this. I don't want to make your cake, go to another cake maker. You think they should be set before this court? Yes or no, it's not a trick question.

McGinn: Well, honestly that would be legitimate discrimination. They're offering their services to the public.

Ibbetson: So, if a landlord says, I got an apartment here and I don't want to rent an apartment to you because you told me your, partner or whatever is another guy. Two guys want to get into an apartment then you think they (business owners) should be brought before this court?

McGinn: Well, if they allow non-married cohabitating...

Ibbetson: They have no choice but to allow the others (homosexual couples), is that what you're saying?

McGinn: If they allow non-married heterosexual couples to do the same then yes and that just gets into well what if a pagan comes to a Christian landlord and says they want, should that landlord be able to discriminate against them. Paganism is certainly a choice and it certainly disagrees with the moral teachings of Christianity.

Ibbetson: Well, if you look at the cake maker, let's start back at the cake maker. If the cake maker has a business but they are known in the community and their business is based on their name. That is usually how it works in small communities. The business is, that's Earl's shop or that Joe's business. A lot of folks would say that the quality of your name as a business owner is important to the viability of your business and your standing within the community.

McGinn: Right.

Ibbetson: If your cake maker is a Christian and their known to be Christians, maybe they play a little gospel music in shop, you know. And they feel that to start selling products, to be making up these gay weddings or gay unions, or gay blow outs is going to be against their beliefs, that it is going to be detrimental to them within the community, that people may silently or not, just bypass their business, your saying that they must, and should take the business brunt, the personal brunt of that or be subject to this trial thing?

McGinn: I am not sure what they would face because they would be opening their doors to more...

Ibbetson: Oh I don't know either, I am not sure what they might face, I am not for sure if they know but if they feel it's going to be negative. If they feel it's going to be sullying their name. You know if people go around the community saying I am a gay basher that may reasonably have some effect on me, I don't know how much. But, I don't want to be known as that. I also don't want to be...

McGinn: Right, now you have a place to go to be exonerated whereas before you didn't.

Ibbetson: I think you have a kangaroo court.

McGinn: Well it's better than rumor.

Ibbetson: I don't know about that, because with the kangaroo court you will always be the one that was accused and brought into this trial thing. Let alone if you are convicted and you can only go as an appeal to the district court after it is done, and you may have this thing looming over you and your business for 4-6 months. So, for 4-6 months you are the accused.

McGinn: That can happen with any case. So, if you have a problem with the overall ordinance, or you have a problem with protecting against religion, or race, or marital status or ethnicity then that's a problem with the entire ordinance. Not just a problem with sexual orientation or gender identity and that's where I, it's hard for me to understand why people seem to single out those two while they don't seem to single out the others which still require them to tolerate some things that may be against their religion and it still might cause their name to be sullied in the community if they are falsely accused. I feel like people's names are already sullied in the community but know they don't have a way to exonerate themselves and this gives them an opportunity to do that in front of basically a jury of their peers and if that is not found just then they can go to court and prove it. Instead of how it works now which is basically rumor and then there is no way to settle these issues. But like I said, most of these issues are settled by city staff before they get to the hearing phase.

Ibbetson: You're telling me this on something that has never been tried in Kansas so you don't have any credibility....

McGinn: Well there are letters from Iowa from Colorado...

Ibbetson: Were not in Iowa Josh, were not in Iowa.

McGinn: How different is Iowa than Kansas?

Ibbetson: This is the Bible belt, this is the heartland.

213

McGinn: Iowa is very evangelical too.

Ibbetson: You're making the fallacy (ecological fallacy) that they talked about in college with statistics of trying to apply a local issue to somewhere else and say it's all the same.

McGinn: Much of the population of Kansas is demographically similar to the population of Iowa and that includes religion. So I just, there are so many evangelicals Christians in Iowa and they may have a problem with the fact that they allow gay marriage there now but I don't think, like I said, their state department of human rights has sent a letter to the city that says that this has not been an issue for all of the complaints that have been discussed in this whole process.

Ibbetson: I guarantee you in Iowa had this been put in front of them; voters would want to have a shot at this as well. Why can't voters have a voice on this discrimination ordinance in Kansas?

McGinn: Well, that just gets, I mean I just think that it's of, I will make another comparison...

Ibbetson: I mean just tell me, tell me why you don't like it, I mean why not?

McGinn: I don't like it because LGBT people have been a historically vilified community. There have been many lies spread about that community throughout history. There has been much violence done to that community.

Ibbetson: Are the people of Manhattan, Kansas, villains?

McGinn: I am saying that the LBGT community in particular has been vilified and so it is wrong to vote on a minority like that when they only make up 2-5% of the whole population. Who do you think is going to win when the, that community has been tarred and feathered and all sorts of distortions have been made about LGBT people throughout the centuries about how immoral they are, do you think that that's a good, a good situation in which to call a vote? Because the same thing...

Ibbetson: So what you are saying is, Josh...

McGinn: Apply it to the south in the 1960s...

Ibbetson: But Josh (laugh)...

McGinn: Would they have voted for the civil rights act? They wouldn't, they would still be segregated.

Ibbetson: So in other words what you are saying is, the citizens of Manhattan, Kansas cannot be trusted with this vote, and that they owe this 2-5% (homosexual community) for centuries of injustice and so they should have no voice in it and we should let a minority tell a majority how to live!

McGinn: Within our system, we have set it up so minorities cannot be trampled on by the tyranny of the majority and that goes back to our Founding Fathers.

Ibbetson: The majority are tyrants. We were villains, now we are tyrants.

McGinn: I am not saying that you are tyrants.

Ibbetson: Well, you are telling me Josh that this (city wide voting) just doesn't happen. That we have a system where this (voting) just doesn't happen but I'm telling you, look at the history in Kansas. All the time we put initiatives on the ballot and guess what, we let people vote on it. So, it's not something new or something that has never been done or I am trying to create something radical, this idea of letting people vote on initiatives that are going to affect their lives. I am surprised that when you talk about equality for people, the betterment for society that you don't want to let society in on it.

McGinn: I am just saying that there is also a very long tradition that it is wrong to vote on the human rights of a minority and that had we had done that in the 1960s that the south would still be segregated.

Ibbetson: Hmmm.

McGinn: Do you disagree do you think that the south would have changed on its own if the federal government had not established this and allowed people to see that hey, it's not that big of a problem and to let it work. Do you think that would have just happened on its own?

Ibbetson: I will tell you this, I think slavery was bad, I was against slavery. I have never owned a slave, nor has my dad or his dad.

McGinn: I am not just, I am not talking about slavery I am just talking about discrimination and I am not saying that this is going to solve discrimination...

Ibbetson: And it's not Josh...

McGinn: No law ever solves any problem...

Ibbetson: Josh this is going to bring more problems to not only heterosexual people but homosexual people because it's an inflammatory law. It's a law that allows preemptive judgments when you say...

McGinn: It doesn't allow preemptive judgments. It allows the process to start...

Ibbetson: Yeah it allows it to start, to be accused and thrown into court that is appointed, you know the people just have nothing, no say in the while process....

McGinn: They do, they elect representatives to the city government and we have a representative form of government that is what our country is based on. We have a republican democracy which means representative government and that form of government determines, because the Founders understood that having a direct vote on everything wasn't necessarily the best way to solve our nation's complicated issues.

Ibbetson: Well, I give you this Josh that we voted in a liberal majority in Manhattan, Kansas, that made a 3-2 vote on this. I'll give you this no doubt. They (the liberal majority) came out, and with political fiat just announced that we were going to have a gay and lesbian, bi-sexual, transgender awareness month, all this they did. But I tell you this ordinance I believe is going to get repealed and I tell you that because I think because the council was so bent on not listening to the majority....

McGinn: Well there were a lot of people...

Ibbetson: Now hold on Josh, just let me finish. I know there were people within the community (supporters of the ordinance alteration) but you have already told me that the side that wants this ordinance alteration, this 2-5% and I agree with you. That just makes me say the 95% are going to have opposition with this, they are going to repeal this thing. In my opinion Josh and I say it respectfully; I think this whole ordinance is not about discrimination, I think this whole ordinance is the gay community wanting mainstream America to legitimate their lifestyle. To say what you're doing (sexual practices) is ok, what you are doing is acceptable with our standards, and that is what I really think. They (LGBT community) want to be legitimated and while I can treat you respectfully, if the university fell in and you were hanging off the roof, I would pull you up. But when it comes to validating homosexuality, saying that it's alright, I will never be able to do that because the Bible tells me different. It would be the same as renouncing God, I couldn't do that...

McGinn: Well, I disagree. It doesn't only effect 2-5% of the population it effects our families it effects our friends. There are hundreds of heterosexual Christians, thousands that do support this ordinance. There were more people that spoke in support of this ordinance at the city meetings when the hearings were held then people that spoke against it.

Ibbetson: Well, then put it to the vote. If that's the case, if I'm outdated, if I am just an angry old dinosaur clinging to my Bible over here, and there is all this support. This is what they (the homosexual community) said in 2005 on the marriage amendment. They said there was a big giant support and you guys (Christian community) are just a bunch of fire worshippers and we don't need to put it to a vote. Finally, the churches of Kansas got together and forced it to a vote, and 70% of Kansas voters voted for traditional marriage, between a man and a women. You didn't have the votes then and I respectfully say you don't have the votes now. But if I am wrong, then put it to a vote.

McGinn: Can we agree that work and equal opportunity is different than marriage. Can we agree to that because this is all this is about. This is about equal opportunity and establishing that standard in our community it's not about validating any sort of sexual practice as you imply.

Ibbetson: It's about traditional values Josh.

McGinn: It's about equal opportunity which is a traditional conservative value if there ever was one and if you deny that then you are denying one of the founding principles that this country was founded upon and what makes it great and that really distresses me. That you would deny that equal opportunity is a great value and it should be supported in our city.

Ibbetson: I don't, but I don't think you get it in this ordinance. I think what this ordinance does is create a Christian witch hunt. You might be able to hide in your churches but once you step out...

McGinn: Well it hasn't happen anywhere it has been put in place.

Ibbetson: Well, we are going to see what is going to happen in Kansas. My prediction Josh is that this thing is going to get repealed. I know it is going to be more bloody going the other direction (repealing the ordinance) because it was originally done by political fiat.

McGinn: I think it is really condescending that you would think that all the LGBT community here in Manhattan is set upon doing witch hunts. I think that that is very condescending.

Ibbetson: I don't, Josh I didn't say that.

McGinn: You said that this would create witch hunts.

Ibbetson: Josh, what you have to understand is, what I said is it "create". Which I am saying is that the inevitable outcome will be something very negative. Probably much more negative than what LGBT or your human rights group or the city's liberal majority thinks. You know, good intentions are the perfect cure-all for what actually happens in the end, the outcomes can be very negative.

McGinn: Well that outcome has happened few and far between across the land in states very similar to Kansas and I feel that that is just very misleading to tell people that that is what is going to happen when that's not generally what's happened in any other place it has been applied. I think that it gives businesses an opportunity to exonerate themselves. If any cases are brought, which hopefully there are not. Hopefully there is no discrimination in this community I would be just as happy with that result.

Ibbetson: (laugh) You're telling me there already is. Logically we know this (Manhattan ordinance) is going to be used. The whole idea to validate it is that it needs to be there because incidents are happening.

McGinn: Well, discrimination has occurred but hopefully with education that will not happen in the future but now no one has a place to go to either prove that it happened or it didn't happen. So, it's like having to prove that we need a law before it exists by saying that, oh well, how many times has the law been broken. Well, it hasn't been broken because it hasn't existed yet but yet there are a lot of cases that have been brought up that have been very suspicious that have indicated that people in this community are not being treated completely fairly in public regardless of what they do in private that is not important to this amendment. It's about what people do in public and how they run their business and we are just trying to set a high standard in this community that people will be judge based on the merit and merits alone.

Ibbetson: Josh McGinn of the Flint Hills Human Rights Project, I appreciate you coming on the show and talking with me. Hopefully you feel I gave you an adequate chance to say your say. I don't agree with you and I am going to oppose this ordinance, but I want you to know that I appreciate you coming on the show and talking with me. Hopefully folks will get a chance to listen to both sides and make their own decisions.

McGinn: Thank you and I really appreciate having this discussion with you and I do appreciate the work you do in your community, and in this community. I know that this is just one issue that we disagree upon and I hope that there are many others that we can work together to improve this community. So, I appreciate your work.

Ibbetson: Alright Josh, have a good day bye-bye now.

McGinn: You too, bye.

Debate concludes.

Appendix B
Bible Verses

Included in this appendix are the Bible verses used in this book. I hope they will be helpful in the arguments you will make for a conservative movement in this country. One thing for certain is that the Bible contains many more passages on marriage, homosexuality, and abortion than what are included in this appendix. I recommend that a person delve deep into scripture to find additional guidance on these issues. The Bible is truly a survival manual. These verses should only be seen as a beginning point. I am using the New International Version in this appendix simply because I feel this version is easier to understand. I was raised reading the King James Version. Find the version that works best for you, but most importantly, read the Bible! A conservative movement will have many moments of uncertainty from the big to the small. When this happens, the Bible will be the primary guide to weeding out right from wrong, and for making good decisions. A conservative movement is primarily a movement to follow God, to do what is pleasing in his eyes. The verses in this appendix are arranged in the order they are found in the Bible. Nothing fancy here, simply God's powerful word.

Genesis 2:21-24. But for Adam no suitable helper was found. So the LORD God caused the man to fall into a deep sleep; and while he was sleeping, he took one of the man's ribs and then closed up the place with flesh. Then the LORD God made a woman from the rib he had taken out of the man, and he brought her to the man. The man said, "This is now bone of my bones and flesh of my flesh; she shall be called 'woman,' for she was taken out of man." That is why a man leaves his father and mother and is united to his wife, and they become one flesh.

Leviticus 18:22. Do not have sexual relations with a man as one does with a woman; that is detestable.

Jeremiah 1:4-5. The word of the LORD came to me, saying, before I formed you in the womb I knew you, before you were born I set you apart; I appointed you as a prophet to the nations."

Romans 1:21-27. For although they knew God, they neither glorified him as God nor gave thanks to him, but their thinking became futile and their foolish hearts were darkened. Although they claimed to be wise, they became fools and exchanged the glory of the immortal God for images made to look like a mortal human being and birds and animals and reptiles. Therefore God gave them over in the sinful desires of their hearts to sexual impurity for the degrading of their bodies with one another. They exchanged the truth about God for a lie, and worshiped and served created things rather than the Creator—who is forever praised. Amen. Because of this, God gave them over to shameful lusts. Even their women exchanged natural sexual relations for unnatural ones. In the same way the men also abandoned natural relations with women and were inflamed with lust for one another. Men committed shameful acts with other men, and received in themselves the due penalty for their error.

1 Corinthians 6:9-10. Or do you not know that wrongdoers will not inherit the kingdom of God? Do not be deceived: Neither the sexually immoral nor idolaters nor adulterers nor men who have sex with men nor thieves nor the greedy nor drunkards nor slanderers nor swindlers will inherit the kingdom of God.

1 Corinthians 7:2-15. But since sexual immorality is occurring, each man should have sexual relations with his own wife, and each woman with her own husband. The husband should fulfill his marital duty to his wife, and likewise the wife to her husband. The wife does not have authority over her own body but yields it to her husband. In the same way, the husband does not have authority over his own body but yields it to his wife. Do not deprive each other except perhaps by mutual consent and for a time, so that you may devote yourselves to prayer. Then come together again so that Satan will not tempt you because of your lack of self-control. I say this as a concession, not as a command. I wish that all of you were as I am. But each of you has your own gift from God; one has this gift, another has that. Now to the unmarried and the widows I say: It is good for them to stay unmarried, as I do. But if they cannot control themselves, they should marry, for it is better to marry than to burn with passion. To the married I give this command (not I, but the Lord): A wife must not separate from her husband. But if she does, she must remain unmarried or else be reconciled to her husband. And a husband must not divorce his wife. To the rest I say this (I, not the Lord): If any brother has a wife who is not a believer and she is willing to live with him, he must not divorce her. And if a woman has a husband who is not a believer and he is willing to live with her, she must not divorce him. For the unbelieving husband has been sanctified through his wife, and the unbelieving wife has been sanctified through her believing husband. Otherwise your children would be unclean, but as it is, they are holy. But if the unbeliever leaves, let it be so. The brother or the sister is not bound in such circumstances; God has called us to live in peace.

Ephesians 5: 21-33. Submit to one another out of reverence for Christ. Wives, submit yourselves to your own husbands as you do to the Lord. For the husband is the head of the wife as Christ is the head of the church, his body, of which he is the Savior. Now as the church submits to Christ, so also wives should submit to their husbands in everything. Husbands, love your wives, just as Christ loved the church and gave himself up for her to make her holy, cleansing her by the washing with water through the word, and to present her to himself as a radiant church, without stain or wrinkle or any other blemish, but holy and blameless. In this same way, husbands ought to love their wives as their own bodies. He who loves his wife loves himself. After all, no one ever hated their own body, but they feed and care for their body, just as Christ does the church—for we are members of his body. For this reason a man will leave his father and mother and be united to his wife, and the two will become one flesh. This is a profound mystery—but I am talking about Christ and the church. However, each one of you also must love his wife as he loves himself, and the wife must respect her husband (NIV: Bible Gateway, 2011).

References

Allen, Jonathan. (2011, March 24). Kinetic military action or war? *Politico*. Retrieved from http://www.politico.com/news/stories/0311/51893.html

Bair, Brant. (2009, March 17). Terrorism is a Man Caused Disaster? *Fox News*. Retrieved from http://www.foxnews.com/story/0,2933,509597,00.html

Bible Gateway. (2011, March 30). Bible: New International Version. Retrieved from http://www.biblegateway.com/passage/?search=

Blackstone, William. (1979*) Commentaries On the Law of England 1765-69 (Volume IV)*. Chicago Ill. University of Chicago Press.

Burkeman, Oliver. (2009, March 25). Obama administration says goodbye to 'war on terror.' *Guardian*. Retrieved from http://www.guardian.co.uk/world/2009/mar/25/obama-war-terror-overseas-contingency-operations

Cosgrove-Mather, Bootie. (2005, July 28). Adoption's New Frontier: Snowflake' Babies Adopted For Personal, Political Reasons. *ABC News*. Retrieved from http://www.cbsnews.com/stories/2005/07/28/national/main712541.shtml

Doma Watch. (2011, May 13). Defense of Marriage Act Information. *Alliance Defense Fund*. Retrieved from http://www.domawatch.org/amendments/amendmentsummary.html

Dujan, Kevin. (2010, December 11). Is Fred Phelps a Democrat? *HillBuzz*. Retrieved from http://hillbuzz.org/2010/12/11/questions-is-fred-phelps-a-democrat-is-westboro-baptist-a-democrat-organization-why-did-fred-phelps-and-westboro-baptist-picket-elizabeth-edwards-funeral-on-december-11th-2010/

Hillbuzz.com. (2010, December 11). Is Fred Phelps a Democrat? *Hizzbuzz*. Retrieved from http://hillbuzz.org/2010/12/11/questions-is-fred-phelps-a-democrat-is-westboro-baptist-a-democrat-organization-why-did-fred-phelps-and-westboro-baptist-picket-elizabeth-edwards-funeral-on-december-11th-2010/

Ibbetson, Paul. (2011, May 10). Bin Laden Death Photo: Obama Breaks from History, America Losing Spine. *Renew America*. Retrieved from http://www6.renewamerica.com/columns/ibbetson/110510

Ibbetson, Paul. (2011, May 3). Osama bin Laden killed by U.S. forces, America should celebrate. *Renew America*. Retrieved from http://www6.renewamerica.com/columns/ibbetson/110503

Ibbetson, Paul. (2011, April 25) Liberals Struggle with Tea Party Reality. *GOPUSA*. Retrieved from http://www.gopusa.com/commentary/2011/04/25/ibbetson-liberals-struggle-with-tea-party-reality/

Ibbetson, Paul. (2011, March 20). Mexico: Your Spring Break Death-stination, *Renew America*. Retrieved from http://www6.renewamerica.com/columns/ibbetson/110314

Ibbetson, Paul. (2011, March 4). Christians Push Back against Gay Agenda in Kansas, *Renew America*. Retrieved from http://www6.renewamerica.com/columns/ibbetson/110304

Ibbetson, Paul. (2011, February 17). LBGT and Rainbow Justice. *Canada Free Press*. Retrieved from http://canadafreepress.com/index.php/article/33463

Ibbetson, Paul. (2011, February 11). Abortion in 2011: From Tax Breaks to Heartache. *Renew America*. Retrieved from http://www6.renewamerica.com/columns/ibbetson/110211

Ibbetson, Paul. (2011, February 4). Analyzing the Open-Border Mentality. *Renew America*. Retrieved from http://www6.renewamerica.com/columns/ibbetson/110204

Ibbetson, Paul. (2011, January 31). The Pet Rock versus Obamacare. *GOPUSA*. Retrieved from http://www.gopusa.com/commentary/2011/01/31/ibbetson-the-pet-rock-versus-obamacare/

Ibbetson, Paul. (2011, January 21). Democrats Look to Dupe GOP at State of the Union Address. *Renew America*. Retrieved from http://www6.renewamerica.com/columns/ibbetson/110121

Ibbetson, Paul. (2011, January 11). The Do's and Don'ts of Sheriff Dupnik: Another Ploy to Silence Conservatives. *Renew America*. Retrieved from http://www6.renewamerica.com/columns/ibbetson/110111

Ibbetson, Paul. (2011, January 6). The Barack Obama Presidency: When Being Unbelievable is the Best Defense. *Canada Free Press*. Retrieved from http://canadafreepress.com/index.php/article/31853

Ibbetson, Paul. (2011, January 3). Ibbetson: The Repeal of DADT - To March or to Sashay into the Future? *GOPUSA*. Retrieved from http://www.gopusa.com/commentary/2011/01/03/ibbetson-the-repeal-of-dadt-to-march-or-to-sashay-into-the-future/

Ibbetson, Paul. (2010, December 23). Love, Hate, and a Dry-Eyed look at the Future of the Country. *Renew America*. Retrieved from http://www6.renewamerica.com/columns/ibbetson/101223

Ibbetson, Paul. (2010, December 12). LGBT: Kansas, you're not in Kansas Anymore. *The Land of The Free*. Retrieved from http://www.thelandofthefree.net/conservativeopinion/2010/12/12/lgbt-kansas-you%E2%80%99re-not-in-kansas-anymore/

Ibbetson, Paul. (2010, November 30). Taxes and Punishment: Why Attacking Achievement Hurts Everyone. *Renew America*. Retrieved from http://www6.renewamerica.com/columns/ibbetson/101130

Ibbetson, Paul. (2010, November 23). Political Correctness and Your Body: Why TSA Security Measures Won't Fly. *Renew America*. Retrieved from http://www6.renewamerica.com/columns/ibbetson/101123

Ibbetson, Paul. (2010, November 15). Oklahoma: When Sharia Comes Sweeping Down The Plains. *GOPUSA*. Retrieved from http://www.gopusa.com/commentary/2010/11/15/ibbetson_oklahoma_-_when_sharia_comes_sweeping_down_the_plains/

Ibbetson, Paul. (2010, November 11). Stewart and Colbert: Laughing with the Left until it Hurts. *Post Chronicle*. Retrieved from http://www.postchronicle.com/cgi-bin/artman/exec/view.cgi?archive=238&num=332511

Ibbetson, Paul. (2010, October 30). National Public Radio and the Skinny Fat Man. *Renew America*. Retrieved from http://www6.renewamerica.com/columns/ibbetson/101030

Ibbetson, Paul. (2010, October 23). California: the Gateway Drug State. *Renew America*. Retrieved from http://www6.renewamerica.com/columns/ibbetson/101023

Ibbetson, Paul. (2010, October 16). Westboro Baptist Church and the Ten-Mile Proposition. *Renew America*. Retrieved from http://www6.renewamerica.com/columns/ibbetson/101016

Ibbetson, Paul. (2010, October 8). Death Before Truth: Political Correctness in America. *American Daily*. Retrieved from http://americandaily.com/index.php/article/4556

Ibbetson, Paul. (2010, October 1). Mid-term Elections in Venezuela: Did Revolution Make It On The Ballot? *Renew America*. Retrieved from http://www6.renewamerica.com/columns/ibbetson/101001

Ibbetson, Paul. (2010, September 24). Values Voter Summit: Why winning Is Not Enough. *Renew America*. Retrieved from http://www6.renewamerica.com/columns/ibbetson/100924

Ibbetson, Paul. (2010, September 20). Embryonic Stem Cell Research: The Blood Trail of Progress. *GOPUSA*. Retrieved from http://www.gopusa.com/commentary/2010/09/20/ibbetson_embryonic_stem_cell_research_-_the_blood_trail_of_progress/

Ibbetson, Paul. (2010, September 11). Just Relax Your Throat: Liberals and Their Need to Force-Feed America. *The Conservative Crusader*. Retrieved from http://www.conservativecrusader.com/articles/just-relax-your-throat-liberals-and-their-need-to-force-feed-america

Ibbetson, Paul. (2010, September 2). Lt. Col. Allen West: A Voice for the Leavenworth 10. *Renew America*. Retrieved from http://www6.renewamerica.com/columns/ibbetson/100902

Ibbetson, Paul. (2010, August 27). Classic Monster Politics. *Renew America*. Retrieved from http://www6.renewamerica.com/columns/ibbetson/100827

Ibbetson, Paul. (2010, August 15). Gay Marriage: Court Decisions from Sodom and Gomorrah. *Publius Forum*. Retrieved from http://www.publiusforum.com/2010/08/15/gay-marriage-court-decisions-from-sodom-and-gomorrah/

Ibbetson, Paul. (2010, August 5). Too Dangerous to Print: Liberal University Bias. *Renew America*. Trieved from http://www6.renewamerica.com/columns/ibbetson/100805

Ibbetson, Paul. (2010, July 30). Mega Mosques and the Territorial Mark. *Renew America*. Retrieved from http://www6.renewamerica.com/columns/ibbetson/100730

Ibbetson, Paul. (2010, July 23). Obamaca: Reshaping Society Through Government Control. *The Common Conservative*. Retrieved from http://thecommonconservative.com/?p=557

Ibbetson, Paul. (2010, July 16). The "Barefoot" Culture and the Promotion of Deviance. *Renew America*. Retrieved from http://www6.renewamerica.com/columns/ibbetson/100716

Ibbetson, Paul. (2010, July 9). Barack Obama: Securing the Border, One Sign at a Time. *Renew America*. Retrieved from http://www6.renewamerica.com/columns/ibbetson/100709

Ibbetson, Paul. (2010, July 2). Burning Drudge, Burning Weigel: A Fiery View from the Washington Post. *Renew America*. Retrieved from http://www6.renewamerica.com/columns/ibbetson/100702

Ibbetson, Paul. (2010, June 23). Get Out of my Tent! Fruming Over the Tea Party Movement. *GOPUSA*. Retrieved from http://www.gopusa.com/commentary/2010/06/23/ibbetson_get_out_of_my_tent_fruming_over_the_tea_party_movement/

Ibbetson, Paul. (2010, June 17). Let's Hear it for the Girls! Women and the Conservative Movement. *Canada Free Press.* Retrieved from http://canadafreepress.com/index.php/article/24393

Ibbetson, Paul. (2010, June 10). Ron Paul, Whose Side Are You On? *Renew America*. Retrieved from http://www6.renewamerica.com/columns/ibbetson/100610

Ibbetson, Paul. (2010, May 29). When I was a Child, I thought like the Obama Administration. *Renew America.* Retrieved from http://www6.renewamerica.com/columns/ibbetson/100529

Ibbetson, Paul. (2010, May 23). Roman Polanski, Pay Your Debt to Society. *Capitol Hill Coffee House.* Retrieved from http://chch2.ws/index.php/article/206

Ibbetson, Paul. (2010, May 14). America and Greece: Beware the Path of the Black Cat. *Renew America.* Retrieved from http://www6.renewamerica.com/columns/ibbetson/100514

Ibbetson, Paul. (2010, May 7). Illegal immigration: is it kind to be cruel? *Renew America.* Retrieved from http://www6.renewamerica.com/columns/ibbetson/100507

Ibbetson, Paul. (2010, April 29). The National Day of Prayer: The Value of Offending. *Capitol Hill Coffee House.* Retrieved from http://capitolhillcoffeehouse.com/more.php?id=8481_0_1_0_M

Ibbetson, Paul. (2010, April 23). Barack Obama: Another Grasp at the Crown? *Renew America.* Retrieved from http://www6.renewamerica.com/columns/ibbetson/100423

Ibbetson, Paul. (2010, April 15). The Westboro Baptist Church: In the Footsteps of the Pharisees and Sadducees. *Renew America.* http://www6.renewamerica.com/columns/ibbetson/100415

Ibbetson, Paul. (2010, April 8). Techno-politics: The War for Downloadable Supremacy. *Renew America.* Retrieved from http://www6.renewamerica.com/columns/ibbetson/100408

Ibbetson, Paul. (2010, March 25). Hanks for the New Memories: A Look at the Skewed Mentality of Hollywood. *The Conservative Crusader*. Retrieved from http://www.conservativecrusader.com/articles/hanks-for-the-new-memories-a-look-at-the-skewed-mentality-of-hollywood

Ibbetson, Paul. (2010, March 19). Protection and Reward: The Case of 1st Lieutenant Michael Behenna. *Renew America.* Retrieved from http://www6.renewamerica.com/columns/ibbetson/100319

Ibbetson, Paul. (2010, March 11). Khalid Sheikh Mohammed: Terrorist Trial Space For Rent? *Renew America*. Retrieved from http://www6.renewamerica.com/columns/ibbetson/100311

Ibbetson, Paul. (2010, March 4). Ron Paul and the "Cujo" Effect. *Right Side News*. Retrieved from http://www.rightsidenews.com/201003048910/editorial/us-opinion-and-editorial/ron-paul-and-the-qcujoq-effect.html

Ibbetson, Paul. (2010, February 18). Palms, Knuckles, and Fingertips: A Rich Assessment of Palin Hate. *Renew America*. Retrieved from http://www6.renewamerica.com/columns/ibbetson/100218

Ibbetson, Paul. (2010, February 11). Give Me the Ball! Entitlement in the Political Field. *Renew America*. Retrieved from http://www6.renewamerica.com/columns/ibbetson/100211

Ibbetson, Paul. (2010 February 4). Stone Soup: What Liberals Are Cooking Up for 2010. *Canada Free Press*. Retrieved from http://canadafreepress.com/index.php/article/19699

Ibbetson, Paul. (2010, January 30). America and Israel: You Got a Friend in Me? *Renew America*. Retrieved from http://www6.renewamerica.com/columns/ibbetson/100130

Ibbetson, Paul. (2010 January 21). Pilfering the Dead: Barack Obama at the Pulpit of the Vermont Avenue Baptist Church. *Right Side News*. Retrieved from http://www.rightsidenews.com/201001228284/editorial/us-opinion-and-editorial/pilfering-the-dead-barack-obama-at-the-pulpit-of-the-vermont-avenue-baptist-church.html

Ibbetson, Paul. (2010 January 14). A Thankful Observance of the "Iron Lady." *Renew America*. Retrieved from http://www6.renewamerica.com/columns/ibbetson/100114

Ibbetson, Paul. (2010 January 7). Presentation vs. Taste: Why Barack Obama is Cooking Up Disaster in the War on Terror. *Renew America*. Retrieved from http://www6.renewamerica.com/columns/ibbetson/100107

Lee, Ken. (2007, August 24). Nicole Ritchie Surprised by Early Release. *People*. Retrieved from http://www.people.com/people/article/0,,20053292,00.html

Marsh, Wendell. (2011, March 18). House Votes to Cut Funding to Public Radio. *Reuters*. Retrieved from http://www.reuters.com/article/2011/03/18/us-media-npr-idUSTRE72H51O20110318

Mataconis, Doug. (2010, August 10). Ann Coulter Booted From World Net Daily Conference For Speaking To Gay Group. *Outside The Beltway*. http://www.outsidethebeltway.com/ann-coulter-booted-from-world-net-daily-conference-for-speaking-to-gay-group

Miller, Dave. (2011, May 13). The Founders on Homosexuality. *Apologetics Press*. Retrieved from http://www.apologeticspress.org/apcontent.aspx?category=7&article=1126

Mitchell, John. (2011, March 11). Rev. Al Sharpton: 'You Cannot Fight for Freedom Without Fighting for Freedom for Everyone.' *Pop Eater*. Retrieved from http://www.popeater.com/2011/03/22/al-sharpton-russell-simmons-glaad-media-awards/

National Right to Life Committee. Abortion History Timeline. *(2011, March 26)*. Retrieved from http://www.nrlc.org/abortion/facts/abortiontimeline.html#1959

NewsMax. (2011, March 28). Exclusive to Newsmax: Donald Trump's Birth Certificate. *NewsMax*, Retrieved from http://www.newsmax.com/InsideCover/donaldtrump-birthcertificate-newsmax/2011/03/28/id/390930?s=al&promo_code=BF5E-1

Parker, Star. (2011, February 12). 'Gay Conservative' is an Oxymoron. *The Examiner*. Retrieved from http://washingtonexaminer.com/opinion/columnists/2011/02/gay-conservative-oxymoron

Real Clear Politics. (2010, April 16). Obama On Tea Partiers: You Would Think They'd Be Saying Thank You. *Associated Press*. Retrieved from http://www.realclearpolitics.com/video/2010/04/16/obama_on_tea_partiers_you_would_think_th eyd_be_saying_thank_you.html

Spencer, Robert. (2009, September 24). Latest Jihad Plot Shows Need to Know Koran. *Human Events*. Retrieved from http://www.humanevents.com/article.php?id=33673

Summers, Juana. (2011, May 12). Ron Paul wouldn't have approved Osama bin Laden operation. *Politico*. Retrieved from http://www.politico.com/news/stories/0511/54822.html#ixzz1M9acZFTe

William Blackstone, *Commentaries on the Laws of England*, Book the Fourth, Oxford: Printed at the Clarendon Press, 1769, Book IV, Chapter XI, pp. 205ú217.
Rictor Norton (Ed.), "Blackstone's Commentaries, 1769," *Homosexuality in Eighteenth-Century England: A Sourcebook*. 26 November 2006 http://rictornorton.co.uk/eighteen/1769blac.htm

The Good Fight

Paul A. Ibbetson

Published By:

Eternal Light and Power Company

PO Box 1533 Smethport, PA 16749

ISBN-13: 978-1466216280

ISBN-10: 146621628X

For information on publishing your book, contact Eternal light and Power company at:

www.YahBible.Com